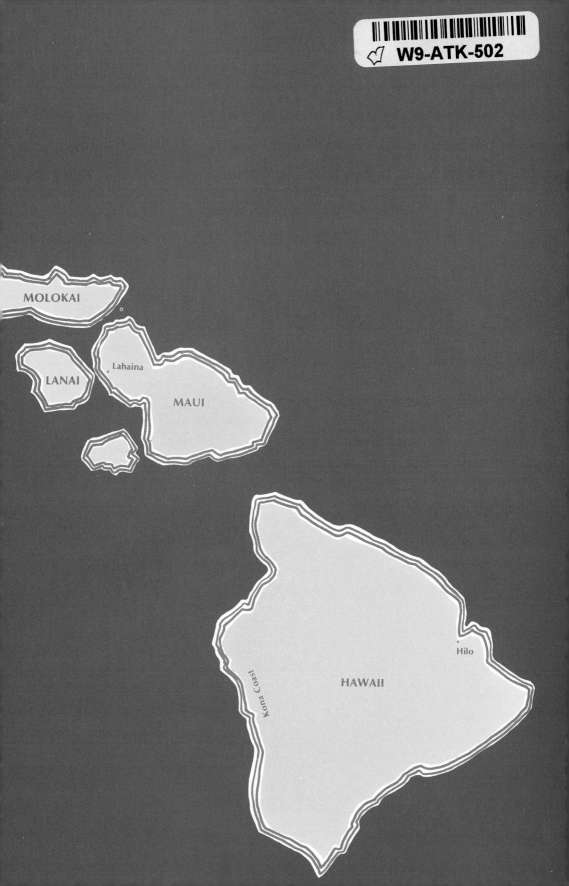

MOLOKAI

LANAI

Lahaina

MAUI

Kona Coast

HAWAII

Hilo

From Land and Sea

The Story of Castle & Cooke of Hawaii

From Land

and Sea

The Story of Castle & Cooke of Hawaii

By Frank J. Taylor, Earl M. Welty, and David W. Eyre

Chronicle Books, 870 Market Street,
San Francisco, California 94102

Foreword

We believe every business organization that has played an important role in the life of its community and area for a long period should have its history recorded.

Coincidentally, the nation's bicentennial year, 1976, is also the 125th anniversary of the founding of Castle & Cooke, Inc. We believe it an appropriate occasion for the publication of this company history.

Over a period of years, three authors have contributed to the research and writing of the manuscript—the late Frank J. Taylor, the late Earl M. Welty, and David W. Eyre. Their names appear on the title page. All were asked to tell the story impartially and objectively. We hope the result reflects that approach. Their manuscripts have been blended and brought up to date by the staff of Castle & Cooke's public relations department.

D. J. KIRCHHOFF
President

MALCOLM MACNAUGHTON
Chairman of the Board

Acknowledgments

Many people besides the authors have contributed to the production of this history of Castle & Cooke, Inc. Among those deserving special thanks are:

Elizabeth Larsen, Lela Goodell, Margaret Schleif, and Mary Jane Knight of the Hawaiian Mission Children's Society; Agnes Conrad, Hawaii state archivist; librarians at the Bishop Museum, the Hawaiiana collection at the University of Hawaii, and the Hawaii State Library; Gwenfread Allen, writer of Hawaii history during World War II; J. C. Condé, Hawaii railroad authority; Barbara Dunn, Hawaiian Historical Society; Albertine Loomis and David Forbes, historians; and the Hawaiian Sugar Planters' Association and the Pineapple Growers Association.

Recognition also is due to the many officers and directors of Castle & Cooke, members of its public relations department, and others within the company—past and present—who have contributed to this history. And special thanks go to Jean B. Stevens, assistant secretary of the company, who has participated in the research on all three manuscripts as well as the final effort that produced this book.

Last, but certainly not least, is recognition of the work of the many company secretaries who over the years have typed, retyped, and re-retyped the manuscripts and their many, many revisions.

Table of Contents

The Missionary Years

1837-1851

Chapter 1

Toward Heathen Shores

IT WAS THE POLYNESIANS who first discovered the Hawaiian archipelago, about A.D. 800 or perhaps earlier. But a thousand years more passed before European man arrived in the shape of British explorer Captain James Cook, who in 1778 named the islands in honor of his English patron, the Earl of Sandwich. Seafaring merchants and adventurers from all over the world soon followed, bringing with them the white man's civilization—and his diseases.

In 1819 the American whaling fleet from New England "discovered" Hawaii once again. It was, by coincidence, the same year the Hawaiian monarchy abolished much of the islanders' ancient religion. A year later the first American missionaries from Boston arrived to introduce them to a new one. In 1837 the Seventh Reinforcement of missionaries arrived in Hawaii. The group included Samuel Northrup Castle, Amos Starr Cooke, and their brides of less than six months.

> Saw about 10 o'clock the distant tops of the mountains of Oahu. About 12 could distinguish natives walking on the shore and native huts. The mountains and all the land wears a desolate appearance but I am not disappointed in the least. I should have been, had it looked beautiful. This is to be my home—welcome Oahu.

These first impressions of Oahu, recorded by Juliette Montague Cooke upon her arrival off Honolulu Harbor Sunday morning, April 9, 1837, were part of a letter to her mother back in Sunderland, Massachusetts:

I wish I could describe Oahu as it presents itself to us . . . . It is one long line of mountains spread around in a picturesque manner. Along the shore is a plain where the village of Honolulu is built. At the right of the village is a mountain that looks to me as if it might have been, ages ago, a volcano . . . . These mountains are not much green. Indeed, all the land wears a barren aspect. There are some fertile spots, bushes, grass, etc. on the mountains—some forests. It does not look much like New England but, of course, better than I expected.

Juliette was the bride of Amos Starr Cooke. Two of their companions on the long journey around the Horn from Boston were Samuel Northrup Castle and his bride, Angeline Tenney Castle. They were lay members of the Seventh Reinforcement numbering thirty-two souls, the largest group of missionaries ever sent to the Sandwich Islands by the American Board of Commissioners for Foreign Missions in Boston. They had made the 16,000-mile journey in 116 days, the fastest trip from New England to Hawaii up to that time.

SAMUEL NORTHRUP CASTLE was an impressive young man—tall, slender, and unusually well-read for his twenty-eight years. Born in 1808 in the town of Cazenovia in central New York state, he came of sturdy stock. His father, who had migrated westward from Connecticut to New York, was known as "Deacon" Castle in the First Presbyterian Church of Cazenovia, which he helped organize. Deacon Castle composed hymns and sang them while he drove his cows in from pasture. He was a strict fundamentalist who allowed no deviation from doctrine. The Sabbath in the Castle household lasted from sundown Saturday to sundown Sunday. This intense religious atmosphere molded the character of young Castle quite as much as did the stern chores of his young life.

His mother, Phoebe Parmelee, descendant of a Belgian baron who had fled his homeland in 1570 to escape religious persecution, became an invalid after bearing nine children. Northrup, as he was called when a child, was number five.

For years, young Castle arose at four in the morning to prepare his mother's food, a diet of eggs beaten with molasses. A constant reader, he cheated on his sleep and memorized much of the Bible, *The Pilgrim's Progress,* and *Paradise Lost.* Once, in his teens, when an especially devout aunt and uncle visited the Castles, Northrup amazed everyone by identifying the book, chapter, and verse of every biblical quotation they tossed at him.

Young Castle taught school two winters, disliked it, and at eighteen landed a job as a store clerk for $6 a month and keep. This fitted him first for a $50-a-month clerkship in Buffalo and then for a still better job clerking in a Cleveland bank when the family migrated again in 1830 during the westward surge into the Ohio Reserve. Whatever his salary, he saved something each month.

He grew into a tall, wiry, angular man with a prominent nose, sensitive mouth, heavy eyebrows, and deep blue eyes that sparkled radiantly when he smiled. When he was twenty-three, a momentous event occurred—he was "converted" at a revival meeting. Five years later in 1836 when the American Board of Commissioners for Foreign Missions called for volunteers for foreign service, he was ready for "giving himself to the Christian cause."

By then, he had quit the bank for a better job in a mercantile house, had become a lieutenant in the militia, and had earned recognition as one of the promising young businessmen of the booming city of Cleveland, population six thousand. He was engaged, but when his fiancée refused to join him as a missionary, he gave up the girl instead of the call.

Castle's appraisal of himself in the letter he wrote the secretary of the Mission Board on April 13, 1836, is revealing:

Dear Sir: In looking into the Missionary Herald for March, I saw a statement of the number of missionaries, physicians, teachers and printers which you wished to send into the field the coming season—and also a statement of the number already obtained. In looking upon the wants of the dying world and seeing how few were willing to deny themselves and make even the slightest sacrifice required for the salvation of souls, I felt my heart bound within me and ready to say, Here, Lord, I am, send me—and in view of the subject, I am induced to offer myself to the Board to go forth as teacher to the Sandwich Islands, Singapore, Southern India or Syria, provided the Board should think that I was suitably qualified.

I am rather inclined to think the Sandwich Islands, in respect to climate, would be more congenial to my health than any of the above named situations, but of that, the Board will judge.

My education is, I suppose, something better than what is termed a common English education. My present occupation is bookkeeping. I have, however, taught a common school for several seasons with tolerable success. I am in the 28th year of my age but single—but shall expect, should I go, to take a companion suitable for the work . . . .

I shall expect to procure the most satisfactory testimonials from clergymen. As to the character of my piety and talents—my reading has been general—and I suppose that, with about 1½ or 2 years study and attending two courses of lectures, I might prepare myself for the practice of medicine—as I have read medical works to a considerable extent. I had thought, however, that I should be enabled better to promote the interests of the common cause in which we are engaged by entering upon the duties of teacher than by delay.

Please favor me with an immediate answer, stating your personal views or the views of the Board—as it is to me, from the nature of my present location and business, of importance to learn as early as possible what course to pursue.

> I am respectfully
> Your Brother in the Lord
> SAM'L N. CASTLE

The Board sent a questionnaire to Castle and among the questions was: "Why do you think it your duty to offer yourself to this work?" He replied:

Because God has said go Ye into all the world and spread the gospel to every Creature—and I see at this period of the world that the injunction has not been fully obeyed. I see 600 million of the human race without the light of the blessed gospel, which only is able to make them wise unto Salvation. I see this vast multitude hastening onward to the retributions of Eternity unprepared because there is Salvation in no one save Jesus Christ . . . .

After checking his credentials, the Board members concluded that Sam'l N. Castle was a man they needed, not as a schoolteacher but as a bookkeeper, to help straighten out the Honolulu mission's fiscal affairs. But first, they informed him, he had to marry "a suitable companion."

Castle was advised, on a visit to Oberlin, Ohio, to check "a certain pious young lady deeply interested in the cause of foreign missions." With his sister, Mary, he hurried over to see the young lady, whose name was Angeline Tenney of Plainfield, New York. She, too, happened to be visiting in Oberlin.

"We talked for an hour and the matter was arranged," Castle reported to the Board. "I have found a suitable female."

He wanted to get married immediately, but the Board restrained him until Miss Tenney's piety could be checked. After several anxious weeks, she was approved, and the Female Missionary Society of Cleveland gave them a send-off party and a purse of $30. The couple was married in the bride's Plainfield home November 10, 1836, then hurried to Boston to get ready for sailing within a month.

AMOS STARR COOKE had spent three years in New York City as a bookkeeper and more than two years of study in preparation for Yale to train for the ministry when he heard "the call." He was born in Danbury, Connecticut, in 1810, eighth and youngest child of Joseph Platt Cooke, a farmer whose home was exceptionally devout. Young Cooke labored on the family farm "in preference to studying" until age sixteen, when he went to work as a clerk in a village store. Having learned bookkeeping, he moved to New York in 1830 to keep ledgers for a firm of commission merchants.

His real ambition was to become a Presbyterian minister, but before he could enter Yale, young Cooke heard the summons for missionary duty. Writing to the American Board, he outlined his talents modestly and offered himself "as a teacher to the Sandwich Islands Mission." And he added, "Silver and gold have I none but such as I have, I willingly offer."

The Board replied: "Scores of men, possessing good common sense, a plain solid education and devoted piety are urgently needed to go and labor far out in the Sandwich Islands." They asked to see his letters of recommendation.

His pastor wrote: "He is regarded by all his acquaintances as enlightened, consistent, zealous, discreet and judicious, a Christian . . . . I believe from the kind of talents he possesses, his good judgment, sound mind and maturity of character, he will make just such a teacher as the Board wants."

Another added: "I can freely say that no one in the circle of my acquaintances of his age and standing promises so much. I know of no one who answers more fully the . . . definition of perseverance. It is to 'take hold, hang on and never let go.' I wish the Board had more of such spirits to send forth."

His former New York employer added: "His talents are considered fair, not showy, but sound . . . . We should think his capacity for teaching good and that his patience and perseverance would enable him to do more good in teaching the ignorant than many possessing more showy qualities."

Cooke was accepted as a teacher but, again, with the admonition that he find a wife. The Board even recommended one—a Miss Juliette

Montague of Sunderland, Massachusetts, who, they said, was a young woman eminently qualified. He went to her home and, to his joy, found her sweet-voiced, musical, and generally pleasant. Among her physical assets, he noted a straight nose and a prim, firm mouth. She had lived for thirteen years on the family homestead until her father died, leaving her mother to rear four children. Juliette supported herself by taking up dressmaking.

To advance her education, she attended lectures at Amherst, becoming one of the first women permitted to do so. She later taught at Ipswich Seminary with Mary Lyon, who went on to become founder of Mount Holyoke College. In 1833 she publicly professed her faith in Christ and added her soprano voice to the village choir.

The following testimonial was sent to the Mission Board:

> In relation to her education, she is in a measure self-taught, but well taught. She has the right kind of education for a missionary. She is not only apt but a pleasant teacher; she has a sweet natural disposition. Her domestic qualifications are all suited for such a station. She is a good tailoress and dressmaker. She has not been brought up in the parlor only but is acquainted with every part of the house. She is remarkable for the improvement of her time and has a heart to do good. She has a full share of common sense to discover the best way and time to do good to others. She is happy in securing the confidence of others and retaining it when gained. Lastly, her Christian character stands untarnished.

Now she was being approached by a slight young man with a thatch of dark hair, dark blue eyes, and a sensitive mouth who "wanted to settle the affair of matrimony" in order that he might take a bride to the Sandwich Islands. Making up their minds in a relatively short time (over the protests of her family, who considered the "romance" much too fast), the couple hurried over the Connecticut border by horse and chaise since there was too little time to publish the banns required by Massachusetts law. They were married at the bridegroom's Danbury home just in time to sail with the Seventh Reinforcement.

MR. AND MRS. CASTLE AND MR. AND MRS. COOKE "honeymooned" on the bark *Mary Frazier* (288 tons), which set sail from Boston Harbor December 14, 1836, at ten o'clock on a cold, clear morning. Their destination was Hawaii, then called the Sandwich Islands, half-way around the globe. None of the thirty-two missionaries aboard expected to see New England's coast again. Someone struck up a hymn, "My

Native Land I Love.'' It was sung with hearts in throats, followed by a few cheers to bolster courage.

But Mrs. Cooke was happy. On the eve of departure, after having met the other members of the Seventh Reinforcement, Juliette wrote to her mother: "I find Mr. C. a very kind friend, think I would not exchange with any of the ladies. He sends much love to Mother."

Chartered especially for the voyage, the *Mary Frazier* actually carried to heathen Hawaii the eighth group of missionaries dispatched by the American Board. The original group had arrived aboard the brig *Thaddeus* on April 4, 1820; subsequent groups were described as "reinforcements." Although in principle nondenominational, the aggressive board was made up largely of Congregationalists and Presbyterians.

Those aboard the *Mary Frazier* were young, strong, and eager, filled with the will to spread the gospel, along with the strict New England Puritan code of living, to the children of the sun in Polynesia.

"I find myself on the way to the heathen," Juliette wrote in her shipboard journal. "Bless the Lord, oh my soul, for His goodness in permitting me to go with my face towards heathen shores."

In the Seventh were four ordained ministers and one doctor. The rest were teachers and secular assistants, including wives. But the titles "Mister" and "Missus" were left behind in Boston. Now it was "Brother" and "Sister."

As the shoreline of Massachusetts slipped away, the voyagers began organizing life aboard the ship that was to be their crowded, rolling home for the next four to six months, depending on the force of the wind in the sails. The cabins, 5½ by 6 feet, were too tiny to hold even half the chests, trunks, rocking chairs, bedding, and books that constituted personal cargo—and they were too dark for reading. Within hours after weighing anchor, most passengers were too seasick to care.

But by the third day, when the fifteen couples and two maiden ladies regained their health on calmer waters, shipboard routine was tackled with enthusiasm. Living conditions were better than anticipated. The ship was clean and the captain considerate. For breakfast there were mackerel, "minced victuals," hasty pudding, warm Indian cakes, sea crackers, coffee, tea, and cold water—"or, rather, warm water not warmed by artificial heat," as Juliette described it. For dinner there were boiled potatoes, turnips, carrots, or rice; boiled ham, beef, or fowl; always puddings or pies; and sometimes apples, pickles, or horseradish.

As the ship sailed into tropical waters, cabins grew hot and stuffy, so the missionaries spent most of their days under an awning reading, writing, working, talking, studying, singing, or gazing at the flying fish that skimmed over the sea. Two Hawaiian seamen, Joseph and Levi, led classes in the Hawaiian language. For recreation there were rope-skipping and mast-climbing contests for men and strolls around the deck for women.

Each day dawned and ended with prayer, and the evangelists were pleased to find that the souls of the officers and crew of the *Mary Frazier* needed saving, especially the first mate's. But he was a rugged seafaring man who refused to see the light, even after all the missionaries had worked on him in relays. He'd never done harm to anybody, he said bluntly, and he considered himself as good as his unconverted father, whom he stubbornly refused to believe had gone to hell.

Others of the crew were easier targets. Captain Charles Sumner soon showed signs of conversion, and so did the second mate. Juliette Cooke wrote in her diary, "We have a trembling hope that the steward has been converted." Later she recorded in triumph, "The Captain ordered the cook to prepare no puddings on Sabbath nor pies, and to bake no warm bread. We have him now. . . ."

Cape Horn was rounded on the sixtieth day in weather unexpectedly calm. The captain, who on earlier trips had sometimes spent whole months getting around the grim cape, admitted that such fine weather just might be due to the earnest prayers of his passengers.

Like shipboard passengers on any trip, certain couples on the *Mary Frazier* paired up, and the Castles and the Cookes developed an affinity that was to lead eventually to a business partnership. Juliette wrote about the Castles in her diary, "Himself and wife are such as I should select as favorites if I were to have any such . . . . Everything they say and do has a peculiar beauty and propriety in it to my eye."

Once in the Pacific, the *Mary Frazier* picked up the trade winds and sped on. On April 6, 1837, Juliette wrote, "All hurly burly today, the staterooms in confusion, the cabin a perfect babel. Cause? Getting ready to land if land should appear. Truly we are a mouldy set."

The next day, Friday, April 7, the cabins and deck were bustling with excitement. Several passengers thought they could see the mountains of the Hawaiian islands. As the journey neared its end, Captain Sumner shook $108 out of his officers and men for the Christian cause, putting in $40 himself. Although the second mate gave $10 and the steward and all the sailors contributed half a month's pay, the bullheaded first mate (whom Sister Cooke described as "stupid") gave nothing.

Saturday evening the island of Maui was visible—a dark mass with a cloud hanging over it—and on Sunday morning the islands of Molokai and Lanai came into sight. At 10 A.M. the long-awaited mountaintops of

Oahu took shape. Because of a strong wind, it was impossible for the *Mary Frazier* to enter Honolulu harbor, but even if she had docked, the passengers would not have disembarked. To do so would have been blasphemous on the Sabbath.

Anchored offshore, the ship was surrounded by scores of canoes, manned by natives wearing only breechcloths. Although the missionaries had been warned to expect near-nakedness, it was shocking, particularly to the women. Some went below deck to weep, suddenly realizing how far behind they'd left their kind of civilization. One native brought several bottles of milk, and the passengers were "right glad to taste something fresh again."

The restless missionaries had plenty of time aboard ship that day to study Honolulu. The town occupied a treeless plain with several burned-out volcanoes in the background. They could make out many grass huts (like so many haystacks on a New England farm), a few stone houses, a fort, and two churches whose bells occasionally rang.

"The sound gladdened our hearts," said Juliette, "and made it seem as if we were in our native land."

On Monday the king's barge lightered the missionaries ashore, and for the first time in 116 days they walked on land.

"I feel to praise His name that He has placed me on heathen ground," Juliette exulted.

If many young missionary husbands and wives were virtual strangers to each other before they sailed off to carry salvation to the Pacific, the people they were to save were equally unknown to them. There is no evidence that the American Board in Boston provided much briefing about the islands for the evangelists, despite the fact that missionaries had been stationed in Hawaii for seventeen years.

Although the Cookes and others had taken a short course in the Hawaiian language from Levi and Joseph aboard the *Mary Frazier,* their journals mention no concentrated study on the history of the islands or the customs of their people.

These New Englanders were basically provincials when they arrived, a fact demonstrated with naïveté by Sister Cooke on her first day in Hawaii. Visiting a school briefly, she observed: "The children behaved very well, considering they are heathen. Their filthiness, disheveled hair and monstrous shell combs made them look not very lovely, but they have precious immortal souls within."

ALTHOUGH HISTORIANS ARE NOT CERTAIN when Hawaii was first inhabited, they believe the first Polynesians came originally from the Marquesas and the Society Islands in double-hulled canoes. They brought with them the pig, the chicken, and the dog—and bananas, coconuts, sweet potatoes, breadfruit, sugarcane, yams, gourds, ti, and taro. The root of the taro plant was pounded into a pulp to produce the basic Hawaiian food, poi. They brought their fishhooks and poi pounders, made a bark cloth called tapa, and started fires in typically primitive fashion. Their life was pagan and filled with numerous gods and taboos, all of which continued until the year before the first missionaries arrived.

When Captain James Cook discovered Hawaii in 1778, the natives welcomed him and his crew, believing they were white gods. But a year later, on his second visit, Cook was killed by the Hawaiians in a violent encounter.

At the time of Cook's arrival, each of the six major Hawaiian islands was governed by a hereditary chief. It was not until 1790 that King Kamehameha I had united five of the islands under a single rule. Although he won his authority by force, he mellowed with the years and sought protection and justice for his people. He died in 1819—one year before the arrival of Hiram Bingham and the original missionary group.

The ancient Hawaiians worshipped many gods and goddesses, all personifications of their nature-oriented religion. These included Kane, God of Light and Life, patron of sunlight, fresh water, and all living creatures; Lono, God of the Harvest, deity of rain and all growing things; and Pele, Goddess of the Volcano. And there was Ku (Kukailimoku), God of War. Despite the fact that Hawaiians are known as a basically fun-loving, easy-going people, they could at that time be as warlike as almost any race in history. The Hawaiians built great temples of worship, using the lava rocks that cover the islands, and human sacrifices were not uncommon.

Upon the death of Kamehameha I, Liholiho, his son of highest rank, became Kamehameha II. He soon outlawed much of the ancient Hawaiian religion and left the Hawaiians in a state of confusion. Whom should they worship? To make matters worse, the white man had taught them how to brew a rather tasty liquor (later called *okolehao*) by boiling the root of the ti plant. Thus the first missionaries found the Hawaiians to be heathen indeed—and, to Puritan eyes, in dire need of salvation.

There were fourteen missionaries and five children in the original group that left Boston on the *Thaddeus* on October 23, 1819, for a 164-day journey to Hawaii. Upon their arrival Liholiho granted them permission to reside in Hawaii on a trial basis. Initially, the party detailed to reside in Honolulu was lodged in three thatched houses that belonged to foreign sea captains. Soon a site for a mission compound was chosen on a barren plain about a half-mile from the village. There, the missionaries lived in grass huts built for them by the king.

But they would change that shortly. On Christmas Day a ship arrived with fresh supplies of lumber and prefabricated construction material, including fireplace mantels. The mantels were installed in the parlors—but without fireplaces, which were unnecessary on the warm, low-lying Honolulu plain.

The missionaries brought their rocking chairs and their melodeons and their English bone china and their children's dolls. However, the dolls had to be put away for a while because the natives thought the children were worshipping small idols, a practice newly forbidden in Hawaii.

The missionary life-style in faraway Hawaii was described by Sister Cooke in replying to questions posed by a curious aunt:

> People at home seem to think that missionaries live like the savages among whom they are, but they have not correct ideas upon the subject. It is no object of the missionary to teach himself barbarianism. On the contrary, he should, by example, endeavor to teach the natives civilization, its benefits, comforts, and pleasures.
>
> Therefore, missionaries consider it a duty on this account, as well as for the good of their families, their own health and the honor of their country, to live in a decent, respectable manner. We have comfortable apartments which we endeavor to keep in order and cleanly, so that when we are called upon by English or European noblemen, we need not blush for ourselves or put our friends, our patrons or our country to the blush for us.
>
> The same regard to dress. Some people will send out, for us to wear, old things which would not be fit to be seen in America . . . . We eat, drink, sleep, live and dress somewhat like the manner of Americans at home. Please throw away all that mysticism and romance which is so apt to infect the mind on the subject of missions, and consider the missionary as a humble, fallible being, endeavoring, with the help of God, to do his duty among the unevangelized of the earth.

As THEY TOUCHED on Hawaiian soil, members of the Seventh Reinforcement were greeted by natives who had come to stare. The native dress was astonishing. Some wore vests, others shirts, others hats or pantaloons—but few possessed more than one of these articles.

When the new arrivals reached the dock, the welcoming committee advised them of the amenities of the day. First, they were to go to a huge grass house to pay their respects to Kinau, the premier of the Kingdom. She was the largest woman Juliette Cooke had ever seen, dressed in a loose black silk gown, her hair held in a pile by an enormous shell comb. Her throne was a lofty stack of mats; chairs, sofas, and other articles of furniture adorned the apartment.

This dignitary invited any missionary who was weary to rest awhile in her adjoining room, and Juliette accepted the offer, partly out of curiosity. She found a room with a double bed, curtains, and a pile of mats on the floor. There lay a small boy, a young chief, and two men were by his side waving small *kahilis* (feather brushes) "to prevent a fly from looking at him."

With official pleasantries completed, the missionaries made the dusty half-mile walk to the mission settlement. It was easy to get a picture of the town as they walked along. Honolulu in 1837 had about six thousand people, about the same size as the Cleveland that Brother Castle had left. But here the citizens were largely natives who lived in grass huts. The colony numbered three hundred fifty Caucasians (*haoles* in Hawaiian), including missionaries, traders, and a raggle-taggle of stranded sailors.

When the Seventh's members arrived at Hiram Bingham's house in the mission settlement, they found their predecessors assembled to bid welcome. Bingham expressed gratitude to God for this large accession to their numbers. Then everyone sang "Blest Be the Tie That Binds," said prayers, and listened attentively while Bingham sang several verses of his own composition.

The new arrivals were assigned to temporary quarters, and conditions were incredibly crowded. At times as many as twenty people were residing in one small house, eating and sleeping in communal style with practically no privacy. The Castles were assigned to live with the Levi Chamberlains—Levi ran the mission warehouse, and Samuel was to assist him—while the Cookes moved in with the family of Brother Dimond, a bookbinder.

The mission compound of 1837 consisted of twelve coral and wood buildings with a few gardens. One building contained the type and press used for printing the scriptures in Hawaiian. The first printing ever done in the islands had come off the mission press fifteen years before, in 1822.

The melodic Hawaiian language consisted of five vowels, seven consonants, and one glottal stop. Committing it to paper was a tedious task and required countless interviews between natives and missionaries, spanning many years. But the job was eventually conquered, and the printing house later produced hundreds of thousands of pages of Christian writings in Hawaiian.

The mission house of worship was a huge grass shelter large enough to hold four thousand people. (A few of the chiefs boasted stone houses, and eight other stone buildings had been erected by traders and consuls in the business district.) Another important part of the compound was the Mission Depository, a combination store and warehouse that supplied the material needs of the missionaries throughout the islands. It was a long, low stone structure, fitted with iron doors and barred windows.

Such was the Hawaii the *Mary Frazier* contingent was joining—a fantastic change from the life they had known. Resolute though they were, they must have gulped hard and said an extra prayer. Their morale was undoubtedly heightened by the fact that the Seventh's members found themselves celebrities of sorts. They had created a sensation among the resident missionaries because they had been the first to convert a sea captain and crew.

Captain Sumner and several sailors even endured the taunts of other seafarers by appearing at Honolulu gospel meetings to testify how good they felt to be "saved."

THE REIGN OF Kamehameha II (Liholiho) lasted less than five years. In 1823 he and his queen, Kamamalu, sailed to London to see how the outside world lived. There the British entertained the dark-skinned monarchs with all due respect and courtesy at theater parties, diplomatic dinners, and other social functions.

Suddenly, Kamamalu contracted measles and died; six days later, on July 14, 1824, Liholiho was dead of the same disease.

For Hawaiians, measles and the rest of the white man's dread diseases frequently were fatal. Isolated throughout their history, they had never developed any immunity to the common illnesses of the western world. Measles killed tens of thousands of Hawaiians in the decades following the arrival of the white man. Epidemics of cholera, smallpox, and plague also ravaged the native population until, by 1837, the number of Hawaiians had been reduced to about one-third of the estimated 300,000 that had inhabited the islands when they were discovered by Captain James Cook some sixty years earlier.

The introduction of the white man's "ways" was also taking its toll. Juliette wrote home:

This people is in a deplorable condition—so much of sin, oppression and degradation that they are evidently decreasing very fast. It is estimated that in 30 years, they will be no more unless the missionaries can, by enlightening them and endeavoring to do them good, stop them in the ways of vice in which they are so swiftly traveling. Oh, how can American citizens of our own native land come here and sow the seeds of sin?

Chapter 2

Princely Pupils

AMOS STARR COOKE, accepted as a teacher by the American Board in Boston, was assigned with his wife to a school in Honolulu following their arrival in 1837. The school was one of several that had been established by the earlier missionaries to educate the children of Hawaii.

Initially, the Cookes' teaching was under the direction of the Reverend Lowell Smith, and their first months in the islands were spent in learning the Hawaiian language. Eventually, Amos became schoolmaster for thirty native girls in morning classes. Perhaps because of her greater educational experience, Juliette had an even larger class of girls, plus twenty-five boys in the afternoons.

In 1837, the Hawaiian chiefs were becoming increasingly aware of the need to be educated in order to function effectively, now that western civilization had reached them. They became convinced that both knowledge and diplomacy were urgently needed if the Hawaiian kingdom was to be maintained. The chiefs themselves were already requesting instruction "in political economy and jurisprudence and all matters connected with government."

Two years later, the royal rulers petitioned the Hawaiian mission to establish a school for their children, and they selected the Cookes as teachers. The invitation, translated from the Hawaiian, read:

Greetings to Mr. Cooke:
    Here is our thought to you that you become teacher for our royal children. You are the one to teach wisdom and righteousness. This is our thought to you.

The curriculum was to be taught in English. Dr. Gerrit P. Judd, the mission physician, was appointed by the chiefs as trustee and school doctor. The school was to be known as the Hawaiian Chiefs' Children's School. (Later the name was officially changed to the Royal School.)

The concept of a special school for children of Hawaiian royalty became highly controversial within the missionary community. Several members of the mission, including Brother Castle, considered the plan undemocratic and preferred that the royal children be taught along with other Hawaiian children. However, all were in general agreement that because Hawaii had been a feudal kingdom, the islands' future kings and queens had to be educated in western ways if they were to deal intelligently with other nations.

It was a momentous and remarkable undertaking for the Cookes, considering their recent arrival and relative inexperience in the art of instruction. Amos was twenty-nine, Juliette twenty-seven, and they had a year-old infant, Joseph. Young couples of lesser courage and conviction quite probably would have ducked the responsibility for any excuse available, but not Amos and Juliette.

The royal pupils were an impressive student body, including five future rulers as well as others who were to play significant roles in the future of Hawaii:

Prince Moses, grandson of the first Kamehameha and hereditary governor of Kauai, who died during a measles and whooping cough epidemic at the age of nineteen.

His brother, Prince Alexander, later to become Kamehameha IV.

Their brother, Prince Lot, who would become Kamehameha V.

Their sister, Princess Victoria Kamamalu.

Emma Rooke, who would become the wife of Kamehameha IV—and the dowager queen after his death.

William Lunalilo, who would be Hawaii's first elected king.

David Kalakaua, who became the last king of Hawaii.

Lydia Kamakaeha, David's sister, who became Queen Liliuokalani, the last of all monarchs in the islands.

Bernice Pauahi, great-granddaughter of Kamehameha I, who twice refused the throne of Hawaii. She married an American, Charles R Bishop, a name famous in the islands today.

ON THE SCHOOL'S OPENING DAY in June 1839, the first six students arrived—a spoiled, ornery, bewildered band of youngsters ranging in age from ten downward. They were accompanied by a retinue of doting *kahus* (personal servants) who took care of their every need and desire, and were almost as unruly as their charges. The many problems of the bold new venture and the grave concern of the Cookes regarding the undertaking are revealed in their journals and letters of that time. Within days after the school opened, Amos wrote:

"My labor for my scholars has scarcely any cessation. They are in my mind by day and by night and every day and every night, I feel to pray with Solomon—give me wisdom that my concerns may be managed with discretion." Two weeks later he added, "Yesterday I became a little more stern with my scholars—and had to discipline Moses [ten years old] to make him mind. Today punished Alexander [five], and Moses replied he was a Child of the Chief. I replied I was King of the School."

After six weeks Juliette described in a letter home the first visit to the school by the royal parents: "Enjoyed with them an interesting conversation upon the education, etc. of their children. The King [Kamehameha III] has all the ease and dignity of a well-bred gentleman . . . . There is one thing remarkable about him, which is that he, mid all his wanderings and the reproofs from the Mission, has never forsaken us, but always esteemed the missionaries as his best friends."

She also described the problem of hosting Hawaiian royalty at that time: "We have none of us sufficient furniture to entertain such a party, so our fashion is to send around to our mission neighbors and get a few chairs in one place, a few spoons in another, a waiter in another, a few tumblers in another, and so on until we get furnished."

Several months later, Amos added triumphantly, "Our school of chiefs' children still lives. The parents are becoming more and more interested . . . and give us almost unlimited control over them."

Six months after the school began, Juliette expressed concern over the chiefs' decision that the project should be converted from a day school to a boarding school: "It is a very interesting school on the whole. But I dread to have them [the pupils] come into the family. They are troublesome fellows, having been accustomed to have their every wish gratified as soon as made known. It is a hard and new lesson for them to learn that they must sometimes be denied."

"Our scholars have entered the family this day," Juliette wrote when the royal students moved into the school on May 5, 1840. "You have no idea, my mother, what a task we have undertaken. From the numerous attendants, these little ones have received all their pleasures. Now they feel so totally lost, they cannot find out what to do with themselves. We were not prepared with amusements and things to interest them, having come in haste and commenced before we were thoroughly settled."

But Amos noted, "They are growing more fond of their books, and I take much pleasure in instructing them, not only in their books, but teaching them principles. Heretofore, parents and children, chiefs and people, have been governed by feelings rather than by principles. When I think of it, I see more and more the herculean task before us, and cry out, Oh! for wisdom from above."

Amos also recorded in his journal:

"Tonight no 'kahus' came, and we have had little or no trouble. William [five] was the worst of the company. Moses acts like a man in all the confusion. I asked at the table tonight who was going to cry. Moses replied, 'I no cry.' They are now locked in sleep."

Three days later, Juliette lamented to her mother:

"We have been in the habit of having everything so very quiet that I have felt as if I could not endure it. Oh, my dear Mother, it is more than I feel as if my weak nerves could undertake to bring up in a proper manner these headstrong princes! I have been thinking it over tonight till it seems as if my heart would burst." And in another letter shortly afterward: "I am exceedingly fatigued having had more than usual to do today. We have been killing a hog, and as natives have no idea of economy or of our way of preserving all parts, I have to attend to such things myself. This, with being a mother to so many children [eight scholars, plus one of her own], attending to calls of strangers and friends, all of it makes me feel rather old. To rest me I have just seated myself and read your two last letters. I wish you could know how much good it has done me, and how much I wish you were here. A young mother needs some old experienced grandma close by."

And a week later: "How we succeed in managing our unruly ones [now increased to eleven scholars], I do not know, but I assure you I feel some like the 'old woman who lived in a shoe and had so many children she did not know what to do.' All the gold of the Indies would not compensate for the loss of all the quiet hours of one's life. But we are not to live for ourselves or for our own happiness. I am obliged to keep this constantly in mind, lest I sink under the accumulating load."

Again in another letter, shortly after she had recovered from a brief illness: "But they need a mother with firmer health, stronger nerves, more skill and more everything . . . . We are obliged to discipline them, sometimes by shutting them up in a room by themselves, sometimes by inflicting pain. If we act judiciously, we do not apprehend [anticipate] any difficulty with their parents."

Juliette missed chilly New England. She wrote: "We frail, frail beings. If only we could find a good cold winter to brace us up . . . . You asked what you shall send me. I would thank you for a snowball."

Amos and Juliette had brought to their assignment the utmost sense of public duty, piety, and deep sincerity. In practice they acted as father and mother, as well as instructors, to their pupils.

The Cookes quickly learned that children of royalty were basically just plain children. Amos noted: "This morning just before school, the children were playing in their yard, and some of them threw dirt into Mrs. Dowsett's yard and some went into the house and some struck her and fell into some bread she was making for breakfast."

And the kahus were no help at all. They kept the young scholars in a turmoil of fear and nightmares by telling them ghost stories.

Juliette wrote: "We have thirteen children in our family [two were her own] and brought up in such a way that you will judge that we have a great many difficulties to settle. It is teaching, endeavoring to correct, to fix principles of right and wrong, etc., from dawn until evening. People who say, do you have only so many, I would beg to undertake the task one day. Six of our family are under six years of age, and I wish they all were. I think we should have more rational hope of success."

The royal pupils had more than their share of bumps and bruises: "At noon, Alexander [six] fell into the well, now digging. It is a wonder he was not hurt . . . . William [five] fell and bruised his head so that a bunch [bump] was made nearly as large as an egg."

Broken bones were frequent in falls while horseback riding. With the horses, it was always something. Juliette wrote: "We had a sad fright this afternoon. A horse . . . proved too high spirited for his rider [William Lunalilo, later to become King Lunalilo] and ran half a mile with him . . . . The boy was only six years old but he acted like a man. He held the reins as tight as he could [and] did not cry . . . . We all felt grateful to God for his preservation. We expected to see him brought home with broken bones."

His ability to educate the royal youngsters was of major concern to Amos:

"Yesterday and today read a hundred pages in Abbott's 'How to do Good' respecting children . . . . O! to be better qualified in my work, and to sustain the responsible task assigned to us in training these children!"

Six months after the children had been living at the school, the older boys began to develop their personalities: "Moses [eleven] and Lot [nine] were bad, and we gave them no supper." And a few weeks later: "Moses was guilty this afternoon of very improper conduct, and I sent him from the school room to his own."

Later the girls showed that they too could misbehave: "They— Moses, Lot, Alexander, Jane and Abigail—have been guilty of improper conduct . . . . O Lord make me faithful.''

Added to the young schoolteachers' trials and tribulations was the task of tending to the youngsters' invariable illnesses:

"One of the children [Victoria, age two] has been attacked with the chicken pox, and I suppose it will have to go through the family.''

Yet the Cookes were making significant progress with the education of their students. Gradually they advanced their charges through reading, writing, and arithmetic to Parley's history, Olney's geography, Smith's grammar, and, as a reward for work well done, the Rollo books.

On January 1, 1841, Juliette invited Moses and Lot to write brief notes to accompany a letter to her sister.

Moses wrote: "Mrs. Cooke says I may write a little in her letter to you, and I think I will wish you a Happy New Year, for she has been telling us that such is the custom in her country on the first of January. I know but little English, but I hope to know more by and by. I wish very much to see what my teachers tell me about snow, riding in sleighs, and many other things.''

From Lot came this: "I suppose my teachers have told you about their school and scholars. We are happy that we have a school to attend. It gives us great pleasure to have Mr. Cooke say to Mrs. Cooke that we have studied hard today, and it makes her very happy, too. I do not think lazy boys are happy.''

In addition to classroom teaching, Brother Cooke supervised considerable outdoor activity, such as sailing, swimming, kite-flying, hiking, and horseback riding.

The school was financed by the chiefs, but it seemed to be a case of feast or famine, depending on how regularly the royal parents remembered to send provisions or money. A year after the school opened, Juliette wrote home, "I will tell you what we will have for dinner. For meat we have fried fresh pork, for vegetables boiled kalo [taro] and sweet potatoes. Then we have a dessert of boiled rice. A pretty good dinner, we think. Each child also has at his place a bowl of poi.''

However, several months earlier, Amos had noted, "Today Alexander is seven years old. We did not succeed in having much of a dinner on the occasion; indeed, I had nothing but poi and fish.''

Later, Queen Liliuokalani, looking back on her life in the school (where she was known as Lydia), commented, "When I recall the instances in which we were sent hungry to bed, it seems to me that they failed to remember that we were growing children. A thick slice of bread covered with molasses was usually the sole article of our supper.''

Amos was also concerned for the morals of his young pupils: "Called on Bro. Armstrong and had some talk about . . . how we should get along in reference to keeping our boys and girls separate. He advised having locks on the doors.''

In his first annual report to the Mission on the Chiefs' Children's School, Amos stated: "The general good health among our scholars has greatly contributed to our school in making it popular with the parents. We have taken special pains to preserve health, knowing that much depended upon it . . . . When they [the children] first came, they were anxious to be eating between meals, but we discouraged it by giving them only some cold kalo or potato. They found soon that their meals were sure at a given time and ceased to ask for anything between meals, except occasionally for some sugar cane [to chew on] . . . ."

Regarding governing the school, he wrote, "This has been a kind of patriarchal one. We have acted the part of a father and law giver and judge, and the children have been more ready to yield to our authority than we had any reason to expect, considering they hardly knew what it was to be governed. All things considered, they have been remarkably docile in learning the importance of obedience and the propriety of submitting all their difficulties to our decision. When we thought the case demanded it, we have not hesitated to use the rod, taking them alone and conversing with them awhile before we applied it, and the result has generally been a happy one . . . . In conclusion, allow us to say we are tired *in* the work but not *of* it. Tho our number has been small, we have endeavored to benefit them the more.''

Despite his strict puritanical beliefs about raising and educating children and about life in general, Amos occasionally revealed a warm spot in his personality: "This has been David's birthday [David Kalakaua]. He is today 5 years old. By referring to my diary, I find that five years ago today, I was on my way from Plymouth to Springfield to see Miss Montague.''

For Juliette, life frequently seemed to be just work, work, work: "The children get thoroughly dressed in dirt by noon. It is no small thing to keep fourteen children [the scholars] looking decent. I have domestics, but I can place no dependence upon them. They are sick or lazy or want higher wages . . . . We have to act the part of a parent, and of a child, of teachers and scholars, advocate and judge, chastizing at one time and comforting at another, giving food to the hungry and medicine to the sick . . . .''

In early 1842, Amos was still perplexed by the magnitude of the task at hand: "Oh! for wisdom from above. Ever since we commenced our school, we have felt as if we were treading on eggs.''

School outings were frequent but could occasionally turn into agonizing tests of endurance for the Cookes. In the spring of 1842, they and the royal students were invited by King Kamehameha III and his chiefs for a visit to Lahaina, then the capital of the kingdom. As Juliette described it, the trip was anything but a pleasure cruise:

"We had a pretty brisk wind, and, of course, all were very sick. I know of nothing so like to what I think one must feel when near to death as that dreadful faintness caused by seasickness. I had a horrid time of it . . . . First I took one of the berths . . . but the air was intolerable. The place was too small, the cockroaches made a road of me, it was intolerably hot, it seemed like being laid in a coffin. I staid there the first night, and then rolled out upon the floor. There found better air, but was exposed to view a little too much . . . . Mr. Cooke was so sick as not to be able to render the least assistance."

While in Lahaina, Juliette added: "Today it has been raining. The children have made me almost crazy, and the red mud has been carried from garret to cellar."

At last, a month later, she confided: "Find myself in Honolulu again in my own home. It never looked as pleasant before, but it brings its redoubled cares . . . . There are sixteen children in all, four under four years of age."

In November, Juliette's spirits were brighter: "I felt very bad about undertaking this work [the school], there seemed so little chance of success. Almost everybody prophesized failure. It seemed a difficult business but we now have some hope of success."

However, a week later, Amos noted in his journal: "Heard today that Moses [thirteen] feigned himself mad yesterday and scared all the 'kahus.' Reproved him for it. I find Moses very much inclined to purloin and to answer back. I am disposed to correct it in him."

And a month later: "Last night after we had retired, John [John Ii, royal 'kahu' for the school and invaluable assistant to the Cookes] came to us saying that Moses had made an attempt to go into ———'s room [one of the girls] . . . . J [Juliette] conversed with [the girl], and I with Moses. He was rather sulky, but by and by, I conversed with him freely and warned him of his danger."

Despite the apparent setbacks, progress was being made, and at the end of the third year, Amos recorded: "Find our scholars have done nobly during the year just elapsed."

A year later, in May 1844, a fellow missionary commented on a visit to the school by Kamehameha III, "The King, on surveying the happy group and noticing their improvement, remarked: 'Wished my lot had been like yours. I deeply regret the foolish manner in which I spent my years.' And, I would venture to add, that the King has more reason to be proud of his chiefs' school than of anything within his dominion."

The American Board in Boston added its commentary: "We are very glad to receive so full an account of the interesting school under your care, and to hear of the progress of those in knowledge and sound moral discipline who are to be the future magistrates and rulers among their people. It is highly creditable to the chiefs that they can see the advantages of subjecting their children to such a course; and it holds out a promise of good in regard to the people, that such preparations are making to supply them with intelligent and upright rulers for the next generation.

"May all that the chiefs or the Mission anticipate from this school be more than realized, and may yourself and wife be richly compensated for all the care, responsibility and labor which it brings on."

Conducting a school for children of royalty seldom left the Cookes with any privacy. When the king and his court came to Honolulu for a week of festivities, the Cookes decided on one of the days to stay home and get some peace and quiet—but it was not to be: "Friday evening as we were about retiring, his majesty and suite called on us, accompanied by martial music. The parlor and court were filled. They said their object was to hear the piano, so the children played and sang, 'Sparkling and Bright,' and several other tunes. We passed cake, pie, grapes, figs, etc., such as we happened to have on hand, and no one would have supposed that they had just come from a feast . . . . The queen is a very pleasant woman, and were it not that she is about as large as a barrel, she would be quite pretty. The children said she completely filled two chairs!!''

As the children grew older, the need for discipline naturally increased. But Amos was sensitive about its proper application: "This morning Dr. Judd called . . . . He took that opportunity to tell Mrs. C. that he thought we were governing too much now-a-days by force. After he was gone, Juliette told me, and I have felt very bad about it ever since. This afternoon John Ii accompanied the children, and I stayed at home. I could not eat any dinner. Have read 150 pages in 'How Shall I Govern My School.' ''

Shortly afterward, he added: "This evening I feel like giving up the ship. The children are disaffected, and I have reason to fear the parents are also, and why should I sacrifice my life, and my wife's and our children's eternal good for those who have no heart to improve by it."

But Juliette had come to see the brighter side: "We are still toiling away according to the best of our abilities for the good of our youthful charges. They are pursuing their studies and pleasures with all the happiness common to children . . . . They all have a decided taste for music. Several play on the accordion and piano; all sing. They very often assemble together and imitate a band. We encourage their finding amusement in music as it prevents idleness and gives a taste for rational pleasures.''

Maintaining the school's rigid discipline on the older boys proved trying at times. In mid-1845, Amos recorded: "Last night about 2 o'clock Sarai [wife of John Ii] awoke us, saying some of the boys were gone. Sure enough, Moses [sixteen], Lot [fourteen] and Alexander [eleven] were gone. I sent John Ii to look for them. They very soon returned . . . . After breakfast we talked to each of the culprits separately, and found that Moses had been out many times to go for wine, and that they drink it frequently.''

And a month later: "Last Thursday morning I heard bad reports of our children being out again at night. I made some inquiries and found it too true . . . . I made preparations to lock them up, each in his room. That night we had native watchmen on duty.''

But despite the many problems, the students were getting an education—and a fine one indeed. A composition written by Alexander was later described as being "remarkable for its diction and penmanship. Alexander, at this time, was eleven years old. When he had entered the school five years earlier, he read but words of one syllable.'' In 1846, a visiting naval captain from Denmark elaborated:

> Mr. Douglass, the head teacher [the Cookes now had some assistance], commenced such an examination of knowledge that I listened in astonishment of the learning that these children had acquired. They were only children as far as age was concerned. Moses was a boy of seventeen or eighteen years. Miss Bernice, pretty and more bright in her complexion than the other ones, was fifteen years old and was absolutely full grown; Jane Loeau, a daughter of Liliha, who was a heathen to her death, was older than the others.
>
> They were especially trained in the English language, grammar, reading aloud and declamation, mental arithmetic, exchange and commercial arithmetic, in geography, geometry, astronomy, etc. Mathematics seemed to be the main subject, and the young princes understood as well as the most clever business man how to write and endorse a bill of exchange . . . .
>
> They also entertained us with one of their teetotalistic drinking songs, praising the Lord and beginning with these words: "Nothing is so good for the youthful blood as clear sparkling water. . . ." I could not help but ask Prince Moses . . . when we were alone, if he did not prefer to sing "Sparkling champagne." And he confessed

quite frankly that I was right, but asked me for Heaven's Sake, not to speak about it. I hope that this indiscretion, that I make here, will not bring the good Moses into any disrepute . . . .

It is to be regretted that the school is under the special direction of the missionaries and in this way got a special puritanical colour, but that should not be considered when examining critically this enterprise, for the reason of its great usefulness. It would certainly do the young men no harm that they are brought up as "teetotalists." However little I approve of such absolute physical measures for the irradication of moral errors, I am convinced that here, if anywhere in the world, it is the right thing in the right place.

In January 1847, the Cookes lost the first of their royal students— Moses, who was finally expelled by order of the Royal Privy Council for his repeated misdeeds of drinking and carousing at night. Shortly afterward, two of the older girls left. Meanwhile, Lot, Alexander, and William had progressed to bookkeeping, trigonometry, survey, natural philosophy, Euclid, and chemistry. Amos boasted a bit in a letter to Mother Montague in late 1847: "We think our school would not suffer in comparison with some schools we were acquainted with while in the States."

In the fall of 1848, Juliette repeated a frequent lament to her mother: "I feel very much worn by fatigue and anxiety. . . . Our children are all down with whooping cough and measles, and our scholars, too."

The measles and whooping cough epidemic killed thousands of native Hawaiians, including Prince Moses, the Cookes' former pupil. "All the carpenters are constantly employed in making coffins," Juliette wrote. But although the royal scholars were ill, they all survived.

Later Juliette wrote: "I do not think that we shall stay in the school more than a year longer. As our scholars grow up, we find it more difficult to restrain them . . . . I tremble to see them enter on the stage of action with uncircumcised hearts. But they seem hardened on religious subjects. They are more like New England hardened sailors than like Hawaiians."

At the end of 1848, Lot [eighteen] and Alexander [fourteen] graduated from the Royal School to go to work as bookkeepers. Before they departed, Amos offered some fatherly advice, albeit the New England puritanical type:

Before retiring, I had an opportunity to testify to Alexander our great anxiety about him and Lot, our great disappointment of

Moses, and that if he and Lot turned out as Moses did, Mrs. C. and I would give up the school and return to the States, and that I did not believe there would be a native King after the present one unless he or Lot were prepared for it . . . that a ship all sail and no ballast would soon be on her beam's end, that they should seek wholesome advice and friendship.

I also said that few princes would have submitted to teachers as they had, and stated that if my discipline had seemed too severe, I was sorry. I said that he and Lot ought to keep a journal, and finally besought them to attend to religion now.

In early 1849, Amos wrote:

Juliette has been baking all the morning and turned out twelve loaves of bread, twelve squash and mince pies, three ginger cakes, two puddings, besides the turkey.

But she is beginning to feel as if she would like to be released from so many cares, especially as the result of them in our scholars is not so encouraging as formerly, and she cannot do so much for her own children [four by then] as duty requires . . . .

The probability is that we shall be released from our labors the coming spring. Most of the scholars . . . will, by that time, have gone out. There are no other children of the chiefs, the only two remaining having died during the epidemic.

Later he added:

We continue to reside [at the school] with them principally for Bernice's sake. She is very anxious to have us remain till she can have a home of her own, and as we have brought her along so far, we cannot bear to leave her till she is lodged in safer hands than those of her own parents, who are kind enough, but who are ignorant of what civilization consists, and wish their daughter to be great in their way. Pray for the poor girl!

As 1849 WORE ON, Princess Bernice Pauahi became the Cookes' only remaining royal pupil. And she had become engaged—to a *haole* commoner, Charles Reed Bishop, who had arrived from the States some two years earlier. He had recently been named collector general of customs.

The romance was conducted in the Cookes' parlor, and Amos and Juliette soon found themselves embroiled in a year-long confrontation with Bernice's parents, Chief Paki and his wife, Konia, both of the Kamehameha line. They were tolerant of the affair at first but later became bitterly opposed. Before long, the governor of Oahu, the rest of the chiefs, the missionaries, and seemingly half the population—foreign as well as native—were involved in a debate on the issue.

Governor Kekuanaoa told Bernice she must quit seeing Bishop and marry within the royal family. He ordered her to marry his son, Prince Lot.

"I do not like Lot and I won't stop seeing Mr. Bishop," Bernice replied. Amos recorded progress of the romance:

> This afternoon Bernice wrote a letter to Lot requesting that he come to see her. She told him of the wishes of her parents and said she would marry him, in accordance with their commands, but she knew it would make her unhappy, for he did not love her and she did not love him.
>
> After this she wrote the governor and her parents and said that, if they wished her buried in a coffin, she would submit to their authority. That she would as soon they buried her as promise to marry Lot. The governor replied to it, saying she was deceiving herself.
>
> Lot, seeing the letter to the governor, wrote that he exonerated her from all her promises in her youth, that he would not be the means of rendering her unhappy, that he knew he was unworthy of her.

But her parents still objected. Amos wrote, "She has not gone out today, so she commenced reading Hannah More's Life to Mrs. Cooke, who is ill . . . . She has read much for Mrs. Cooke 'and well I may,' she says, 'for all I am—and hope to be—I owe to Mrs. Cooke.' "

Finally, in May, the young couple decided to get married right away. Cooke went to Bernice's parents to invite them to the wedding.

"What wedding?" they growled and once again lectured him for letting Bishop get so close to their daughter.

Bernice was sad when she learned her family would not be present at the wedding. But undaunted, the eighteen-year-old princess, wearing a gown of white muslin and a wreath of jasmine, wed Charles Reed Bishop on June 4, 1850.

Amos's journal noted the event succinctly: "At 8 o'clock Mr. Bishop was on the spot, and Bro. Armstrong married them, no stranger being present but the parson and his wife. After the ceremony, we sat down to tea, and at 9 o'clock they went in a wagon to Judge Andrews' where they are to board.''

(Bishop went on to become Hawaii's pioneer banker. On August 17, 1858, he founded the Bank of Bishop, now the First Hawaiian Bank. Bernice, as a direct descendant of Kamehameha I, later inherited extensive property, equal to 9 percent of all the land in the islands. She died of cancer in 1884. In her will, she left her vast real estate holdings in a trust—the Bishop Estate—with instructions that the proceeds from her property were to support the Kamehameha Schools for Hawaiian Children, which she had founded. These handsome schools still operate today, supported by the proceeds from the property managed by the Bishop Estate.)

Two days after Bernice's marriage to Bishop, the Cookes left the Royal School. With the aid of a yoke of oxen, a cart, and four men, they moved their possessions to Mr. Bingham's place, Hawaii's first frame house, built in 1821.

Although they had taught for ten years, they felt no great satisfaction about what they had accomplished. ''During those ten years, we did twenty years work,'' Amos observed. ''The good actually done is not so apparent as we could have wished. There is much to regret . . . but if we had to do it over again, we very much doubt whether we could do it better.''

Chapter 3

Hard Times

WHEN SAMUEL CASTLE WAS ASSIGNED to the Mission Depository in 1837, his boss was Levi Chamberlain, an old-timer within the ranks of the gospel pioneers. He had been in Hawaii since 1823, three years after the arrival of the *Thaddeus*.

Chamberlain's task was ordering, unloading, and distributing the supplies that mission families needed—supplies that had to be brought thousands of miles. Because ships came and went with uncertainty, orders were compiled two years in advance.

Logistics could be exasperating. Sea travel often ruined cargoes, and the usually soft-spoken brothers and sisters didn't hesitate to raise their voices to scold the secular brothers at the depository:

"The flour was horrible—a mass of life—sour and musty. If you get any new, send another barrel, but don't send any more of this."

"You did not send the saleratus [baking soda], and Wife calls for it."

"The large bundle of books was nearly all spoiled. They appear to have lain in water and mud a considerable time and are quite wet and mouldy."

"I find myself forced to return the 2½ yards of cloth which you have sent . . . . By no contrivance of ours can a pair of pants for myself be got out of it."

These were the details and complaints that became Castle's daily routine. He was, in fact, shouldering a large part of the responsibility for the entire depository operation, as Levi Chamberlain was ailing with tuberculosis.

Castle quickly came to know most of his fellow missionaries, through personal contact and the large correspondence that saddled him. And almost as quickly, he became the center of continuing controversy among the missionaries. It often seemed to Castle that his "customers" were more emotional than practical and more suspicious than understanding of his efforts on their behalf.

During the first six months on the job, Castle spent hundreds of hours catching up on correspondence and bookkeeping, for Chamberlain had managed to keep abreast of only the most urgent business. Castle would get to work at four in the morning, and his day often didn't end until late at night. He kept innumerable records in a round, legible script, and his letter-writing to both the Board in Boston and the Hawaii missionaries was prolific. He also unloaded and checked all shipments as they arrived and was usually surrounded by preachers and their wives who gathered promptly to witness opening of boxes and barrels. Each was intent on getting what he wanted before the needs of brethren at outlying stations were met.

Brother and Sister Castle once grew so weary of these pressures that they decided to visit the neighboring islands in an effort to get some rest. The trip also offered an opportunity to understand better the problems of missionaries at outer stations.

One of those encountered was Titus Coan of Hilo, an ardent revivalist who, during 1837 and 1838, baptized 7,500 souls. His meetings were so full of hell-fire that the sobbing and shouting in the congregation often built to tremendous peaks, and small children, frightened by the tumult, had to be carried from the assemblage. Castle had reservations about many of Coan's "instant religion" techniques but nevertheless held great admiration for his zeal.

Missionaries at other stations also had qualities that displeased him, especially those who were extremely narrow-minded. Once, for example, he booked passage for himself and his wife on a schooner from Lahaina, knowing they'd reach Honolulu on a Sunday. Otherwise, they might have had to wait weeks for another ship. It was a decision for which he was soundly condemned. One Lahaina missionary asked, "Does it not seem a clear and perceptible violation of God's rights? Do, Brother, write me a full and explicit recantation of all you tried to say in favor of starting from Lahaina when there was a moral certainty that you would occupy a part of God's day. We shall all rejoice to see your names to such a paper."

Although the Castles did not recant, they managed somehow to retain the respect of even the zealots.

Brother Castle, who continued to spend many hours as corresponding secretary for the entire missionary group, frequently called on Brother Cooke for help with the depository's ledgers. Castle had high regard for Cooke's skill with figures.

Early in 1840, Cooke wrote in his journal, "Yesterday and today I was at work all day on the books . . . . Have probably saved Mr. Castle a week's time. He pressed me to leave my school and come into the depository. I told him I should leave no post until they removed it, for then I could be censured by them."

Castle was a man to get involved in the affairs of his community, and his voice was heard on many subjects. He thought the islands should become self-supporting as soon as possible. When Ladd & Company was pioneering Hawaii's first sugar plantation on Kauai in the late 1830s, he wrote arguing in favor of the project, "It will promote industry among the people, because it makes the income of each individual to depend solely upon his perseverance and also to develop the pecuniary resources of the country."

Castle also became one of the founders of Honolulu's Punahou School, the first preparatory school west of the Rockies. One of the nightmares of the missionaries was that while they were carrying the gospel to the heathen Hawaiians, the native children were carrying the "Hawaiian gospel" about life to the missionaries' offspring. Many missionaries threatened to abandon their posts and return to New England in order to rear their children in a more rigid atmosphere. The solution was Punahou School, made possible from the sale of land given to the Reverend Hiram Bingham by the Hawaiian king. The school opened in 1841 with fifteen students, all of them children of the missionaries. Later it opened its door to nonmissionary children and became one of the outstanding private schools in Hawaii.

Brother Castle served as treasurer and trustee of Punahou for forty years. "So carefully had he watched over the funds of the institution," says the one hundredth anniversary history of Punahou, "that not a dollar had ever been lost by unwise investment at the Islands."

BY NOW THE CASTLES occupied their own home. Angeline described it as "a good house" made of coral blocks and with a shaded yard. But the Castles had lived long enough with the Chamberlains to expose Angeline to Levi's tuberculosis. Now she, too, was ailing.

Despite her illness she opened a small school for girls but was forced to quit after their daughter, Mary, was born. Later she tried living in several different locales, hoping the change of climate would help. For a while she lived in Honolulu's damp Manoa Valley; then she moved to Ewa, which is extremely dry. But nothing helped.

The Castles' marriage of convenience had become one of devotion. A letter to "My Dear Companion," written by Samuel to Angeline when she was living in Ewa, expressed great tenderness: ". . . I came in at the time of supper and no wife to welcome me with a smile . . . . No companion to share my bed, no precious little daughter to take from the cradle into my arms and carry upstairs—I should learn by deprivation more fully to appreciate the inestimable blessing of an affectionate wife and innocent babe—although my heart may be and I fear now is more wedded to them than to my Savior."

Angeline's health continued to decline, and the islands' missionaries sought to buoy her spirits with "happy" letters about the afterlife she was going to find. "I can weep and rejoice with Sister Castle in the ineffable glories before her," Titus Coan wrote from Hilo. "Hers is an enviable lot. But the Husband! The Child! 'Tis the survivor dies!"

By now a complete invalid, she asked to be carried outside one day to get some fresh air and to look across the water. She whispered to her husband, "Those clouds look like land beyond the water."

Angeline died on the morning of March 5, 1841, and was buried the next day in the small mission cemetery. The United States consulate flew the flag at half-staff, and the people of the church colony mourned. Angeline's life in Hawaii had spanned but four years.

ALTHOUGH SPINSTERS were regarded as safe moral risks, single men were not tolerated in the mission. Castle sought permission to return to New England to seek a new "companion." With his three-year-old daughter, Mary, Castle sailed December 2, 1841, on the *William Gray,* a slow and leaky packet that encountered storms, ran low on food, and barely escaped wrecking on a rocky shore. The miserable voyage ended in Salem, Massachusetts, on April 19, 1842.

Leaving his daughter at the Tenney home in West Exeter, New York, Castle embarked on a six-thousand-mile trip around the United States to make personal reports to relatives about their missionary kin in the Pacific. Not until he had completed what he felt to be his solemn missionary duty did he begin to look for a new "companion."

On her deathbed, Angeline Tenney Castle had talked dispassionately to her husband about another companion to carry on in her place. Castle had asked if Angeline's sister Mary would make a suitable wife. Angeline replied, "Yes, if she is a Christian." Castle talked everything over with the Tenney family before writing to Mary in Oberlin to ask if she'd accompany him back to Hawaii. Mary was receptive. "I regard your proposal as a chart brought to me by the hand of God," she replied, and accepted on the spot.

But the couple had to wait many weeks while the American Board decided whether to approve Mary Tenney, who was recognized as a devout and pious Christian but admitted occasional doubts about details of the dogmatic Calvinistic doctrine. The delay dragged on so long that Castle decided to remain in America if the Board failed to approve his fiancée. The Board finally gave approval, and the couple was married on October 13, 1842, nineteen months after Angeline's death.

They honeymooned in Boston, and Castle took time to give the Mission Board a refresher course on conditions in the Sandwich Isles. On November 7 they sailed for Hawaii on the bark *Behring*. The Castle household would, henceforth, have two Marys.

WHEN THE *Behring* REACHED Honolulu four and a half months later, Castle and the other passengers were shocked: a British flag was flying over the town. Lord George Paulet, commander of the British warship *Carysfort*, had at the instigation of the local British consul seized the Sandwich Islands in the name of "Her Britannic Majesty," ostensibly to protect British subjects.

Some four years earlier, in 1839, the French had briefly held Honolulu under the pretext of remedying injustices resulting from the Hawaiian monarchy's refusal to accept Catholic priests as missionaries, and a French warship had extracted a bond of $20,000 from Kamehameha III as a guarantee against future "injustices."

Now the British apparently had taken over the tiny kingdom in the middle of the Pacific. Again the action, following investigation, appeared to have been based on alleged injustices against British residents, according to the local British consul.

It turned out that the primary motivation for the appearance of Lord Paulet was to thwart renewed French attempts to annex the islands. But Paulet had gone beyond the instructions given him by his superior, Admiral Richard Thomas, chief of the British Pacific fleet. Not only had Paulet raised the British flag, he had bypassed his superior and sent word directly to London seeking approval for his action. When Admiral Thomas heard of this, he sailed to Hawaii and shortly after his arrival ordered the British flag lowered and apologized to the Hawaiian kingdom.

The events involving both the French and British attempts to establish their sovereignty over Hawaii were described in detail in a letter written by Castle in 1883, forty years later. (The letter was intended to support continuation of the Reciprocity Treaty of 1876. It wound up as testimony in the U.S. Congress in 1894 in support of Hawaiian annexation to the United States.)

Castle's letter gives an insight into his reasons for supporting annexation at various times during that forty-year period:

I have deemed the aggressions made by both the British and French in former times to enforce demands having in my opinion but little foundation in justice, as part of a system of encroachment, having for its ultimate object the appropriation or possession of these Islands.

Indeed, it has been stated to me that the French consul said that had they, the French, supposed that the [Hawaiian] Government could have raised the $20,000 demanded, [the French naval captain] would have placed the sum so high that it could not have been raised, and he would have taken possession . . . .

In the case of the British, Castle pointed out, the main reason Admiral Thomas had ordered the return of the islands to the Hawaiian monarchy was his irritation with his subordinate, Lord Paulet, for not having gone through proper channels—that is, through the Admiral instead of directly to London:

My belief that the flag would not have been restored but for this informality rests partly on the past practice of the British, and the statement made to me by Mr. Richards [the Reverend William Richards, one of the King's advisers, who had been sent by Kamehameha III to England to resolve the problem] that the Earl of Aberdeen, the Foreign Secretary, or Mr. Addington, the Under-Secretary, told him that if Admiral Thomas had not restored the flag, the British Government would not have done so . . . .

The United States had already recognized the independence of Hawaii, the first of the major nations of the world to do so. This was done in a presidential message to Congress on December 31, 1842. Thus, the Hawaiian mission to France and Great Britain was able to secure a treaty, signed by both powers on November 28, 1843, in which they agreed to recognize Hawaii as an independent nation and, according to Castle's own words, "never to take possession, neither directly or under the title of protectorate, nor under any other form, of any part of the territory of which they are composed."

By 1849 the French finally got around to returning the $20,000 bond extracted from the Hawaiian kingdom ten years earlier. Even then, however, the French warship returning the bond sought to make trouble at the instigation of the French consul. Considerable damage was done to Hawaiian property, and the French even ordered the governor of Oahu to pull down the Hawaiian flag. But he refused to do so. As Castle recorded, "They [the French] did not do it themselves [remove the Hawaiian flag] out of respect to the treaty of November 28, 1843." They may also have been moved to prudence by the fact that an American warship was anchored in the harbor as a potential witness to the deed.

Following the departure of the British in 1843, Kamehameha III asked Castle to sit on a special board appointed to settle the claims arising from the incident. The appointment marked the start of Castle's many years of service as an adviser to the monarchy—informally at first, then in later years on an official basis.

His appointment to the Claims Board produced criticism within the missionary community, however. The critics pointed out that such service was absolutely improper for Castle in view of a ruling by the American Board in Boston that missionaries should not engage in any manner whatsoever in politics or government. Because of this, Castle for years refused any official position with the government, although he gave freely of his time and advice when asked.

A few years later, Castle was again criticized by many of the missionaries, because of his advice to the king that Hawaii be placed under the protection of the United States, a petition that was rejected by Washington. It was his belief that the kingdom was too weak to resist what to him appeared to be repeated attempts by the French and British to annex the islands—as those powers were doing elsewhere throughout the Pacific. But Castle's missionary critics were not as farsighted.

In 1850, following the second French incident, Kamehameha III dispatched Dr. Gerritt P. Judd, one of his advisers, to Paris to straighten out the diplomatic snarl. It was decided to send Prince Alexander and Prince Lot along as well to acquire some international polish. In Europe the princes were extended every courtesy because of their rank. They were momentary social lions, entertained constantly, and even found time to study French and fencing. Europeans were surprised that they spoke such good English (thanks to the Cookes).

One woman asked, "And where did they acquire their court manners?"

"We have a little court of our own," Dr. Judd told her.

Continuing his reforms, Kamehameha III recognized the need to establish more workable and democratic laws, especially those affecting the ever-increasing numbers of foreigners.

In 1848 a council composed of the King and the chiefs, together with their foreign advisers, announced what is now called the Great Mahele, a distribution of the king's lands on a democratic basis. Prior to this action, the king had sole right to the ownership of all the lands in Hawaii; the chiefs held land in fief as retainers of the king. The Great Mahele permitted the common class within the Hawaiian population to own land for the first time. It also permitted foreigners who had been residents to take title to lands previously granted by royal dictate. In 1850 all foreigners, including newcomers, were given the right to purchase land in the islands.

Because of certain details of these new laws, the American commissioner in Hawaii became involved in a controversy with the king, who finally demanded his removal. Castle was urged as his replacement. However, the American Board in Boston, continuing its rigid policy of noninvolvement by missionaries in government, refused to grant permission to Castle, and another applicant was chosen instead. The king then urged Castle to become his collector of customs and serve as his representative on land problems. In deference to Boston and his fellow missionaries, however, Castle declined the invitation.

EVER SINCE HIS RETURN from Boston in 1843, Castle had found himself again working long hours at the depository, as Levi Chamberlain, his superior, was by now totally incapacitated by tuberculosis. One of Castle's duties was to make inspection trips to the mission posts on the neighboring islands. On one trip in 1847, he took along his wife, Mary, to share the escape. They traveled to Lahaina and on to Kohala on inter-island sailing vessels so crowded with seasick Hawaiians that it was impossible to sit down. Adding to the congestion were the pigs, dogs, chickens, and other family possessions that the Hawaiians invariably took along on such trips.

Reaching Kohala, at the northern end of the island of Hawaii (called the "Big Island"), the Castles walked overland to the rugged Hamakua Coast, covering twelve to fifteen miles a day. From Laupahoehoe they took an outrigger canoe, traveling by night to Hilo, where they mounted horses for a trip to the volcano crater at Kilauea.

Castle visited missions along the way, glad to use the opportunity to measure the work of the brethren. The missionaries, for their part, enjoyed the opportunity to become better acquainted with Brother Castle, who more and more was becoming their link with the American Board. Mission members needed a practical, no-nonsense advocate, and Castle was to be their champion.

This he soon became when the Board arbitrarily cut the salaries of missionaries in Hawaii to $500 a year, while those in Ceylon received $666 and others in China were paid $1,000. He protested, with dignity yet forcefulness—albeit in vain. Some missionaries meekly accepted these pay cuts and remained at their stations. Others resigned in frustration. Still others engaged in some form of "moonlighting." The Cookes, for instance, took in boarders.

To add to the missionaries' economic woes, prices in Hawaii were high—pushed up by the pressures of California's gold rush. Castle lamented in a letter to a friend in 1850, "You will like to know how we live in these times. Well, I will tell you something of how we live—or, rather, how we don't. We have not bought a bunch of bananas in many months . . . . Much of the time we have neither Irish nor sweet potatoes . . . . Almost every species of fruit is beyond our means."

The Castles occupied the same house Samuel had shared with Angeline in 1840. There were some changes, mainly a gradual increase in the number of rooms to meet the needs of a growing family. They eventually had ten children, plus Mary from his first marriage. Fidelia Coan, wife of the Hilo missionary, once wrote to Mrs. Castle, "I must thank you, too, for your hospitality to my dear husband, when lately in Honolulu. It must be quite a convenience to the visiting public to have one family in Honolulu so large that an addition of one more don't make any noticeable difference!"

The house was so crowded that younger children slept in a trundle bed in their parents' sleeping quarters. For bathing, there was a tiny outhouse containing an oil cask into which water for the bath was pumped from a shallow well. For many years, water for all purposes was obtained from this well and from one in the cellar. Water was so scarce that bath water was drained through a trough to the gardens.

But the hard-pressed missionaries had not yet seen the worst. In January 1849 news arrived from Boston that the American Board had decreed that henceforth the Hawaiian mission should get along without any financial help whatsoever. Become self-supporting, the Board said, or come home and be disbanded. Obviously the missionaries, some of whom had been on the scene more than twenty-eight years, would have to find new ways to earn a living.

Cooke wrote to relatives in Connecticut, "The propositions are . . . to allow us to possess property, and get a part of our support, and finally the whole from the natives or our resources." A humble man, not given to overestimating his ability, he urged his kin, "Pray for me! I love to preach, but, you know, my talents are limited. I left a mercantile life to prepare to preach, and shall I now leave the prospect of preaching to return to my former work?"

As Levi Chamberlain's health continued to fail, Castle had been urging Cooke to join him at the mission supply base. By now—it was 1849—Cooke's duties at the Royal School had diminished considerably, and he searched his soul for guidance. Should he join Castle at storekeeping or return home to America? There was only scorn waiting in New England for men who had gone abroad to till the Lord's vineyard and came back while still in their prime of life.

At that point Edwin O. Hall, an assistant at the depository, resigned to become editor of the *Weekly Polynesian*. This helped Cooke reach a decision. He recorded in his journal in May, "The question, Who should occupy his [Hall's] place in the Depository was agitated, and by an unanimous vote [of the missionaries in general meeting], I was invited to take it." But for a time he continued his duties at the Royal School.

After Levi Chamberlain died on July 29, 1849, Castle came up with an idea for earning a livelihood. Discussing it with Cooke, he pointed out that the depository's future was uncertain because of Boston's decision. How about forming a partnership—Castle & Cooke—to take over operation of the storehouse as a private enterprise? Under such an arrangement they could supply the mission posts at cost and still make a profit from trading with the community at large.

Why not? According to W. R. Castle, Jr., Castle's grandson, "Cooke was a competent accountant, a good mind for detail, conservative and accurate. Castle, on the other hand, had a broad vision, was willing to take risks, and seldom missed an opportunity . . . . Mrs. Cooke happened also to be an excellent businesswoman . . . ."

When Samuel and Amos discussed the proposition one evening with Mary and Juliette, the wives agreed it was worth trying. In such conversations, Brother Castle and Sister Cooke often led the discussion, while Brother Cooke and Sister Castle made good listeners. After resolving to explore a partnership, the four joined in prayer for the success of the new venture. Next the proposal would have to be placed before the Board in Boston.

Some of the Honolulu brethren voiced objections to the proposed partnership, fearing that missionaries would be at the mercy of two secular members who would be beyond Board control. One even argued that, human nature being what it is, Castle & Cooke might charge more than the missionaries could afford—a cynical suspicion, indeed.

In fact, it was the Mission Board itself that balked at Castle's offer to supply the missionaries at cost. It even suggested that, if the depository were to be kept open, a 5 percent surcharge be added on all goods sold to missionaries to cover overhead. Castle protested, vowing that the missionaries were finding it difficult enough to live on their incomes already. As a counter offer he proposed that he and Cooke would quit the mission, give up their salaries, continue acting as disbursing agents, and earn what they could in trade with the public.

Negotiations continued via slow mail for two years, until well into 1851. Meanwhile, on June 5, 1850, the Cookes officially severed their ties with the Royal School.

The two men decided that, inasmuch as they intended to be permanent residents of Hawaii, they should become citizens of the kingdom. In 1850, Cooke wrote to the minister of the interior, "Sir: Having been, for some time past, residing in this Kingdom, and intending to remain in it permanently, I am desirous of becoming a naturalized subject of his Hawaiian Majesty." That same year Castle also took the oath of allegiance.

Waiting for Boston's decision required considerable patience, but the two men were not dismayed. Indeed, they became increasingly determined to become partners, no matter what the Board decided, and prepared accordingly. On May 30, 1851, Cooke wrote:

> During the week, Mr. Castle has drawn up articles of agreement for a partnership.
>
> June 3, 1851. Today obtained our licenses to sell wholesale and retail.
>
> June 5, 1851. Today signed our articles of partnership. [The articles were retroactive to June 2.]

The following week the firm's first advertisement appeared in *The Polynesian*. It read:

> The undersigned, having asked a dismission from the service of the A.B.C.F.M., take this method to inform the public that they have formed a co-partnership for conducting the mercantile business, under the style of Castle & Cooke, and would respectfully solicit a share of public patronage.
>
> S. N. CASTLE
> A. S. COOKE

The partnership was launched—but Castle & Cooke were merchants without merchandise of their own. They continued to operate the depository as before until January 1852, when they finally received word from Boston. The partners were to have their release as requested but would be employed as agents for the mission at an annual salary of $500. They could have another store if they wished, could acquire at cost any merchandise not wanted by the mission, and could use depository funds as initial working capital. But—the Board still insisted or charging the brethren 5 percent for service.

"We have no responsibility for the loans out, nor for goods in the Depository," Cooke reported. "At first I felt very much like quarreling with the new plan . . . but it may turn out for the best. It has certainly relieved us of a great burden—respecting debts, bad stock on hand and bills receivable and, last but not least, the brethren cannot find fault with our percentage as it is not from whence we derive directly our support . . . ."

Thus, the partnership of Castle & Cooke, begun June 2, 1851, became a reality on January 1, 1852. A sign reading KAKELA ME KUKE (Hawaiian for "Castle & Cooke") was installed at the entrance to the depository.

Samuel Northrup Castle was twenty-eight years old when he arrived in the Sandwich Islands to become a missionary bookkeeper. He was a tall, wiry man with deep blue eyes that sparkled when he smiled. His first wife, Angeline Tenney Castle (below), died of tuberculosis in 1841. The following year Castle married her sister, Mary, during a trip home to New England.

Amos Starr Cooke, two years younger than Castle, had been trained as a bookkeeper but was assigned to the Hawaii mission as a schoolteacher. He was slight of build with dark blue eyes. For ten years, he and his wife, Juliette Montague Cooke, operated a special school for the children of Hawaiian royalty. Five of their pupils became monarchs of the island kingdom.

Accommodations were meager aboard the bark Mary Frazier, *which carried the Seventh Reinforcement from Boston to Hawaii. The passengers' cabins measured 5 1/2 by 6 feet. They are numbered 1 through 17 in the floor plan above, drawn by S. N. Castle. Below is a watercolor sketch of the* Mary Frazier.

This wood sculpture depicts Kukailimoku, Hawaiian god of war.

King Kamehameha III, Hawaii's reigning monarch when the Seventh Reinforcement arrived, is considered by some historians as one of the kingdom's most farsighted rulers.

Grass huts with thatched roofs were typical of the dwellings found in Hawaii in the early days of the missionaries. Some of the early arrivals from New England initially lived in these structures. By 1837, however, the mission compound in Honolulu included twelve coral and wood buildings.

The palace of King Kamehameha III is depicted in this sketch following the transfer of the Hawaiian kingdom's capital to Honolulu from Lahaina in 1845. The structure was replaced by the more elaborate Iolani Palace in 1882.

During the 1840s and 1850s, Honolulu was dependent on shipping, principally whalers, for its commerce and livelihood. At times, as many as one hundred vessels were anchored in the harbor, and night life along the waterfront was usually boisterous. When the Seventh Reinforcement arrived in 1837, Honolulu's population was six thousand, of whom a mere three hundred fifty were Caucasians.

Honolulu's famous Kawaiahao (Stone) Church was known as the Missionary Church. Built in 1842, it is still in regular use today, although the wooden steeple top, destroyed in a storm, was never replaced. The Polynesian was the community's early newspaper. In 1851, the Royal School, successor to the original one operated by the Cookes, opened its doors to the public.

The Mission Depository, depicted in this painting, became Castle & Cooke's first place of business when the partnership was organized in 1851.

May.   After passing a sleepless night with my feverish little boy I rose to commence another days labour.
Found my little boy better to day through the kindness
of my merciful Father. He has been about to day
though not quite as well as usual.

You can have no idea my mother what a task we
have undertaken. From the numerous attendants these
little ones have recieved all their pleasures — Now they
feel so totally lost, they cannot find out what to do
with themselves. We are not prepared with amusements
and things to interest them having come in in haste
and commenced before we were thoroughly settled.

Mrs Thurston & family called on us to night she
expressed great pleasure in the prospects of the children — lamented that the expected heirs of Hawaii
had not been gathered into such a school as it was
too late. They are now married though young, their
habits are fixed and are not improved at all by their
intercourse with civilization & religion. He has declared his intention of being a Catholic because he says they
are not so strict as the protestants. He can be religious & go to heaven & retain his sins into the bargain. His wife is not much better a young person
of 18 She is said to be a ring leader of wickedness.

These young chiefs have grown up under Mr & Mrs
Thurstons eye — that is they used all the influence
and did all they could for them while surround
by such deleterious influences the larger part
of the time — I feel very much as I used to some time
when teaching school for a few first days — I used
to look on the time with so much dread — that in the
morning it seemed as if I could not live through another

"You can have no idea, my mother, what a task we have undertaken." Juliette Cooke wrote in 1840 shortly after the Chiefs' Children's School became a boarding school. She went on to say about the royal students, who were now living with the Cookes, "From the numerous attendants, these little ones have received all their pleasures. Now they feel so totally lost, they cannot find out what to do with themselves. We were not prepared with amusements and things to interest them, having come in haste and commenced before we were thoroughly settled."

In addition to the royal pupils, the Cookes were starting a family of their own, and Juliette told her mother about the illness of her firstborn, Joseph, "After passing a sleepless night with my feverish little boy, I rose to commence another day's labour. Found my little boy better today through the kindness of my merciful Father. He has been about today, though not quite as well as usual."

She also wrote about a young chief (identity unknown) and his wife, lamenting the fact that they were too old to attend the Cookes' school. "He has declared his intention of being a Catholic because he says they are not so strict as the Protestants. He can be religious & go to heaven & retain his sins into the bargain. His wife is not much better, a young person of 16. She is said to be a ring leader of wickedness . . ."

Below is a photo, believed to be their wedding picture, of Princess Bernice Pauahi and Charles Reed Bishop. A great-granddaughter of King Kamehameha I, she was the last of the Cookes' pupils at the Royal School. The couple was married in the Cookes' parlor. Bishop became Hawaii's pioneer banker.

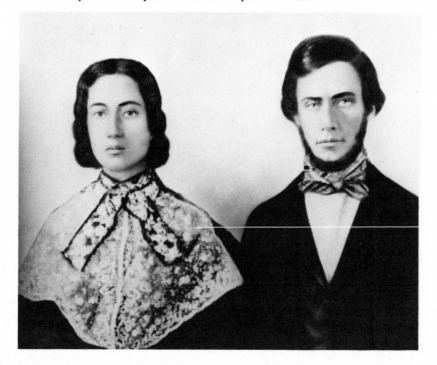

Downtown Honolulu in the 1850s (upper left) shows the architectural influence of the white man. The firm of J. T. Waterhouse, shown in the photo, was organized in the same year as Castle & Cooke. The Cooke family home, known as the Mission House (lower left), is shown as it looked about 1865. Three of the Cookes' children are perched on the roof. Built in 1821 and since restored, the house borders King Street and today is part of Hawaiian Mission Children's Society complex. The Castle home (below, circa 1895) was built in 1832 on King Street adjoining the Mission House and the Mission Depository. Following Castle's death in 1894, Mrs. Castle established a home for orphans and a kindergarten on the property.

PALAPALA AE.

—◦•◦—

E iki auanei na Kanaka a pau, *ua hana o*

Castle & Cooke

e like me ka olelo ma ka Haawina mua o ka Mokuna 2 o ka Apana mua o ke
Kanawai i kapaia he Kanawai hoonohonoho o na hana i haawiia i na Kuhina o
ke Hawaii Pae Aina; nolaila, ua ae ia ku *oia* e malama i hale kuai kukaa ma

Honolulu ma ma ka Mokupuni o *Oahu* a ua

aeia ku *bana* e kuai kukaa malaila i na ukana, a me na waiwai, a me na mea kuai o ia
ano aku ia ano aku, aole nae na wai ikaika, a me na waiwai pale dute, a me na mea
e ae i papaia ma ke Kanawai. Aole hiki ke hoolilo i keia palapala ia hai.

Pau keia *June 2d 1852*.

Na ko'u lima i hana i keia a kau i ka Sila o ka Oihana
Kalaiaina, ma Honolulu, i keia la 2 o *June*
1851

Keoni Ana

---

*The partnership of Castle & Cooke was authorized to begin business on June 2, 1851,
by this royal license granted by the Kingdom of Hawaii. Issued in the Hawaiian
language, it translates, "License [Palapala Ae]. Know all Men, That Castle &
Cooke . . . are hereby licensed to open and keep a place of business in Honolulu,
Island of Oahu, where they are at liberty to sell all manner of Goods, Wares and
Merchandise at Wholesale excepting . . . prohibited articles and articles imported
contrary to law, or the duties upon which have not been paid or secured. This License
is not transferable, and expires June 2, 1852." The license was signed by Keoni Ana
(John Young), who was then the premier of the kingdom, second in power to the king.*

OURNAL.

ONOLULU.

ved.

asty, constwise
ker, 14 ds fm San Francisco.
Williams, 20 ds fm do
Gillispie, 80 ds fm Sydney.
0 ds fm Auckland.
ting, 17 ds fm San Francisco.
, Morrice, 16 ds fm do.

red.

asty, for San Francisco.
Sherman, Tahiti.
y, Calcutta.

in Port.

rham.

cation having been made
Esqr. Chief Justice of
wis Haalelea for probate
nohi, late of Honolulu de-
given to all persons whom
lay, the 9th day of August
e forenoon, is a day and
g proof of said will, and
offered thereto, at the
of Honolulu.
    HENRY RHODES,

The Partnership

1851-1894

Chapter 4

Large Gilt Letters

"THERE SEEMS TO BE NO DANGER of their getting rich," Juliette Cooke wrote in a letter home two years after the young partnership of Castle & Cooke had started in business. And rich they weren't for years to come. Castle was even tempted in 1852 to accept the post of Hawaiian minister of the interior, which the king had offered at a salary of $4,000. "Bro. Castle said something about leaving," Cooke wrote, "and if he does, I do." But neither left; they felt an obligation to keep the depository open for the mission families.

A new mission depository had been built in the spring of 1846. The coral block structure, about twenty by fifty feet, stood on the ocean side of the Levi Chamberlain house, very close to what is today known as the Mission Cemetery. The Cooke and Castle residences were nearby. The second story, reached by an outside stairway, was used as a store and countinghouse, and here Castle and Cooke had their desks.

Cooke wrote in his journal:

I am seated at my desk, with J. [Joseph, the Cookes' oldest son] near to wait on customers if any come. Mr. Castle sits facing me, having his desk and my own turned back to back. He is writing to the Missionary House for various things, among which are a harness and wagon for me, also "Arnold's patent washing machine."

Here we have a delightful prospect towards the sea, harbor, and indeed all around . . . . Our door is at my back, and if I look out at that, I see Diamond Point, around which all our vessels come when they arrive, either from North, South, East or West.

By this time, the gardens in the mission compound were greener, thanks to a pipe system that brought water from nearby mountains. Now there was a vegetable garden, and Mary Castle and Juliette Cooke could set a better table.

Beef was cheap, but fish was hard to get, an ironic island circumstance that still persists today. There was usually taro and sweet potatoes, and bananas—often cooked and eaten as a vegetable—had become plentiful. The boys milked the cows in the mission herd. Hash (the most practical use for yesterday's leftovers) was common for breakfast. Dinner at noon was meat and vegetables and a simple dessert. Guests were served homemade guava jelly. There wasn't much variety, yet both the Castles and the Cookes had reputations for being good hosts, and guests were frequent at their tables.

Sister Castle and Sister Cooke—and all the other missionary women—dressed simply, even when styles got fancier at the palace in the late 1850s. The Bible was all-pervading. There were family prayers mornings and evenings, and grace before meals. The missionary families went to church twice on Sundays and to midweek prayer meetings.

Some of the missionaries, as a matter of courtesy to the king, attended the royal receptions, which became more and more elaborate with the passing years. The palace was a modest establishment, as palaces go, but it was slowly acquiring the accouterments of royalty. An English butler and a French chef were eventually added to the staff. Dancing was often enjoyed at palace social events, and although the New Englanders strongly disapproved anything resembling a waltz, they bit their lips and watched, not wishing to offend the king.

The missionaries objected to nearly all forms of entertainment. Castle once read a paper on "Duties of Christians Respecting Theatres and Circuses." The message: stay away! But he didn't always follow his own advice. Writing of his grandfather's life, William R. Castle, Jr. tells of a time in the 1850s when Brother Castle took his children to see a circus that had come to Honolulu. Everybody thought it would be fun to see an elephant, the first ever to visit the islands. But that meant attending the show. Castle, after some hesitation, walked slowly to the entrance. The acrobats and the bareback riders didn't seem very wicked. After a while, he sat on a bench with the children. Mary, his oldest, suddenly realized where she was and fled in terror of eternal damnation, but the other children were only too delighted to remain and see the circus. Very serious and much interested, Castle sat in silence until the end of the performance; he never spoke of the episode afterward.

Why had he gone? His grandson theorizes: "Probably, brought suddenly face to face with reality, he realized that much of what he had said and thought of sin—such sin as this—had been a mere matter of words. He was already broader than most of his fellow missionaries in the mere matter of attending the parties of the King where dancing was allowed. On this day, he simply took another step forward. It was an example of his growing tolerance toward such things as were not definitely laid down by the Bible as intrinsically evil."

In 1845 the capital of Hawaii was moved from Lahaina to Honolulu. By the 1850s the town sprawled over a square mile, and the dusty plain of pioneering years was now covered with palms, algarroba, banyan, eucalyptus, and the bright flowers and shrubbery that had been imported from foreign lands.

Dwellings were still largely thatched, but new business houses of coral blocks were going up. New churches were being built, too. One of them—the Fort Street Church—was founded in 1852 with the assistance of Castle (years later it merged with another to form the Central Union Church). By 1853, Catholicism in Hawaii had eleven thousand converts, and the first Mormons had arrived three years earlier. The Mormons were led by George Q. Cannon, who translated the Book of Mormon into Hawaiian and proclaimed the revelation that the Polynesians were descendants of the Lost Tribes of Israel.

Fleets of whaling ships sailed into the harbor twice a year, turning the waterfront into a roaring place of sin and degradation. Their visits were supplemented by occasional calls of clipper ships.

The merchant-traders worked long hours at their high bookkeeping desks. It took a lot of pen-dipping because the material requirements of both islanders and whalers still had to be figured months, and even years, in advance. Adding to the problem of doing business was the fact that there were no banks, no foreign exchange, not even a Hawaiian currency. Individual missionaries began sending their meager savings to Castle for investment. Before long, Castle & Cooke had become bankers as well as traders. Many ships reached port battered and destitute. Whether whalers or traders, they had to be provisioned and refitted, often on risky long-term credit. In their partnership, Castle and Cooke shared in these gambles.

In 1852, the first year of business for the young partnership, Castle left Honolulu for a trip to Washington, New York, and Boston. In Washington, as a representative of the Hawaiian government, he negotiated the first postal agreement with the United States Postmaster General, providing for twenty-four cents postage on letters between San Francisco and Honolulu. In New York, he lined up Castle &

Cooke agency agreements for sewing machines, patent medicines, and other commodities. In Boston, he sought to clarify the new policies established for the Hawaii missionaries, abandoned in what the American Board considered a mid-Pacific paradise.

Cooke handled affairs in Honolulu while Castle was away. His quill pen scratched with modest pride:

> When he first left us, I was afraid I should not get along very well, but I have done everything that I could expect and much more than he calculated I should do. I have posted up our books twice . . . answered all letters and orders from the Mission . . . taken more than $1,000 monthly from sales to foreigners and natives, on our own account . . . collected and disbursed some $20,000 and received three large shipments from the United States . . . . Our harbor now contains about 150 sails, and more than 100 of them are whalers . . . .

Castle & Cooke was determined to keep faith with the mission community, selling to them for the smallest profit what the partnership could have been selling to others for a substantial sum. Cooke wrote, "Today I have sold 10 bbls. of flour at $24 a barrel . . . . This sale clears us $150. We might have made $750 on 50 bbls. just received, but we chose to let the Mission have what it wanted at $10 per barrel."

He concluded, "Bro. Castle will be greatly surprised to learn the amount of business I have done during his absence."

When Castle returned to Honolulu, the partners had a number of new mission duties. Castle & Cooke was still the agent for the Board, on a commission basis plus a fee. As such, the partners accepted title to lands given to the mission by order of the king. They also operated the *Morning Star*, a sailing ship purchased by the American Board to supply mission posts in the Micronesian Islands far to the south. This proved to be a headache, largely because the Board insisted on issuing the sailing orders from Boston, and by the time the orders reached Honolulu, many staples were ruined by humidity.

In January 1853—a year after the partnership actually started functioning—Castle & Cooke took inventory. The two men wanted an official inventory to forestall the possibility of criticism from the brethren. An outsider took stock: the inventory was valued at $27,073.41; the first balance sheet showed assets of about $7,000; and profits were just short of $2,000.

CASTLE & COOKE'S COMPETITION in 1853 included three mercantile firms, which with Castle & Cooke were to become four of Hawaii's "Big Five" companies. The three were forerunners of C. Brewer & Co., Ltd., Theo. H. Davies & Co., Ltd., and Amfac, Inc. The fifth of the Big Five, Alexander & Baldwin, did not emerge until 1870.

Of the five, only Castle & Cooke was founded by missionaries. Alexander and Baldwin were sons of missionaries, while the other three companies were established by Germans, Englishmen, and assorted sailors and sea captains.

C. Brewer traces its origins back to 1826, when James Hunnewell opened a small store in Honolulu to sell, buy, and barter. Hunnewell first arrived in Honolulu in 1817 as a sailor on a ship en route from Boston to California. Hunnewell's ship returned to Honolulu, and the master swapped the vessel to native chiefs for sandalwood, then much in demand in the China trade. He left young Hunnewell in Honolulu to assemble the sandalwood cargo, take it to China, exchange it for Chinese goods, and bring them home to Boston.

This was the era when adventurous young Americans sought fortunes at sea, and boys became mates and masters at an age that today would find them sophomores in college.

Hunnewell shipped out again in 1819, this time as second mate on the brig *Thaddeus*—the voyage that brought the first band of New England missionaries to the islands. Again, the captain sold his vessel to the chiefs in exchange for sandalwood and left Hunnewell to handle the details. The valuable wood was becoming scarce. Hunnewell was on the beach in Honolulu for four years completing his assignment.

By early 1826, he was off for Honolulu again, this time as master of the *Missionary Packet,* an incredibly small vessel for such a voyage. She was registered at 39 tons—49 feet long and 13 feet wide. In lieu of salary, Hunnewell took cargo space for $3,000 worth of trading goods that he had thriftily accumulated. The *Missionary Packet* was so heavily laden that her deck was barely a foot above water. She was forced to put into port thirty times between Boston and Cape Horn. In nine months she reached the islands—with half the merchandise ruined by salt water.

Undaunted, Hunnewell set up shop in Honolulu. Two years later he added a clerk. Eventually he took his clerk in as partner and sailed back to Boston with assets of $67,000, leaving $20,000 in the business. Later he sold out to his partner, who took in a new partner in exchange for a load of otter skins and a quarter-interest in a trading ship. Then Captain Charles Brewer of Boston bought into the firm, and in 1843, Hunnewell's old concern became C. Brewer & Co. (now 54% owned by IU International Corporation).

Two years later, R. C. Janion, a young Englishman, arrived in

Honolulu, bringing a stock of goods owned by Starkey, Janion & Co. of Liverpool. The venturesome firm had already set up branches in Victoria, British Columbia, and San Francisco. Janion leased from the king a site at the foot of Kaahumanu Street, lamenting in a letter to his partner, Starkey, that the lease was for only 299 years, "that being the best I could do."

The company received and sold goods from England on consignment, and shipped home beef, hides, and tallow. In 1851, Janion became sole proprietor, but he soon obtained a new partner. In 1857, Theophilus H. Davies arrived on the bark *Yankee* with a five-year contract to a clerkship, eventually becoming owner of the business known today as Theo. H. Davies (now owned by Jardine, Matheson & Company of Hong Kong).

Henry Hackfeld, a German sea captain in the China trade, first visited Honolulu in the mid-1840s. Sensing opportunity, young Hackfeld acquired a stock of goods in Bremen, and as captain of his own ship, the *Wilhelmine,* reached Honolulu on September 26, 1849. He brought with him his bride and her eighteen-year-old brother, J. Charles Pflueger. Captain Hackfeld set up shop on October 1, 1849, in a one-story building on Queen Street, west of Nuuanu. Four years later, brother-in-law Pflueger became a partner, and the firm moved to a two-story brick building on Queen Street, which soon sported the sign "H. Hackfeld & Company." A German flavor was now added to the already cosmopolitan Honolulu scene.

During World War I, when Americans renamed the Katzenjammer Kids the "Shenanigans," Hackfeld & Company went through a similar red-white-and-blue metamorphosis. The company was taken over by the Alien Property Custodian, sold to U.S. citizens, and renamed American Factors. At the same time, its B. F. Ehler's department store took the patriotic name of Liberty House. (American Factors has since been shortened to Amfac.)

ALTHOUGH CASTLE & COOKE was getting the mission trade, its location on the fringe of Honolulu convinced its principals that they were missing a lot of downtown business—they needed more of the "walk-in" whaling trade. In late 1852 they entrusted a stock of goods to a man named Charles Nicholson, who ran a tailor shop at King and Bethel streets, two blocks from today's Castle & Cooke headquarters. But Nicholson was no merchant. Within a year, the partners had to take over. They now had a branch store that soon became their main place of business—and business was good, thanks to the California gold rush.

By 1855 new businesses were bringing fresh money into the community. The vegetables that Castle once complained were seldom on his table were now grown in sufficient quantity to ship to gold-rich California. Castle & Cooke shared in a thriving marine trade, risky as it was, and a year later the partnership bought the old *Morning Star* that had been used by the missionaries for trips from Hawaii to the South Pacific. This marked the company's first investment in the shipping industry.

All the minutiae of daily transactions were written down meticulously in the company's records. Twenty copies of *Uncle Tom's Cabin* were received and "sold the same day for a good profit." One missionary ordered a $150 set of false teeth, and it was suggested that the American Board pay the bill. We'll have none of it, the Board replied. But, Castle rebutted, good teeth are essential to good health and, consequently, useful to the mission cause. He lost the argument.

For the store's young clerks, Cooke laid down rules of conduct. These included politeness, accuracy, "putting all money in the till," no credit, no profane or obscene language, and "no visiting Billings" (a saloon down the street).

But a few months later, the small store burned to the ground. Flames had started in an adjacent theater and soon spread to Castle & Cooke.

The next day was Sunday. Castle's son William found his father sitting in the early morning sunshine at the front door of their house with his Bible on his knee.

"Willie," said his father, "did you know that the theater burned last night—and our store with it?"

"What shall we do?" the boy asked.

"We must be very careful," his father replied sternly. "We shall not be able to spend any money for a long time." Then a smile broke over his face. "But we must remember that the Lord gave and the Lord hath taken away. Blessed be the name of the Lord."

There was almost no insurance on the store. However, because Castle was widely trusted in the community, he soon managed to borrow enough to start over again. The partners built a new two-story store that opened for business in 1856. It was the "highest building around us—except for Dr. Buffrem's new Hall on Hotel Street . . . it is safe to say the only higher buildings in town are the churches . . . . You would not know the new store now with its new sign overhead, 'Castle & Cooke,' in large gilt letters." The firm now gave up the depository to concentrate on its downtown location.

For a time it seemed to the partners that the large gilt letters were rapidly tarnishing. Business suddenly turned sour as depression fell across the United States and spread its effects to the islands. It was also a period when the whaling business was suffering one of its infrequent bad years. (Following the discovery of oil in Pennsylvania in 1859, the whaling business would begin a steady decline that would be hastened by the Civil War, when Southern naval vessels captured and burned many of the ships in the whaling fleet.)

By late 1856 doubt was growing in Castle's mind whether the partnership could survive. In November he wrote a confidential letter to his agent in Boston: "I do not feel any confidence that our mercantile business is not pretty likely to fail us as a means of support for our large families." He asked his agent's help in getting an appointment as U.S. commissioner to the islands. "So far as I understand myself, I seek the post for its emolument as affording the means of support and usefulness." He failed to get the post, so struggled on to build stronger props under the shaky young firm. Despite weakening of the economy, Castle & Cooke's 1856 inventory was placed at $51,165, and the partners had saved $5,000.

AS A RESULT OF THE GREAT MAHELE of 1848–50, there was a good deal of action in real estate, and missionaries could buy land at special prices. Recognizing the constant financial problems faced by the churchmen, yet feeling his kingdom owed them something for bringing the gospel and literacy to Hawaii, Kamehameha III ordered his real estate agent to sell land to the missionaries at one-half to one-third off the going price.

Cooke was definitely interested—more so than his partner—as the following letter, written in 1850 to his brother-in-law in Connecticut, testifies, "There has been a great influx of foreigners . . . . They and those already here are buying up lands and embarking in speculations, and not a few are acquiring property. I have an opportunity to invest my means, if here, to almost unlimited amount, and still do my missionary work, as a secular agent; and the inducement is so great that I venture to draw on you, at thirty days' sight . . . for $1,000 to be laid out in goods and sent by the first opportunity."

Early in 1851, Cooke again wrote to his brother-in-law, "Money is loaned these days for 24%, it always commands 12%, has done ever since I arrived . . . . I think I shall draw . . . for about $1,000 more, to be expended in goods and sent on, as I did now just about a year since."

During this period, when several great property fortunes were being founded, the partners picked up but a few of the fast-moving acres off the bargain counter. Hawaii's lands, admittedly cheap, produced too little in cash returns, and besides, the partners had precious little cash for such investments.

Records show that Cooke acquired about 600 acres on Oahu—
some for 50¢ and $1 an acre—which he held for little more than ten years
and sold for a grand total of $1,470. In 1858 he purchased 850 acres on
the Kona Coast of the Big Island for $1 an acre. Two years later, he sold
most of it for a profit of $350. He owned his King Street home site, which
he purchased from the American Board. He had a beach place at
Waikiki, which even then Mrs. Cooke described as "the fashionable
bathing place of the foreigners of the metropolis." Apparently the
beach house was on rented land.

Castle made only one large purchase—five hundred acres in the
Waialua area, which he bought for $125 in 1851 and sold for $250 twelve
years later. He also owned a few small parcels in Honolulu. Castle &
Cooke once took in for a bad debt a hillside near Punahou School.
Cooke made such a fuss over the deal that Castle put up the $600
involved and took the land, but he later sold it to the Judd family for
the same amount.

Yet the impression persists that the Castles and the Cookes, and
the missionaries in general, collected—sometimes connivingly—vast
tracts of valuable property in Hawaii. The preponderance of historical
evidence strongly indicates that this popular notion is unsupported by
facts. Most missionaries left relatively small land holdings to their heirs.

Besides, Cooke, although himself somewhat interested in acquiring land, had reservations about the wisdom of outsiders buying up
Hawaii's soil. "While the natives stand confounded and amazed at their
privileges [to acquire land] and doubting the truth of it all, etc.," he
wrote in his journal, "the foreigners are creeping in among them, getting
their largest and best lands, water privileges, building lots, etc., etc.
. . . The Lord seems to be allowing such things to take place that the
Islands may gradually pass into other hands. This is trying, but we can-
not help it. It is what we have been contending against for years, but the
Lord is showing us that His thoughts are not our thoughts, neither are
His ways our ways. 'The will of the Lord be done.' "

Castle continued to be active in community affairs. During the
early 1850s, when he was convinced that the Hawaiian kingdom was in
grave danger of being seized by the British or French, he urged
Kamehameha III (and later, Kamehameha IV) to seek annexation to
the United States "for the good of the Hawaiian people." He signed
one petition as "Your Majesty's sincere friend and faithful subject,
Sam'l N. Castle." Castle was branded a traitor and turncoat by some
of the missionaries, who were ardent royalists and did not comprehend
the dangers he visualized.

Basically, Castle had the support of most of the missionaries, but there were some who seemed to be forever critical. A few even complained to Boston about the prices of goods supplied by Castle & Cooke and accused the partnership of "making a fortune" off the missionaries.

Still, Castle continued to be the missionaries' champion. Aware that they were being regarded by the Mission Board as leading rather pleasant lives in tropical Hawaii and, in some cases, feathering their own nests, he wrote with seemly humility and propriety, but also with sharpness, to the Board:

> In relation to the grasping or accumulating propensities of the Mission and the concern felt in consequence by the committee at home, I may remark that we cannot be too often admonished or too much upon our guard as members of a fallen race against the dangerous tendency of riches upon the mind or any undue influence, but if Missionaries and Ministers at the islands differ from Ministers in the United States in these respects, it has escaped by observation.

In 1857 the American Bible Society made Brother Castle their Hawaii representative, and he presented a handsomely bound copy to Kamehameha IV. That same year, however, he was summarily removed as corresponding secretary–treasurer of the Hawaiian Evangelical Board by the American Board in Boston. In spite of a caustic protest from a bitter Castle, the Board turned the post over to the Reverend Ephraim W. Clark, who promptly asked Castle & Cooke to do the work without credit or pay! It was not until 1868, after thirty-one years as agent, that Brother Castle's services to the mission were finally severed.

Considering the problems of the 1850s, it is not surprising to find these comments in Cooke's journal: "This is Christmas [1858] and I am at the store . . . . I find I am losing my handwriting and my eyes. I have sent for spectacles. Mother has lost her black hair and she is trying to regain it by using Mrs. Allen's 'Hair Restorer.' Bro. Castle is already using spectacles . . . ."

ON DECEMBER 15, 1854, Prince Alexander became Kamehameha IV. Henceforth Amos and Juliette Cooke would have the unique experience of living under Hawaiian monarchs they had educated in the Royal School.

Alexander's reign was to be a time of increased debate over the constitution of 1840—an argument between those who wanted to strengthen the monarchy and those who hoped to limit its powers.

Alexander was two months short of twenty-one when he ascended the throne on the death of his foster father, Kamehameha III. Historians have generally described the young man as affable and intelligent, but the Cookes, especially Juliette, had some qualms about the new ruler, who had been one of their students for more than eight years.

Juliette said in late 1855, "The young king is not doing well. He bids fair to follow in the footsteps of his predecessor as far as dissipation is concerned, and he does worse in some respects . . . . His companions are wicked foreigners, who have no desire to see him otherwise than he is. But we have ceased to give ourselves uneasiness on his account. He is in the Lord's hands."

Amos, too, was concerned: "Our new King is getting entirely under the influence of the English and the French. The Americans are being removed from office by degrees. We hear that he is to marry Emma Rooke, of English descent, another of our old scholars. She is pretty and modest and a suitable wife for a king. Oh, that they might both become Christians!"

This may seem like a pretty discouraging evaluation of their former students, but Cooke conceded, "All our scholars are doing better than we feared they would, and some much better . . . ."

Alexander did marry Emma—in June of 1856. Two years later a son was born, Albert Edward Kauikeaouli, and there was rejoicing throughout Hawaii. But in 1862 the four-year-old prince—the last child born to reigning Hawaiian royalty—became ill and died. The people of the islands were despondent. In the words of Juliette: "Oh, how dreadful to hear a nation wail!"

Chapter 5

A Taste of Sugar

IN 1858 THE SIX-YEAR-OLD PARTNERSHIP of Castle & Cooke branched out from the mercantile business with its first investment in Hawaii's infant sugar industry. This move marked the company's entry into the food business, although food production as a major company activity was not to flourish for another century. The initial investment was in a proposed plantation to be developed at Haiku on Maui, the Haiku Sugar Company, the first sugar enterprise in Hawaii to raise its initial capital through the issuance of stock.

In the late 1850s sugar was just beginning to receive serious attention from Honolulu's business community. The whaling industry was still strong, but it had its bad years along with its good ones. More and more, businessmen were talking about finding something from the soil rather than the sea to feed the young Hawaiian economy, and sugar was what they talked about most.

Castle wrote an article for the *Pacific Commercial* on sugar as a crop for Hawaii: "With requisite capital, the Islands could produce 50,000 tons of sugar, instead of the 248 tons for 1856." In 1857, Cooke returned from a trip to Kauai, excited about the irrigation systems he had seen which furnished vast amounts of water to the dense cane fields. He sensed that a new era was about to begin. Sugar would be the crop that would sway Hawaii's destiny—and perhaps Castle & Cooke's as well.

Sugarcane is believed to have arrived in Hawaii when the ancient Polynesians first settled there. Boki, the Hawaiian governor of Oahu, introduced cane to Honolulu commercially. In partnership with John Wilkinson, an Australian, he grew seven acres in the Manoa Valley in 1826. It was trouble from the beginning; a shortage of labor, tools, and money, and a deluge of rain plagued the project. When Wilkinson died a year later, Boki took over and began to convert the mill to a rum distillery, an idea that sounded more profitable.

But the missionaries soon put a stop to that. Kaahumanu, the queen regent, and the leading chiefs had been converted to Christianity by now, and they responded readily to the church's plea for temperance. A *kapu* (Hawaiian for "forbidden") was placed on the making of rum, and Kaahumanu ordered the cane fields destroyed. Yet this limited experience indicated that Hawaii's climate and soil, in more favorable locations, could produce sugar.

The sugar industry in Hawaii was pioneered by a collection of rugged, iron-willed adventurers. One was James Campbell, a shipwrecked sailor who was deposited on the beach at Maui by a whaling ship that had picked him up in Tahiti. Campbell started by building houses and repairing ships. With the shoestring capital saved from these labors, he launched a plantation at Lahaina in 1861. By the early 1870s, he and a partner had founded the Pioneer Mill at Lahaina, where they owned the entire townsite. Before long, Campbell bought out his partner and soon he became known among the Hawaiians as *Kimo Ona-Miliona*—James the Millionaire—although nobody in the islands was worth a million at that time.

Another sugar pioneer was Dr. Robert W. Wood, who came to Hawaii in 1839, served for ten years as physician in the hospital for seamen at Honolulu, then bought Koloa plantation on Kauai. One of his neighbors was Valdemar Knudsen, a Norwegian who had panned gold on the Yuba and Feather rivers in California, established a trading business in California, caught Panama fever while returning from a visit to Norway, and came to Hawaii in search of health. He stayed to develop Kekaha and Mana plantations on Kauai.

Another sugar pioneer, Captain James Makee of Massachusetts, arrived in Hawaii in 1843 as master of a whale ship. While his vessel lay in the roadstead off Lahaina, Makee was attacked by the cook, who bashed him with a cleaver and left him for dead. Captain Makee made an amazing recovery and set up a ship's chandlery business in Honolulu. Sugar caught his imagination, and he bought the struggling Torbett plantation on Maui. Later, with King Kalakaua as a partner, he developed the Makee Sugar Company on Kauai. His daughter Rose later became the wife of E. D. Tenney, who was to become one of Castle & Cooke's most flamboyant presidents.

WHEN CASTLE AND COOKE arrived in Honolulu in 1837, a sugar plantation on the island of Kauai had processed its first crop, producing two tons of sugar. Despite those meager results, it was to be the first successful sugar plantation in Hawaii.

Through the 1840s and 1850s, sugar growing and processing spread to other Hawaiian islands, although methods were crude and often ineffective. Rollers were powered with oxen, and juice was boiled in whalers' try-pots. But these early sugar pioneers persisted. They were farsighted enough to realize that the whaling ships might not always return each year to Honolulu and that the islands needed a product of the soil to take the place of the defunct sandalwood trade.

Then a centrifugal separator that whirled molasses out of sugar crystals was invented, replacing the tedious draining process.

By 1858, the steam age had arrived, but steam-driven sugar mill machinery was expensive and called for capital. Cooke noted in his journal, "Bro. Armstrong invited me to take stock in a contemplated sugar plantation in Haiku, Maui." "Bro. Armstrong" was the Reverend Richard Armstrong, who had arrived in the islands in 1832 and taken advantage of the king's offer to sell low-cost land to missionaries. Armstrong was now offering his 1,500 acres on the moist, windward side of Maui for $5 an acre to a group of prospective investors who met at the Castle & Cooke store in May 1858.

Cooke personally offered to take $700 worth of stock, with $100 cash down. After a consultation with Castle, it was agreed to raise the total investment of Castle & Cooke to $2,000.

Haiku's first crop—260 tons—was harvested in 1862. It produced a meager profit of $450. Castle & Cooke had invested in Haiku in the hope that it would be named agent for the new plantation, but the Haiku treasurer's company got the business. Not until 1866, after two shake-ups in plantation management, was Castle & Cooke appointed Haiku's agent.

Three other mercantile companies—C. Brewer, Theo. H. Davies, and H. Hackfeld & Co. (forerunner of Amfac)—were also bidding for the growing sugar agency business. Like Castle & Cooke, they sold hardware and flour, sewing machines and tombstones, calico and boots. Now they were all hopeful they had found a new source of income.

These companies purchased the supplies the plantations needed, recruited labor and handled the storage, shipping, and marketing of the raw sugar and molasses. They also supplied the required financing. Providing all these services constituted the work of an agency, which was paid a commission for its efforts. The system was known as "factoring."

In the early days of Hawaii's sugar industry, communication was by letter, written in longhand, and delivered—if at all—by some wandering missionary or trader. Currency was uncertain. Dollars, pounds, pesos, and scrip were exchanged as come by, but always uncertainly, because proper exchange rates were unknown.

Supplies were optimistically ordered, often were not delivered, and sometimes, frustratingly, arrived below specifications or damaged by salt water. It took a long time to adjust a complaint with a shrewd supplier six months away on the Atlantic Coast. If Honolulu seemed the end of the earth, Koloa on the island of Kauai, Kohala on the island of Hawaii, and Lahaina and Haiku on the island of Maui—all geographic names that figure in the early history of Hawaiian sugar—were like distant stars.

There were labor shortages. Mill parts performed badly. There was concern about the merits of different cane varieties and the cost of guano versus manure. Financing was always difficult, and so was the disposal of molasses.

In all these problems, a Honolulu agent was needed as a point of contact with the outside world. Ladd & Company served Koloa in this respect, raising money, marketing sugar, and seeking to assist the manager in any difficulties with the monarchy over land leases.

Shipping was of prime importance. Then, as now, only a small local market existed for the sugar produced, and there was no scheduled shipping service to carry it elsewhere. Ships operated on a tramp basis, depending on the captain's judgment of where the best cargoes could be found. If the China run looked more attractive than Hawaii's business, the captain went to China.

It also became apparent that shipping, purchasing, and financing weren't enough. It was a hazardous business to sell little-known Hawaiian sugar in competition with Caribbean production, the historic source of American needs. The task of doing a better selling job fell to the Honolulu agents, who, with their banking connections and suppliers, knew their way around the major markets of the United States.

Marketing raw sugar at the best price the U.S. refineries would pay became the most important duty of the agents in Honolulu. Until the sugar was marketed and paid for, the plantations had to call on their agents for such large cash advances to tide them over that the sugar usually belonged to the agents by the time it was milled. Planters invariably underestimated expenses and overestimated returns. Agencies like Castle & Cooke frequently had to borrow money in Honolulu or San Francisco and lend it to the plantations to keep them afloat.

Honolulu agents fought the battle of selling Hawaiian sugar in competition with the rest of the world. It was to be almost another fifty years before an orderly means of distributing the bulk of Hawaii's sugar was achieved.

AT WINDSWEPT KOHALA on the northern tip of the island of Hawaii, the Reverend Elias Bond grieved over the poverty of his native flock, and especially over the urge of young Hawaiians to leave their fathers' land and migrate to the towns in search of work and fun. To Father Bond, as this Protestant shepherd was known, the towns were places of vice and sin. He decided his people needed some way to make a living at home in Kohala.

"It came to me clear as sunshine," he wrote in later years, "that it must be sugar cane . . . . There was no work in the district by which our people could earn a dollar . . . . So far as I know, there was not a successful plantation on the Islands at that time . . . . Yet my figuring . . . led me to believe implicitly that, with proper management, a plantation could be made to pay expenses, whilst retaining our people in the district. [Father Bond apparently had no thought of profit, just to pay expenses, and Kohala became known as the Missionary Plantation.]

"Having thought the matter through, I went to Honolulu . . . . Bro. S. N. Castle heard my story patiently and was inclined to take hold of it. I did not care for any other agents than Castle & Cooke. Bro. Castle's efforts to get the stock subscribed were successful."

The first meeting of Kohala Sugar Company was held in Castle's office in November 1862. It was voted soon after to raise forty thousand dollars in capital stock, and Castle & Cooke was named agent. Father Bond and a neighbor, Dr. James Wight, who ran a small store at Kohala, received stock in return for 3,282 acres of land at a valuation of two dollars an acre. Castle was named treasurer, an office he was to fill for the next thirty-two years.

Despite difficulties, cane was planted and sugar mill machinery from Scotland set up. Sometimes there was too much rain, sometimes there were long periods of drought, and always there was the ceaseless wind that dried out the fields. Once, bundles of dynamite were attached to kites and exploded inside the clouds in a futile effort to create rain for the parched cane. Another year rats destroyed two-thirds of the crop. In addition there were all the problems of mastering a new science, of producing sugar by the ton instead of in small lots. "We have everything to learn by experience," wrote Castle, "and can only feel our way."

Father Bond's strict hand can be seen in company regulations:

1. Said Company shall not distill nor manufacture any spiritous liquors from the products of the plantation.
2. The laborers and all belonging to the plantation are requested to attend church once at least every Sunday . . . .
3. There is to be no card playing.
4. No fighting is allowed under penalty of one dollar for each offense, the money to be laid out on books and papers.
5. No quarreling with or whipping wives is allowed under penalty of one dollar for each offense . . . .
6. No tittle tattling is allowed, or gossiping.

Father Bond and his manager, Captain George Willfong, soon tangled. The manager demanded a full day's work from his laborers, while the pastor demanded they be treated with humanity. In the end, the pastor caught Willfong flogging a native and had him fired.

In January 1865, when Kohala produced its first sugar, flags were hoisted and a cannon fired. But there had been so much trial and error that the plantation owed Castle & Cooke thirty-five thousand dollars. It wasn't until 1875 that the plantation got out of debt and paid its first dividend. Even worse, to Father Bond's disappointment, the younger members of his flock still moved to sinful Hilo and Honolulu. Back-breaking work in the cane fields held no appeal whatsoever for the easygoing, fun-loving Hawaiians.

When it came to finding strong backs to work in the fields, all plantation developers encountered the same problem that faced Father Bond. The Hawaiians simply did not want to work that hard. Solutions to the planters' labor problems had to be found elsewhere. As early as 1852 the Royal Hawaiian Agricultural Society, which Castle helped organize, had experimented by bringing 180 Chinese laborers from Hong Kong. Each was to receive three dollars a month, plus food, clothing, housing, and medical care. This was about twice what they could earn in their homeland, and they lined up to volunteer for the journey.

To critics Castle vigorously defended importation of contract labor. He pointed out that more than half of the people in the American colonies of 1776 had at one time been indentured servants or were descendants of such labor.

The Chinese marked the beginning of a vast importation of

labor—all voluntary—that led to Hawaii's becoming a melting pot for peoples from throughout the Pacific Basin and other areas of the world. The Chinese were followed by the Japanese in 1868, the Portuguese ten years later, Puerto Ricans in 1900, Koreans in 1903, and Filipinos in 1906. By 1900, more than 60 percent of Hawaii's population of 154,000 was made up of these ethnic groups that were imported to provide labor for the expanding sugar industry. That percentage remained above the 60 percent level until as late as 1950 and was still 51 percent in 1960 and 47 percent in 1970.

Chinese came both from the Orient and from California, where many had migrated earlier. Pigtails and bound feet became common sights in Hawaii. The Chinese were considered excellent workers but as soon as their contracts were completed, many of them returned home or moved into Honolulu to become a significant part of the city's merchant community.

The Japanese brought their costumes and customs, adding still a different look to the island scene. They wore kimonos, bowed low upon greeting, retained their Buddhist religious beliefs, and enjoyed their *furo*, a super-scalding daily bath.

"The Japanese want plenty of hot water or arrangements to provide themselves with a hot bath every day," Castle & Cooke advised its plantation managers by memo. "They do not require a full bath but strip and pour it over them. Men and women bathe indiscriminately but this fact is not against their morals, which are high, as any attempt against their women will result in blood and probably death."

As in their homeland, the Japanese were extremely diligent. They worked hard, kept clean, educated their offspring, and retained their ties with Japan. Teahouses and Shinto temples were erected, special schools taught their children the language of their ancestors, and the dead were honored at summer Bon Dances.

Meanwhile the Hawaiian sugar planters continued to look for strong backs. Dr. W. Hillebrand, the physician and botanist who wrote the first *Flora of the Hawaiian Islands*, turned up a manpower source in overcrowded Madeira and the Azores while collecting plants for Hawaii. Castle & Cooke went after its share of these island Portuguese, even as it had with the first Chinese arrivals. In a letter to its plantations, the firm wrote: "The President of the Board of Immigration asked how many Portuguese we could take. We told them 100 to start . . . . Planters must take an average of three children to a family and house them. Planters must take, if necessary, 40% of women. That is to say, if we order 100 men, 40 of these are to be women and 60 men.

"Now we are aware the terms are high, when we consider the

women and children which we may be obliged to take. But when we look upon the project as an introduction of a valuable class of citizens into the country, the planters ought to be willing to contribute something towards the introduction and securing of a permanent and growing population for these Islands.''

The Portuguese set up homes, planted gardens, and found the islands a pleasant place to live. Good workers and good family men, they eventually graduated from manual labor to become *lunas* (Hawaiian for "foremen"). They brought with them their music, the familiar six-stringed guitar and two smaller versions that had never been seen before in Hawaii. One was a five-stringed instrument they called a *rajao*, and the other was a tiny four-stringed novelty, the *braguinha*. The latter was to become the famous *ukulele* (Hawaiian for "jumping flea").

At one period during the 1870s, the plantations also turned hopefully—and with the encouragement of the king, who had some concern about so many Orientals in Hawaii—to the Solomon Islands and the New Hebrides. What resulted was recorded by Mrs. Meta Hedemann, who lived at Hana, Maui:

> These terrible looking laborers were called Levalevas. They were really quite savage with awful looking kinky red hair and when, in the evenings, they lighted a great bonfire and danced around it, naked, beating tins and drums, screaming and yelling (which was their way of singing), it was quite uncanny . . . . They made great holes in the lobes of their ears, carrying anything in these lobes from big flowers to their pipes. We have a picture of one of them carrying a little dead rat in his ear . . . .
>
> They very much liked to dress up in white man's clothes, whether they fitted or not, and were crazy about hats. Some would wear three or four, one on top of the other. They had a kind of religion, of course, and their own idols. When they saw a certain kind of butterfly, never mind where they were or what they were doing, they dropped everything to drop to their knees and pray . . . . They did not stay long on the plantation; I don't think they were very good laborers.

They weren't.

King Kamehameha IV ruled for only nine years. He died of asthma in 1863 and was succeeded by his brother Lot. It was at Lot's request that Castle agreed to run for his first political office. In 1864, he was elected to the Assembly, the lower house of the legislature, and was chosen Speaker. He made the easygoing legislators work hard for the first time.

Later he was appointed by the king to the House of Nobles, a post that involved a lot of work, some honor, but no pay.

Fellow missionaries fought his election, attacking his character and integrity. They proclaimed it a disgrace for anyone having the remotest connection with the mission to seek political office. Some even went so far as to proclaim they would "no longer trade with such a firm as Castle & Cooke, one of whose partners is Castle."

Castle once again had managed to reap the wrath of the brethren. In 1852 he had been one of the first to urge annexation of the kingdom to the United States. Now, thirteen years later, when most missionaries had decided annexation would be a good thing, Castle opposed them. He tried to explain that in 1852 he had felt the Hawaiian government was so weak it was ready to fall either to Britain or France, but now that the government was much stronger, any such action was unthinkable. His explanation did not convince his opponents, but he stood firm and the controversy gradually dissolved. Castle & Cooke not only survived the bitterness but began to prosper anew.

By the late 1860s, Castle & Cooke was branching out into the ship agency business. The company handled shore-side business for a number of trans-Pacific schooners and several interisland vessels. But it was still dependent on its mercantile business for most of its profit. By now, it represented Wheeler & Wilson's sewing machines, the Hall Patent Sewing Machine Treadle, and those universal boons to mankind, Dr. Jayne's Celebrated Family Medicines. The partners also had in their stock such items as ink powder, quills, sadirons, gutta-percha hose, whiffletrees, hooped skirts, corsets, kerosene, blasting powder, cartridges, hair tonic, lumber, saddlery, crockery, spelling books, codfish, linens, and Jenny Lind cakes. In addition, the company represented the New England Mutual Life Insurance Company, rented houses, accepted contributions to churches, and helped build an early hotel to accommodate travelers to Honolulu.

It was even rumored around town that Castle & Cooke was getting into the liquor business! The mission heads promptly sent a delegation to investigate. Castle not only admitted having alcohol on hand but took the men into the back storage room and pointed it out to them.

"There it is—in that leaky cask," he said defiantly. "If you doubt my word, taste it." One of the delegation stuck his finger into the seepage, winced as he put the dampness to his tongue, and confirmed Castle's admission.

"Why don't you take the whole cask back as evidence?" Castle suggested, a twinkle now in his eye. "But be sure to return it to us as we are holding it for trans-shipment to Boston. It contains the pickled body of Captain Blank who died in Micronesia."

The delegation fled the premises.

SOME SUGAR PLANTATIONS of that era never did get out of the red. Castle & Cooke warned planters to hold down costs, pointing out that the company had stretched its credit to the breaking point to finance them. Nevertheless, the firm kept digging deeper for money.

Sometimes Castle & Cooke's dollars did the pioneering, but their rivals got the agency business. Castle's son-in-law, Edward Hitchcock (who married the oldest daughter, Mary), was a founder of Papaikou Plantation on the island of Hawaii. First declining the agency, Castle relented after Papaikou had a disastrous fire, and in 1875 he advanced money for the growers to make a new start. One advance led to another until the plantation owed Castle & Cooke $190,000. Then it merged into neighboring Onomea in 1888, and Castle & Cooke lost the agency to the rival C. Brewer & Co. It had the same experience, on a smaller scale, with the Wilcox Plantation, the Smith Plantation, and the Waimea Sugar Mill, all on Kauai.

However, Castle & Cooke's first sugar venture, Haiku, was to prove another story. After a number of slow years, Haiku's directors in 1870 hired two missionary sons, Samuel T. Alexander and Henry P. Baldwin, to manage the plantation. Haiku also sold a parcel of 600 acres to the missionary sons. The sale launched the Alexander & Baldwin partnership that was to become one of the Big Five.

Samuel Thomas Alexander was born at Waioli, Kauai, where his father, the Reverend W. P. Alexander, who had come to the islands in 1832, was assigned to conduct a mission. In 1864, Sam had married Martha, one of the Cooke daughters. Henry Perrine Baldwin was the son of the Reverend Dwight Baldwin, who had reached Hawaii in 1831 and had been assigned to the mission at Lahaina, Maui, where Henry was born. The two missionary sons became inseparable friends at Punahou School. Baldwin had planned to work in the sugar industry only long enough to save money to go to the United States to study medicine. Instead, he married Alexander's sister Emily and stayed in sugar.

Sam and Henry made an unbeatable team. Sam Alexander was the dreamer and the promoter. He and Henry Baldwin could make sugar grow better than anybody else in the islands. Under their management Haiku boomed. So did the young partnership of Alexander & Baldwin, begun in 1870 and aided in its early years by Castle & Cooke.

Two other missionary offspring backed by Castle & Cooke were

Warren and Levi Chamberlain, sons of old Levi, for whom Castle had worked at the depository. They launched a sugarmaking project in 1864 on lands at Waialua on the northern shore of Oahu. The Chamberlains also owned 588 acres of adjoining land until, after twice going through the financial wringer, their plantation came into the hands of the Bishop Bank.

The bank sold it to O. R. Wood, who borrowed $3,000 from Castle & Cooke and retained the firm anew as agent in 1870. Within a year, Wood faced bankruptcy, and Castle & Cooke had to foreclose, thus taking ownership of the property.

Young Levi Chamberlain ran the plantation for four years until Castle & Cooke was able to unload it for a $30,000 mortgage to Robert Halstead and Henry Gordon. When the latter died in 1875, Halstead bought his interest for his sons, Edgar and Frank, who eventually paid off the mortgage and made Waialua a money-maker—not only for the Halstead family but for Castle & Cooke as well. Many years later, the Halstead plantation became the nucleus around which Castle & Cooke was to build the prosperous Waialua Agricultural Company.

IN DECEMBER 1858 the sailing ship *Syren* left Boston for Hawaii with a cargo of whalers' supplies, general goods, and one passenger, Joseph Ballard Atherton, a frail young man who was making the voyage for his health.

Damaged by rough seas, the *Syren* put into port in Río de Janeiro, Brazil. The buffeting had been hard on the sickly passenger, and the captain's crude doctoring had not helped. It took three weeks to round the Horn, and Atherton twice locked himself in the cabin, preferring to go down with the ship than take to the lifeboats. But the *Syren* weathered the storms and reached Honolulu seven weary months out of Boston.

Atherton obtained a temporary job as bookkeeper and decided not to return to Boston; he had had enough of sailing for a while. Then Mrs. Cooke found a place for him among her boarders. When his employer offered him a permanent job at $1,200 a year, Cooke promoted a job for him at Castle & Cooke at $40 a month, plus room, board, washing, and postage. Atherton accepted the latter offer.

Joe Atherton was soon chief clerk, and although others offered him more money, he stayed with Castle & Cooke for a ten-dollar-a-month raise. A major consideration may have been Julie, the second daughter of the Cooke household. She was engaged to Frank Judd, son of Dr. Gerritt P. Judd, when Atherton joined the family circle.

Within a couple of years, her mother was writing relatives that

Julie "will probably marry Mr. Atherton. Mr. A. is an agreeable young man . . . the backbone of our business at present."

In January 1862, Cooke wrote, "This evening Bro. Castle talked with Mr. Atherton about being a Partner." He also wrote, "Bro. Castle and I decided to keep taking $500 a year salary." And further, "I am feeling more and more feeble." Although he still kept a shaky hand in business affairs, Cooke's health was failing rapidly.

Searching for rejuvenation, he sailed on a missionary vessel through Micronesia. Upon his return, he wrote in his journal that he "weighed 109 pounds. Gained while absent 6 or 8 pounds." A trip to Maui followed. Mrs. Cooke wrote, "He is a little better but not much. His complaints are nervous. The mind is more affected than the body. He can't bear excitement on any subject. I don't think that he will ever do business again. He has been gradually getting worse for several years, and since last January [1863], he has not been to the store at all."

Although he no longer went to the store, he did find the strength to shake everybody's hand at the wedding of Julie and Joseph on June 29, 1865. "Mr. and Mrs. Atherton expect to go to housekeeping in a beautiful cottage about a mile from us on their return [from a honeymoon on Kauai]," Juliette wrote. "Their prospects for happiness seem quite fair. She had about $400 worth of bridal presents, all spread out on the dining room table. Grandma's pretty castor and Aunt Fanny's preserve dish occupied a conspicuous place . . . ."

By 1867, Amos Cooke had become an invalid from his nervous disorders, and a year later Juliette wrote, "Mr. Atherton has been in our family three years and it seems perfectly natural to look upon him as a very dear friend. Joe [the oldest son] being gone [to school in the United States] and Mr. Cooke being ill, I have been in the habit of leaning on him for some time, have always found him ready and willing to do anything possible for our happiness."

On March 20, 1871, at the age of sixty-one, Brother Amos Starr Cooke died.

Referring to him as "Deacon Cooke," *The Friend,* a missionary publication, eulogized:

> We give to him the title of his official position, because it was as a member of the Church of Christ that he always wished to be known. Infirmity had removed him for some years from the active duties of life . . . but habits of a religious nature formed early in life were scrupulously continued up to the last . . . .

> At his funeral we were glad to see many of his old pupils, including Prince William [Lunalilo], the Honorable David

Kalakaua, the Honorables Mrs. Bishop [Bernice] and Dominis [Lydia] and Mrs. Pratt [Elizabeth]. His labors and those of Mrs. Cooke as teachers of the Royal School will long be remembered.

The *Hawaiian Gazette* added: "For the warmth and earnestness and stability of his zeal, he had few equals. As a merchant and as a Christian, he was known and highly esteemed here for many years, as well as a missionary teacher and principal of the Royal School. He leaves a wide circle of friends who will bear testimony to his purity and upright, honorable character."

Chapter 6

Difficult Decade

"IF CASTLE & COOKE DO FAIL, I shall not have much left. We shall all go together."

Those chill words of foreboding were written in the fall of 1873 by Juliette Cooke, widow of two years, in a letter to her sister in Massachusetts. With short crops and extremely low sugar prices that year, Castle & Cooke was struggling to keep alive. During the Civil War years of the early 1860s, the price of Hawaiian sugar had boomed when the northern states' traditional source of supply was cut off. But that was long past. Now an American tariff of two cents a pound on Hawaiian and other foreign sugar was slowly strangling the young industry in the islands.

Other letters from Juliette described the situation:

All the plantations in bad shape. Haiku, which two years ago was almost out of debt, owes $40,000 and, what is worse, owes it to Castle & Cooke, as they have advanced money to carry on the work. They are agents for four other plantations who have not all suffered so much, but still many thousands. We cannot tell what will be the result . . . .

> If C. & C. should fail . . . my home and a little outside prop-
> erty cannot be taken to pay off the indebtedness. However, the
> principal part of my property is in their hands and must take its
> chance with theirs.

When a group of planters offered Castle & Cooke their agency
business in exchange for financial backing, Castle snapped, "We have
all the sugar business we desire . . . we do not intend to risk more."
He did not admit that the firm was so in debt it could not obtain additional financing.

"The truth is," he told friends, "that every line of business has
prospered in the past at the expense of the plantations. The plantations
have paid out $1½ million more than they have got back. They are the
ones who have given measurable prosperity to others but they have
wrecked themselves. Reciprocity will not give back the lost money but
it will enable them to continue . . . ."

Castle, with others, knew that removal of the tariff on sugar was all
that could save the islands and his firm. The need for a reciprocity treaty
was greater than ever. Business was growing steadily worse.

It was becoming clear that the United States would not enter into
any such treaty merely to show friendliness. Benefits must accrue to
both nations. Washington demanded some tangible return—for example, ceding Pearl Harbor for use as an American naval base. Castle said
he would give "far more than Pearl Harbor" to obtain reciprocity.

"It seems to me," he said, "that annexation offers the only remedy
to save the people. It would be so little for the U.S. to give, and the
country [Hawaii] would gradually and naturally slide into its arms. It
must, in a few years, go into other than native hands, for none will be
left, and it is a strategic and important point for the United States in case
of war with any formidable or third rate power . . . ."

Castle's outspoken feelings were considered traitorous by many
Hawaiians. One meeting, headed by David Kalakaua, uproariously
passed the following resolution:

> Whereas, the Hon. S. N. Castle has publicly declared himself an
> annexationist, his advocacy of the annexation of the Hawaiian
> Islands to the United States having appeared in a newspaper called
> the Evangelist of New York, in which he said "on the death of the
> King [Lunalilo] and a vacancy in the throne, the United States
> would have the power to take possession of and annex the Is-
> lands." Resolved that S. N. Castle and his family be banished
> beyond the limits of the Kingdom.

It was an angry proposal, but nothing came of it.

In 1873, William Lunalilo had been elected to the Hawaiian throne following the death of King Kamehameha V. At that time, Hawaii's constitution provided that if a monarch had not appointed a successor before his death, a new king was to be elected by the people, and Lunalilo became the first.

The new monarch acted quickly to seek a reciprocity treaty with the United States to slow down Hawaii's slipping economy, but his efforts were no more successful than those of his predecessors. Slightly more than a year after he became king, Lunalilo died of tuberculosis, complicated by alcoholism. He, too, failed to designate a successor, and David Kalakaua was elected to succeed him.

Kalakaua was persuaded to send a commission to Washington to reopen negotiations for a treaty. Later he went in person to meet President Grant and speak before Congress on behalf of reciprocity, and his goodwill tour was a triumph. The long-sought treaty was finally approved and became effective in 1876. The document was neither long nor complex. It simply provided that unrefined sugar, rice, and virtually all other products of Hawaii were to be admitted to the United States duty-free. In return, a large list of American products was to be admitted free to Hawaii.

The U.S. Senate inserted a clause without which the treaty would have been rejected: it provided that, so long as the treaty remained in effect, the king would not offer the same kind of treaty to other nations and would not "lease or otherwise dispose of . . . any port, harbor, or other territory in his dominion, or grant any special privileges or rights of use therein, to any other power, state, or government." (In 1887 the king granted to the U.S. exclusive use of Pearl Harbor as a naval base.)

Within four years after passage of the Reciprocity Treaty, Hawaii's sugar and rice production had doubled, and prosperity had returned to the islands.

NOW THAT THE RECIPROCITY TREATY had been passed, Sam Alexander and Henry Baldwin came up with a dynamic idea that, if it was successful, could double sugar production at Haiku and their own adjoining plantation. They proposed to build seventeen miles of ditch along the steep windward mountainside of Haleakala to capture millions of gallons of runoff rainwater and channel it down to the Haiku plain. It was a bold, imaginative plan, but speculative.

The ditch could not have been planned for rougher country—the windward face of Haleakala was gouged with deep gulches, some of them miniature Grand Canyons, and the ditch had to skirt the shoulders of these gulches. Laterals would reach up into the draws to tap all possible sources of water, and tunnels would have to be punched through the deepest ridges between gulches. There were only precarious trails into the wild mountainside, but the young partners estimated they could build the ditch for $25,000 to $50,000.

That was a small fortune in those days, and Sam and Henry decided to approach Castle & Cooke for the necessary financing, even though they were so doubtful of their ability to sell the idea to the hardheaded partners of Castle & Cooke that they had already talked to other capitalists in Honolulu who might gamble on the ditch.

The meeting was held at the Castle & Cooke store in August 1876. To the complete surprise of young Alexander and Baldwin, Castle not only considered the project feasible but, farsighted businessman that he was, had already applied to the king for the rights to water from various streams flowing down the mountainside on behalf of Haiku Sugar Company, Alexander & Baldwin, and other plantations in the area—he believed Haiku's neighbors should also benefit. So Castle & Cooke agreed to help finance the ditch.

When construction got under way, Sam Alexander and Henry Baldwin began to find out what a monumental job they had tackled. Torrential rains and landslides plagued the project. Workers had to hack their way through jungle and go over sheer cliffs by rope. When the men balked at the final barrier because of the extreme danger, Henry Baldwin, who had lost an arm in a sugar mill accident, shamed them into returning to work by sliding down a rope over the precipitous cliff, with his one good arm. Day after day he went over the side to inspect progress and help alleviate the fears of the workers.

In July 1877 the first water began flowing through the ditch. It reached the parched Haiku plantation twenty-four hours later—barely one day before the deadline set in the royal grant. All could easily have been lost to forfeiture. Instead, 60 million gallons of water a day were soon running through the new ditch system. But instead of $25,000 to $50,000, the ditch had cost $80,000, and Castle & Cooke had to come up with the additional funds.

At the same time that Castle & Cooke was agreeing to finance the Haiku irrigation ditch on Maui, Claus Spreckels arrived in Honolulu. Spreckels was a wealthy San Francisco refiner of beet sugar who had fought for years to defeat a reciprocity treaty with Hawaii. Having failed, he was now in Hawaii to do business with sugarcane growers— and he moved fast. Within three weeks he bought more than half the sugar crop for 1877 and was laying plans to take over the industry as a one-man monopoly.

Spreckels, a tough-minded German of the thrifty, tenacious merchant class, first arrived in San Francisco when it was a boomtown. He opened a grocery store and decided to brew beer and refine beet sugar after noting that those commodities were the backbone of his retail business. He went back to Germany and took humble jobs in beet sugar refineries to learn the sugar business from the ground up. He was to become one of the West's early financial giants.

Spreckels knew sugar was the foundation of the Hawaiian economy—it was the only collateral the islanders possessed. If he could contract for all of the production to supply his San Francisco refinery, he could eventually dictate the price—he hoped.

But his efforts were thwarted by a letter from Castle & Cooke to the plantations it represented:

> Mr. Claus Spreckels is in town . . . . He is known in California as the "Sugar King" . . . . He wishes to contract for the whole of the crop of 1877 . . . . So far he has expressed himself unwilling to take half of the plantations' sugar crop.
>
> It seems to us if Mr. Spreckels would agree to accept half of the crop, it might be best for the planters to do business with him. But to give him the whole, we cannot see the justice of the measure, either to our California or Oregon friends [by that time the refiners in those two states were the purchasers of much of Hawaii's sugar].

Spreckels watched the Hamakua-Haiku ditch development on Maui with special interest, hoping it would fail so he could pick up the pieces. Having learned what Alexander and Baldwin were doing, he had acquired 8,000 acres of barren plain adjacent to the Haiku and Alexander & Baldwin properties. He had then leased 24,000 acres of crown lands through an agreement with one of the royal family—a deal considered questionable by historians studying that era. It was later declared legal under equally questionable circumstances when Spreckels managed to get title to the once-royal acres.

Spreckels now had land. He needed water, and the water he wanted was from the same general area to which Alexander and Baldwin had prior rights. Kalakaua's cabinet had turned down Spreckels' application for water, but this did not stop him. He went to see his friend, the king himself.

At a post-midnight drinking session, Kalakaua dismissed his recalcitrant cabinet and appointed new members who would take orders. By breakfast, the new cabinet had granted Spreckels rights to water from Haleakala. Spreckels knew that the Hamakua-Haiku ditch agreement contained a clause that said all rights would revert to the monarchy if the ditch were not completed by a specified deadline. Because of his influence with the king, he figured all such rights would come to him, since his water lease covered the same general area as that of the Haiku project, subject to "prior and vested rights."

But Alexander and Baldwin beat the deadline—barely. Disappointed but undaunted, Spreckels went on to build his own thirty-mile ditch and develop his Maui lands into a great and profitable sugar plantation.

BY 1875, PROFITS HAD FINALLY COME to Kohala; the first dividends that year amounted to 75 percent of the original investment. For the next three years, the dividends amounted to 100 percent, 300 percent, and 225 percent on the investment. In 1879, Kohala increased its capital to $480,000 out of surplus by declaring a twelve-for-one stock dividend.

Father Bond, the good pastor who had started the plantation on the Big Island solely to help his native parishioners and whose family of nine children had lived on his meager missionary's salary of $500 a year, a vegetable patch, and a couple of cows, repeatedly gave his share of the profits to Christian charities. When he received a dividend check for $48,000, he was stunned. "That money is not mine," he said. "I never earned it or in any way sought it." He gave it to the American Board in Boston, with the injunction, "Record this as 'From a Friend' only." It was done, with the notation that that year he was the largest single contributor to the Board's funds.

Later in life, he wrote to his children: "If, when my Father calls, I leave more cash than I ought, it will be because time has not sufficed for the carrying out of my plans. I am not my own, nor are my possessions my own."

The dividends from Kohala Sugar were welcomed at Castle & Cooke, but they were far too small to meet the company's new financial needs.

The Hamakua-Haiku ditch turned out to be a mixed blessing. With almost unlimited water, Haiku's acreage was expanded, a move that meant Castle & Cooke had to find the dollars to enlarge Haiku's sugar mill. They also had to advance more capital to Alexander & Baldwin for development of its plantation, and by the following year, 1878, Alexander & Baldwin was $101,650 in debt to Castle & Cooke. In fact, so deeply in the red were they that Baldwin sounded out Castle & Cooke on the idea of selling the plantation to Claus Spreckels. The answer came back:

If you can make favorable terms with Mr. Spreckels by the disposing of the place to him, we would have no objections to the sale, provided you get a good price for your place and they are willing to give written guarantee that we are to act as agents for the next five years. We would much prefer to deal with you and Mr. Alexander; but if you must sell, it seems to us more than fair that in the conditions of sale that our interest should be protected after having seen you through all your "pilikias" [Hawaiian for "troubles"] and supported you with credit when the prospects of sugar planters were in their darkest hours.

Fortunately for the future, Alexander and Baldwin were unable to come to terms with Spreckels. They hung on by their teeth, and with the help of Castle & Cooke funds, but by the next year they were $122,790 in debt. Castle & Cooke was almost bankrupt, too, and was pleading for sugar to ease its own financial position. A letter to Henry Baldwin advised, "Don't be tired if we call for 'Sugar, sugar.' But we have about reached the end of our rope, and we must have sugar to make good our promises. Had we any idea of the tightness of the money market, we would have advised you not to have gone into new works and into new expenses this year."

To another plantation the firm wrote, "Unless it is a dire necessity, we cannot consent to any more outlays . . . . With cash as tight as it is, it is no pleasure to do business . . . . We cannot raise a dollar for you . . . . We are perfectly sick of plantations."

But the water brought down from the side of Haleakala soon began to pay off in bumper crops and bigger dividends. By 1882, Alexander & Baldwin had been able to cut its debt to Castle & Cooke in half. By the end of the 1880s, the company was able to buy up and merge with five smaller plantations. Eventually the Alexander & Baldwin plantation on Maui was to become part of one of the most productive and prosperous sugar operations in the world.

MANY CHANGES HAD COME TO HAWAII since that day in 1837 when Castle and his fellow missionaries in the Seventh Reinforcement arrived in Hawaii. In her descriptive book *Six Months in the Sandwich Islands,* Isabella Bird, world traveler, noted botanist, and the first woman fellow of England's Royal Geographical Society, found the Honolulu of 1873 almost halcyon:

There are coral thoroughfares shaded by trees brought from various parts of the tropical world. Pleasant cottages of coral blocks or of wood are surrounded by verandas, decorated and festooned with flowering vines. There are neat grass houses interspersed with those of the foreign residents . . . . [One sees] Hawaiians sitting at ease outside their thatched homes, enjoying calabashes of poi spread on mats under the trees.

[I found the foreigners] in delightful condition . . . living in pretty cottages under the shade trees . . . eating the lotus and dancing the polka through a perennial summer. The days are filled with gossip after the coming of a mail ship . . . . Carriages, carrying ladies and children, roll leisurely up the [Nuuanu] valley road on afternoons or creep across the plains to the seabeach [Waikiki], returning to hospitable gatherings in the evening . . . and all this without hurry or care; still nights vibrating with the twang of fiddles and the shuffle of quadrilles as merry parties dance away the evening.

Hawaii's isolation of the 1830s had diminished considerably in the following decades. It was no longer necessary to go around the Horn when traveling to New York or Boston. After 1867 the traveler could use the new steamship service to the Pacific Coast of Central America, where he crossed the isthmus to board another ship for the Atlantic leg of the journey. Later it was possible to cross the United States by rail. Letters that had once required months to reach Hawaii from Boston were sometimes received in only twenty days.

The more affluent residents of Hawaii now sent their children to Yale and Harvard. Castle had allowed his older children to make their own choice of college, but he chose Oberlin College in Ohio for his four youngest. In 1877, he took his wife, James, Caroline, Helen, and Henry all to Oberlin so that Mrs. Castle could set up housekeeping there and keep a motherly eye on the youngsters while they were in school.

By 1880 public schools had been built and a YMCA opened; horsedrawn trams traveled the streets, and water carts sprinkled the dust. Buggies were fancier, and the velocipede had arrived. You could even buy ice and ice cream.

Honolulu's population in 1880 had passed the 15,000 mark. The town boasted a new government building and a post office. The business area was not exactly imposing, but it compared favorably with those found in many American towns of equal size at that time.

On the other hand, some of the homes were magnificent. Princess Ruth had a residence called Keoua Hale, a four-story expanse of Victorian gingerbread whose giant scale matched her own portly proportions. Curtis P. Ward, of Kentucky, erected "Old Plantation'' and surrounded it with seven thousand coconut palms. (The site is now occupied by the concert hall of the Neal S. Blaisdell Center.) The Oriental community was also beginning to progress up the economic ladder; Chun Afong, a wealthy Chinese merchant, built a mansion with oriental trimmings, a structure sufficiently large to shelter his sixteen children.

Honolulu's first concert hall was built in 1881, but there had already been occasional cultural events, such as *The Barber of Seville,* under the patronage of the king, and a concert by a quartet of Swiss bell ringers.

Located on land adjacent to the present state capitol was the town's first hotel of consequence—the verandaed Royal Hawaiian (a predecessor of Waikiki's famous Royal). The tourist trade was beginning. Among the visitors were Mark Twain and Robert Louis Stevenson, whose enthusiastic writings about paradise did much to instill curiosity about these faraway lands. Twain's description of Hawaii as ''the loveliest fleet of islands that lies anchored in any ocean'' is still a standard quote in Hawaii's tourist literature.

The fact that opera had been presented under the auspices of the king said a lot about the times. It was the era of the Merry Monarch, David Kalakaua, who had become king in 1874.

He and three of his predecessors were all graduates of those puritanical classrooms ruled by the Cookes at the old Royal School, but the rather sterile regimen of the school had never held much appeal for them. Increasingly, they had indulged in pomp and ceremony and everything that went with it.

When Lot and Alexander visited Great Britain and France in 1850, the young princes were impressed with the royal trappings they observed. They also fancied the rich ornamentation they discovered in Episcopal cathedrals—a sharp contrast to the pristine surroundings of Hawaii's Congregational churches. As a result, when the princes became kings, they were instrumental in the establishment of an episcopate in Hawaii.

The furbelows of office were fanciest during the reign of Kalakaua. Although his days in office were plagued with problems, he still found time to build an elaborate new palace. From the time the monarchy was abolished until 1968, Iolani Palace continued to be used as the territorial and later the state capitol. Since then it has been undergoing restoration and is expected to be opened in 1977 as a historical landmark—the only royal palace in the United States.

The Kalakaua era was a period of gaiety, ostentatious court living, gold-fringed and feathered hats, and elegant wining and dining.

In 1881, Kalakaua became the first monarch of any country to make a trip around the world. The purpose of the voyage was "to recuperate his health and to find means for recuperating his people." Royal honors were extended to him in Japan, Thailand, and India. In the capitals of Europe, he was regarded as generally urbane and gracious, although he was reported to have "tied one on" occasionally along the way.

Kalakaua was decorated impressively as he traveled from capital to capital, and he, in turn, pinned Hawaiian decorations on royal bosoms throughout the world. On his journey he noticed that many monarchs had a lot of things he didn't have, such as jeweled crowns and regal robes, armies and navies, and far-flung empires.

When he returned to his new, $350,000 palace in Honolulu, he announced he would crown himself and his queen, Kapiolani. In 1883, marking the ninth anniversary of his reign, elaborate coronation rites were celebrated in a small pavilion next to the palace. "Cry Out, O Isles, with Joy!" the choir sang. Luaus, dancing, and general celebration filled the better part of the next two weeks.

In 1886, a jubilee celebrated Kalakaua's fiftieth birthday with parades and balls, hula dancing and fireworks—and the illumination of Iolani Palace by the first electric lights to shine in Honolulu.

Kalakaua created a navy flagship from an old copra vessel (it was his total fleet) and started dreaming of a far-flung empire; he would become king of Polynesian Oceania. However, it became apparent that other South Pacific countries wanted no part of his empire.

The way Claus Spreckels manipulated King Kalakaua caused considerable head-shaking, for a lot of drinking and poker-playing often preceded the decisions that increased Spreckels' power in the Hawaiian sugar industry. Kalakaua's style of living soon put him in debt, and he was paying 12 percent interest to his creditors. Spreckels loaned him $40,000 at 7 percent, thus increasing his hold on the king, and was dubbed "ex officio Emperor of the Hawaiian Islands."

Walter Murray Gibson, who, Hawaiian historians agree, had a shadowy background, also endeared himself to the king and soon became premier, a position of power within the government. One of Gibson's initial moves was to engineer the repeal of prohibition for the native population. He also persuaded the legislature to establish an annual license permitting the sale of opium to the local Chinese. The license was sold to the highest bidder, and according to reports, Gibson frequently profited from the transactions.

This type of dealing convinced an organization of some four hundred *haole* businessmen that changes had to be made. Led by attorney Sanford Dole, publisher and attorney Lorrin Thurston and Brother

Castle's son, William, also an attorney, they eventually generated sufficient pressure to drive Gibson from the islands. The king signed a new constitution and set up a cabinet-type government responsible to the legislature.

Four years later, in 1891, weary from political strife and court life, Kalakaua died at the Palace Hotel in San Francisco while on a holiday. "Tell my people I tried," he whispered.

His sister, Liliuokalani, succeeded him on the throne. She was determined to regain the royal power her brother had forsaken, but her reign was to last less than two years. When she attempted to invoke a new constitution in 1893, a bloodless revolution removed her from the throne and established a provisional government headed by Sanford Dole.

Dole, backed by Samuel Castle and just about every other leading businessman in Hawaii, campaigned for annexation by the United States. But President Grover Cleveland was not sympathetic, so the provisional government organized Hawaii into an independent republic, with Dole as president.

AFTER COOKE DIED IN 1871, his widow disposed of her interest in the partnership to her eldest son, Joseph. Actually, Juliette had been the "Cooke" of Castle & Cooke for almost a decade and had proved herself an astute businesswoman. Joseph had first worked for the company in the days when it was just a depository. On the Castle side, Alfred, the eldest son, was coming along, having likewise started in his teens as a clerk behind the counter. However, the careers of both were to be cut short by tragedy.

When Samuel Castle returned from a trip to San Francisco in 1874, his ship anchored in Honolulu harbor before daybreak. He walked home to find his household sound asleep. He tossed a few pebbles against the window of Alfred's room to awaken him. When no one responded, he entered the house and encountered a sleepy Hawaiian servant.

"Where's Alfred?" he asked.

"Alfred dead," replied the servant.

Alfred, who was his father's closest confidant in both business and public affairs, had died of appendicitis at the age of thirty, just as the firm was about to make him a partner. Five years later Joseph Cooke succumbed to a liver ailment. Thus, the eldest sons of both families were gone—and within a year the youngest Cooke son, Clarence, was to die of typhoid fever.

By 1880, Castle was becoming known around Honolulu as "Father" Castle, and at age seventy-two, with white hair and beard, he fit the title. Although he maintained a keen interest in Castle & Cooke, and his business counsel was frequently sought, he was now understandably playing a lesser role in the affairs of the company.

For some time Juliette Cooke's son-in-law Joe Atherton—now known as "J.B."—had been handling the day-to-day responsibility of running Castle & Cooke, while Father Castle devoted most of his time to public affairs. The erstwhile missionary had mellowed considerably in his later years; though he was still a dogmatic fundamentalist, his beliefs were tempered somewhat by a doctrine of charity. He believed that idleness was intolerable; he had never been idle himself nor had he taken a real holiday. And he still practiced thrift. On a trip to visit a friend on Maui, he walked four miles from the ship to his destination. "I carried my saddle bags and overcoat and was perhaps never more weary than when I reached there," he wrote later. The interpretation by his grandson-biographer was that "this hard tramp, over dusty roads, was probably taken to avoid the expense of a carriage."

Though he believed in rigid economy, he gave generously to charity and gambled on experiments to provide new industries for Hawaii.

He had become a walking encyclopedia as he aged into a stately and serious, but no longer somber, old-timer. He knew the islands intimately from his journeys on foot from mission to mission. An enthusiastic agriculturalist and supporter of the Royal Hawaiian Agriculture Society, he never relaxed in the search for new crops for the islands.

In his later years, Castle's main concern was how to steer the Hawaiian kingdom into an affiliation with the United States. Once again he had changed his mind, because the British and French were seizing many of the islands in the Pacific, and he feared the same would happen to Hawaii. He had been a member of the King's Privy Council and a friend and adviser to six of Hawaii's monarchs. He had a horror of revolution, although he tolerated participation by the younger Castles in the conspiracy that eventually led to declaration of the republic.

On July 14, 1894—ten days after the Republic of Hawaii was proclaimed—Samuel Northrup Castle died at the age of 86. He left an estate appraised at $416,000, a handsome sum for the 1890s but modest, perhaps, if compared to the fortune he might have accumulated. Most of it went into the Castle Estate for the benefit of his heirs or the Castle Trust, administered by his sons to help finance missions, colleges, and other charities.

An astute student of men and opportunities, Castle had assumed the risks of a pioneer when others hesitated. Some of the projects he backed, and nearly all of the men, vindicated his judgment. The shrewd, devout Yankee storekeeper had left his imprint on the Sandwich Islands.

He was outlived two years by strong-willed Juliette Cooke, who in her seventy-eighth year took a Chautauqua (correspondence) course, graduated, and went on to get two certificates of distinction. To her last day, she had a say in Castle & Cooke, through son-in-law J. B. Atherton. Mary Castle lived until 1907, devoting her later years to the Castle Trust and other charities.

The annual statements record of the Castle & Cooke partnership was labeled "Especially Private." All financial records, as well as all other accounts, were written meticulously in longhand with a quill pen. At the end of five years in business, the company's inventory was valued at $51,165. Profits for 1856 amounted to $5,000.

Dr.	Wilama	at Mrs. Rogers		Cr.
1851		1851		
Aug. 1	1 pr. Shoes	2 25	Dec. 6 By Cash	2 25
Dec. 20	Balance on pants	1 00	27 " do	50

Dr.	Makulu	Carpenter		Cr.
1851			1851	
July 29	1 Sauce Pan	1 25	Dec. 5 By Cash p. Nife	3 —
Sept. 8	1 Bowl	1 50	20 " do in part	50 00
	1 pr. Table Nutts Nassau	25	31 " do "	12 —
Dec. 20	7 M Cedar Shingts 14,	98 00	1852 Feb. 3 " do in full	36 0
Jan. 3	1 pr. Shoes 2.			

Dr.	Lukia	Mrs Bree woman		Cr.
1851			1851	
Aug.	1 Dress Pattern	1 50	Aug 20 By Cash	1 5
Sept. 15	3 yds. 3/4 Unbld cot.	75	Sept. 19 " do .50 do 25	7
27	9 " Calico	1 50	Oct. 10 " do 1.00 do 50	1 5
Oct. 10	9 " Orange Stripe	2 00	Deck " do. 1. do 1.	20
		6 25		6 2

Dr.	Kahue			Cr.
1851				
July 29	4 3/4 yds. Bro. Holland	1 62		
	1 Woolen Shirt	1 50		
Nov.	1 Rope	50		

Dr.	Kapule	Mrs Bree man		Cr.
1851			1851	
Aug 26	1 pr. Shoes	2 50	Sep. 4 Cash 1. 22d do .50	1
Oct. 11	Balance	1 50	1853 Apl 1 By Cash pd Monks	2
		4 00		4

Honolulu Dec 2. 1851

D' Bro Baldwin

We have looked anxiously by the two last arrivals from Lahaina for the Money due on the rent of the Richards house. We are trying to raise Money for exchange for remittance and we ought to have this for it is long overdue. We have the refusal of exchange for a little time if we can raise the money We hear that Mr Bolles has been successful in obtaining drafts at 15 %

This being the case we will take of him good whalers drafts at 10 % or $1.10 face of draft for every dollar due to us which allows him 5 % commission for purchase. If the draft happens to be larger we will pay Money for the balance at the same rate. We hope on no % that we shall fail of getting drafts or money on this a/c by return of vessel on friday morning

Yours in haste
S. N. Castle

A page from the Castle & Cooke account book for the first six months of the partnership's operation (opposite) illustrates a wide variety of transactions. Typical of the correspondence required in those days is this 1851 letter (above), written by Castle and concerning overdue rent payments.

Honolulu, Nov. 17/52.

H. Hill, Esq. Dear Sir, We wrote to you
on the 5th inst, enclosing first of Exchange on
_____ for Ex'g of New London for $2,000. Your number 2.
_____ we have received yours of _____ Sept. 4
_____ Aug. 17 Sept. 4. Also, Invoice _____
_____ which we have credited on our books
_____ your $99.00 for overcharge on Dep. Invoice
_____ have credited you $ 20. $2. $76. Aug 2
_____ hold, Esq. Balance due you from
_____ should this not be the _____
_____ credit him any _____ balance.
_____ than $699, on acct. Debr
_____ committed to ship
_____ each, consisting to
_____ of 150 M. Shingles.

_____ shipped, per
_____ size:
_____
_____
_____ down
_____

M_____
$1,000_____
to us, _____ for, for
ly, but _____ them as by
in this _____
We were _____
about $1000. _____ from $1,000.
including the _____ _____
Such _____ we paid _____ Bd. per Valparaiso
$600, & Elder M. M. Smith. $250.
Yours truly, Castle & Cooke.

Honolulu, Nov. 17, 1852.

Messrs. Butler, Keith & Hill,
Dear Sirs, A young man
now boarding in Mr. Cooke's family, & just received _____
of an elder brother, wishes us to procure for him
a handsome Marble Grave Stone.
He limits the cost to $30. including your
charges, & wishes the following inscription, viz:

In Memory of
S a m u e l   H a m i l t o n
son of John & Elizabeth Hamilton, Virginia Iron _____
who, after a residence of fifteen da_____
died, of a pulmonary consumption,
at Honolulu, Oahu, Hawaiian _____
Nov. 15, 1852.
Aged 28 years, 10 months, & 7 _____

"Blessed are the dead which die in the _____
Rev _____

Please purchase such a Stone,
by first opportunity, & charge _____
to us. & much oblige
Yours truly _____

J Wilgoss, Kauls   one _____ about 13 yrs & 10 _____
one six candle _____
E H Rice,   one Banker iron Chi_____

The first account book of the Castle & Cooke partner-ship, together with blotter, pen nib and keys to the Depository store, are on display in the executive suite of the company's headquarters in Honolulu. The account book includes copies of all correspondence. The entries on these pages were made in late 1852.

Mr C. is very much occupied in
his business matters. The market is dull
and they are somewhat perplexed with sundry matters. They have some losses. There
seems to be no danger of their getting rich
I trust however that they will be able to gain
enough to satisfy our wants.

There are 30 or 40 whale ships in now
and things begin to assume a busy aspect—
There are two men of war here—All seems quiet. Mr
Alexander is to be married to to Emma.
We have had a long dry summer—no rain for six
months.

Oct 21st We have had rain it is really refreshing—crea-
-tion rejoyces an man sympathizes. Fanny says
that you love flowers and help take care of them
will how many flowers did you nurture and
care for when you had 6 children around you.
— My hands are so full—I have now 6 besides my own
family—All I can do is to just hoe day by day—
tick one tick at a time—do not there to look ahead.

This is such a meagre letter that I am ashamed
to send it but I do not know when I shall
be able to write a better one—So I'll send it
Do not get blue over it— My mind is confused with life's cares—But I have many—
Oh! how many blessings!! I think you

*Mr. C. is very much occupied in
his business matters—The market is dull
and they are somewhat perplexed with sundry
matters. They have some losses—There
seems to be no danger of their getting rich.
I trust however that they will be able to gain
enough to satisfy our wants.*

*There are 30 to 40 whale ships in now
and things begin to assume a busy aspect—
There are two men of war here—All seems quiet.
Alexander is to be married to to (sic) Emma.
We have had a long dry summer—no rain for six
months.*

*Oct. 21st—We have had rain, it is really refreshing—vegeta-
tion rejoyces (sic) an(d) man sympathises (sic). Fanny says
that you love flowers and help take care of them.
Well, how many flowers did you nurture and
care for when you had 6 children around you.
—My hands are* so full*—I have now 6 besides my own
family—All I can do is to just live day by day—
tick one tick at a time—do not* dare *to look ahead.*

*This is such a meager letter that I am ashamed
to send it but I do not know when I shall
be able to write a better one. So I'll send it.
Do not get blue over it—My mind is confused with life's cares—But I have many—
Oh!* how many blessings!! *I think you . . .*

*Above is a verbatim transcription of a full page (opposite) from a letter written by
Juliette Cooke on October 7, 1853, to her mother. Note her somewhat pessimistic
comments about the Castle & Cooke partnership. Her mention of Alexander and
Emma refers to Kamehameha IV and Emma Rooke, both former pupils at the Royal
School. Her reference to having "6 besides my own family" means six boarders in
addition to, by then, six children of her own.*

Honolulu harbor in the early 1850s was the principal port of call in the Pacific for the New England whaling fleet as well as vessels of commerce that arrived from all corners of the world. This sketch shows the waterfront area of downtown Honolulu. Looming behind the town are the Koolau Mountains. Punchbowl, now the home of the National Memorial Cemetery of the Pacific, is at the right, and Nuuanu Valley cuts through the mountains at the left.

Honolulu in 1853, looking toward famed Diamond Head, is detailed in this early lithograph. Kawaiahao, the Native Stone Church still in use today, was then eleven years old. Its wooden steeple was later damaged but never replaced. To the left and rear of the church was the mission compound, including the Mission Depository that housed the Castle & Cooke store. Also visible is the palace of Kamehameha III, with the Hawaiian flag fluttering in the breeze.

Three of Hawaii's monarchs who reigned during the first twenty-five years of the Castle & Cooke partnership were (clockwise): Kamehameha IV (Alexander), 1854–63; his brother, Kamehameha V (Lot), 1863–72; and their cousin, William Lunalilo, 1873–74. Lunalilo was the first elected king of Hawaii. All three were former pupils of the Cookes at the Royal School. Throughout this period, Castle, concerned with affairs of the public as well as business, served as an adviser to the kingdom's monarchs—at first unofficially; later, in an official capacity.

The Nicholson tailor shop (opposite) became a downtown branch of Castle & Cooke in late 1852. Several years later, the partnership left the Depository to devote full attention to the downtown trade. H. Hackfeld & Co. (later to become Amfac, Inc.) was a competitor.

The Reverend Elias Bond sought the assistance of Castle & Cooke in 1862 to organize Kohala Sugar Company to provide work for his native flock.

In the 1880s, the Hawaii Railway Company began carrying sugar (as well as passengers) from the North Kohala mills to the port of Mahukona.

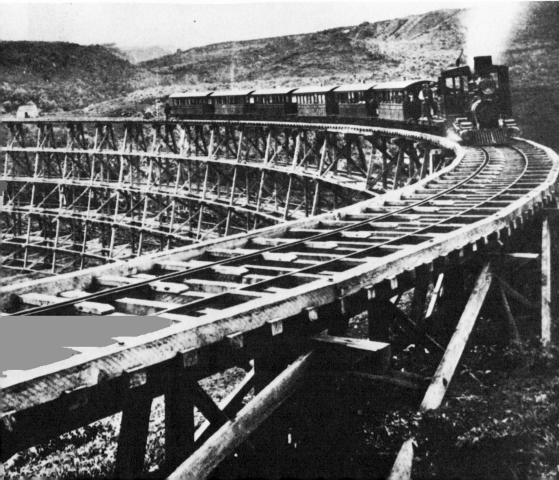

At Kohala and elsewhere throughout Hawaii in the early days of the sugar industry, harvested sugarcane was hauled to the mill by straining teams of bullocks (above). The cut cane was loaded aboard the oxen carts by hand (below). Although Kohala Sugar was profitable in its early years, the plantation was located on marginal land, and finally had to be closed in 1975.

In the early years of the industry, Hawaiian sugar was shipped to San Francisco and other West Coast ports for auction to the highest bidder. In 1905, the C and H cooperative was organized to refine and market Hawaiian sugar.

Honolulu Dec. 17th 1872

Dear Edward & Mary

The mail goes on the Ceylon to day & I have little time to and I inclose for you the childrens last letters I have nothing of note to say Prince William has issued his proclamation for a plebiscitum or vote of the people on the 1st day of Jan 1873. I presume their expression will be in his favor as he is popular. but I fear to place an incorrigible drinker on the throne. The desired to appoint Mrs Bishop as his successor but she did not want it & declined. but she Could be persuaded to take it as a duty to her people for whom she feels for I have talked privately with her but dont speak of it now. If a way can be devised to bring her out with any hope of success it will be done Judge Allen holds my views on the subject, but please you & Mary not drop a hint to any body until further developements. or if there are none Maintain silence. ~~Please burn this~~ ~~letter~~ much love to you all.

Your aff father
S. N. Castle

Castle's continuing concern about Hawaii's rulers is illustrated in this letter written in 1872 to his oldest daughter, Mary, and her husband, Edward Hitchcock, then living in Hilo. He notes that Prince William (Lunalilo) will probably win an election to select a successor to Kamehameha V, but adds that "I fear to place an incorrigible drinker on the throne." Castle adds that Mrs. Bishop (Princess Bernice Pauahi) has declined to be named Lunalilo's successor, but he confides, "She could be persuaded to take it as a duty to her people. . . . I have talked privately with her, but don't speak of it now. . . ." His instructions to "Please burn this letter" obviously were not followed.

King David Kalakaua, the Merry Monarch, raised the pomp and circumstance of Hawaii's royal throne to a peak during his reign from 1874 to 1891. He ordered the construction of Iolani Palace, and he was the first monarch of any country to travel around the world. Unfortunately, his reign was marred by several scandals involving business deals.

King Kalakaua and his staff posed for this photo in 1886 on the steps of Iolani Palace. Impressed with the royal opulence he observed on his world trip, Kalakaua decided to crown himself and his queen, Kapiolani, at elaborate coronation rites in 1883 marking the ninth anniversary of his reign. It was an era of elegant wining and dining.

Queen Kapiolani's crown, bestowed on her in the coronation of 1883, contained Hawaii's first crown jewels. The gold-fringed Kalakaua era ended with his death in 1891 in San Francisco.

Letterheads on the invoices of Hawaii companies during the 1870s were colorful, informative documents. Of the three above, only the name of Castle & Cooke has continued in the world of business.

Hawaiian money and stamps were ornate and colorful during the 1880s and 1890s. The coin, minted in 1883, bears the profile of "Kalakaua I, King of Hawaii." The $1 stamp carries the likeness of Queen Emma (Emma Rooke), who became the Dowager Queen following the death of her husband, Kamehameha IV (Alexander), in 1863. She died in 1885. The signatures on the $20 bill—W. G. Ashley (lower left) and Minister of Finance Sam M. Damon (lower right)—indicate it was issued during the period of the provisional government following the overthrow of the monarchy.

This was the throne room of Queen Liliuokalani, last of the Hawaiian monarchs. She was overthrown in 1893 and confined to her home, Washington Place, still in use today as the official residence of the Governor of Hawaii.

The queen was the sister of King Kalakaua. Both were former pupils of the Cookes at the Royal School, where she was known as Lydia.

Three generations are shown in this Castle family photo taken in the early 1890s shortly before S. N. Castle's death. Standing behind white-haired "Father" Castle and his wife, Mary, are daughter Caroline (Mrs. W. D. Westervelt) on the left, son Henry Northrup with his infant daughter, and daughter Harriet (Mrs. Charles C. Coleman). Perched atop the pergola is grandson Northrup Castle Coleman. Castle had eleven children in all—one during his first marriage, and ten during his second. Harriet was the fourth, Caroline the ninth, and Henry the eleventh.

Five of the seven Cooke children are included with their mother, Juliette, in this family photo, taken in 1874 (three years after the death of Amos Starr Cooke). Seated, from the left, are daughter-in-law Mrs. Charles M. Cooke (the former Anna Charlotte Rice); "Mother" Cooke; son-in-law J. B. Atherton; daughter Juliette (Mrs. J. B. Atherton); and son Joseph. Standing, from the left, are son Charles; son-in-law Samuel T. Alexander; daughter Martha, who was known as Pattie (Mrs. Samuel T. Alexander); daughter-in-law Mrs. Joseph P. Cooke (the former Harriet Emelita Wilder); and son Clarence.

The "streetcar" came to Honolulu in the 1880s when Hawaiian Tramways, Ltd. introduced four mule-powered cars. This one traveled along King Street past Aliolani Hale (House of the Chiefs), on the left, and Honolulu's Music Hall. Aliolani Hale is still in use today as the Judiciary Building.

CASTLE & COOKE LIMITED

INCORPORATED, DEC. 29TH 1894.

CAPITAL STOCK $600,000.

6,000 SHARES $100 EACH.

HONOLULU — HAWAIIAN ISLANDS.

...tifies that Mrs. Mary Castle No. 17 is the owner ...usand eight hundred five — Paid up shares of the Capital Stock of CASTLE & COOKE, LIMITED.

...able only on the Books of the Company by endorsement hereon and surrender of this Certificate

Honolulu, H.I. February 20th 1895

TREASURER.

PRESIDENT.

TREASURER.

J. B. Atherton

PRESIDENT.

Incorporation
1894-1941

Chapter 7

Trying Corporate Wings

On December 28, 1894—five months after the death of Father Castle—the forty-three-year-old partnership of Castle & Cooke was incorporated. Younger members of the partnership had wanted to incorporate earlier, but Father Castle had strenuously objected on the grounds that a man should back up his business judgment with all his personal resources. The only change in the name was the addition of "Ltd.," the standard designation for corporations in Hawaii at that time. ("Ltd." was changed to "Inc." in 1958.)

The capital stock was set at $600,000 (6,000 shares at $100 par value) with privilege of extension up to $2,000,000.

Joseph Ballard Atherton, senior member of the partnership since Castle's death, was elected president at a salary of $400 a month. Three months later at the first meeting of the board of directors, George Parmelee Castle was elected vice-president, and James Bicknell Castle auditor. The two sons of Father Castle had been elected members of the partnership nine years earlier.

As president, J. B. Atherton represented the Cooke family interests in the new corporation. He had joined the company in 1859 and had been made a partner three years later. Juliette Cooke had long regarded her son-in-law as one of her own sons and perhaps felt even closer to him because of his assistance to her during the trying period of Amos Cooke's final years while her own children were still growing up or away at school.

J. B. Atherton was a man of strong prejudices combined with unshakable integrity. Though not of missionary stock, he was more rigid in his religious beliefs than many of the missionaries. When he arrived in Honolulu, he had belonged to the Close Communion Baptists. He was faced immediately with the decision of whether to form a one-man Baptist church—there was none then in the islands—or to join the Congregationalists. He finally concluded that the latter were sufficiently orthodox and threw his energies into the new Fort Street Church (which Father Castle had helped to organize). He collected pew rents and served as treasurer and Sunday school superintendent for twenty-one years.

A strong family man, he conducted his life on a strict schedule. He was at his desk early in the morning, drove a delivery wagon home for lunch, and had his carriage call for him in the evening. He spent much time making "Fernhurst," the Atherton home, a horticultural showplace. After dinner he played sober games with his children until 8 P.M., when he went upstairs to read. His library was one of the finest in the islands.

The Athertons were known for their hospitality. J. B. enjoyed meeting incoming vessels and frequently brought passengers home as house guests. Once he did make a serious mistake in judgment. A young guest pulled a bottle of whisky out of his suitcase! After a hurried consultation with his wife, Atherton asked him to leave at once.

Although he came to Hawaii for his health, Atherton never did become robust. About five feet, eight inches tall, he weighed only 140 pounds. After his terrible trip around the Horn on his journey to Hawaii, he stayed off the sea until 1872, when he finally screwed up courage to take a trip to the United States and England. In spite of his fragile build, Atherton always walked fast, almost running. His doctor used to drive alongside in his carriage and admonish, "Atherton, go slow!"

AT THE TIME OF INCORPORATION, Castle & Cooke was just beginning to see daylight again after another long bout of "financial depression." As in the past, the cause was sugar.

Five years earlier, in 1889, the company had invested in and become agent for another bold new sugar development—this one on the desert plains of Ewa, west of Pearl Harbor on the island of Oahu. The costly project, plagued with trouble, had gone deeper and deeper into debt. In order to provide the huge amount of money needed, Castle & Cooke had sold a large part of its holdings, including its then valuable interests in the Haiku Sugar plantation on Maui. By the end of 1894,

Castle & Cooke was pinning a major share of its hopes for the future on the new Ewa Plantation Company, then still a million dollars in debt.

Ewa was a broad, arid plain covered with scrub and coral—unsuitable, certainly, for growing sugarcane. Its infrequent rainfall provided uncertain forage, even for cattle. The land belonged to James "Millionaire" Campbell. Legend says he won it in a poker game, but the Campbell Estate's records show he bought 43,250 acres for $95,000 paid to John H. Coney.

This barren land intrigued another adventurer, Benjamin F. Dillingham, who had shipped out of Boston at the age of fourteen and become a mate at nineteen. His ship, the *Southern Cross,* was captured and burned by the Confederate raider *Florida,* and Dillingham was dumped ashore in Brazil. Later he shipped for Hawaii as a first officer. He was left on the beach at Honolulu in 1865 with a broken leg, suffered on shore in a fall from a horse.

Dillingham decided to remain in Hawaii, and he landed a job as a clerk in a local hardware store at $40 a month. He married Emma Smith, daughter of the Reverend Lowell Smith, an early missionary who had instructed the Cookes in the Hawaiian language upon their arrival in 1837. By 1869 Dillingham had teamed with Alfred, Castle's eldest son, to buy the hardware store for $28,000, borrowed from Father Castle. Under the name of Dillingham & Company, the firm prospered. After Alfred's death, Ben operated the business for himself and Alfred's family.

But Dillingham had bigger ideas. In 1888, he persuaded the king and the Hawaiian legislature to grant him a franchise for building a railroad on Oahu. The king even agreed to certain land subsidies, provided Dillingham could build the first seven miles of rail and run a train on it. Dillingham talked to Honolulu's businessmen, but most shook their heads at what they referred to as "Dillingham's Folly." When he laid his plan on the doorstep of Castle & Cooke, farsighted Father Castle and his associates agreed to invest $100,000 in stock and bonds in the railroad. It was then easy to raise the rest of the money.

In September, 1889, "B. F." steamed his first train out of Honolulu. The tiny locomotive hauled a string of ten flat cars, equipped with crude seats, out to the Palama rice fields half a mile from town. The ladies' bonnets and the gentlemen's fedoras were sprayed with soot and cinders, but "Dillingham's Folly" had become a genuine railroad—the first in the islands—and Ben was on the way to becoming Hawaii's Commodore Vanderbilt or James J. Hill. This tiny railroad was the forerunner of 160 miles of track on Oahu and another railroad on the Big Island. Ben's railroads were to revolutionize the handling of sugar in Hawaii.

Having launched the Oahu Railway, Dillingham needed freight traffic to make it pay. Sugar plantations could provide ample traffic.

Dillingham had noticed an artesian well that flowed generously at the Campbell ranch house at Ewa. Also, down at Pearl Harbor he had watched cows wade into the ocean to drink. Drink salt water? Not possible. He reasoned that there must be a water table under the plain seeping into the ocean. If that were true, wells could be drilled on the Ewa plain to irrigate the sugarcane that would solve the problem of freight for his railroad. Not one to waste time, Dillingham leased all the lands at Ewa from James Campbell in November 1889.

Then he sold his idea to attorney William R. Castle, Father Castle's second son. William saw merit in the Ewa proposition, discussed it with his younger brother, James, and the two went to talk with their father. With the elder Castle's blessing, they called a meeting of the Castle & Cooke partnership and other experienced sugar men in William's law office on December 11, 1889.

The group agreed to form a $500,000 corporation to develop a 10,000- to 12,000-acre sugar plantation on the Campbell ranch. Charles M. Cooke, second son of Amos and Juliette, was elected president. James Castle was vice-president, and J. B. Atherton treasurer. Dillingham agreed to sub-lease the acreage for the plantation at an annual rent of 4 percent of the gross proceeds from sugar, or a minimum of $5,000, and the right to haul freight to and from the plantation.

Ewa required a water development comparable in magnitude to that achieved by Sam Alexander and Henry Baldwin on Maui. In this case, the rain fell on the Koolau range behind Honolulu and seeped through volcanic rock toward Pearl Harbor and Ewa. The problem was to drill wells and install pumps to collect about as much water as was needed daily for a city the size of San Francisco—if the water was there.

They hit water in abundance, thereby partially silencing the skeptics. But after the first ten wells, the drilling crew ran into trouble with an endless succession of cracked casings, bent pipes, lost bits, and frayed tempers. Castle & Cooke imported a rig and two drillers from California, but they failed. The local drillers went back to work. Eventually they managed to put down seventy-one wells, capable of flooding the dry Ewa plain with 105 million gallons of water a day. The water was lifted from the wells by some of the biggest steam pumps ever used in agriculture. Planting began in 1890.

ALTHOUGH THE WATER PROBLEM WAS SOLVED, the plantation floundered from one crisis to another. The local iron works, which was building the machinery for the plantation's mill, went bankrupt. Ewa's management had to gather up the scattered pieces, and Castle & Cooke was scraping for money to pay the workmen who were building the machinery.

Shortly after Ewa Plantation was incorporated, the McKinley tariff was passed by the U.S. Congress (1890), admitting all foreign sugars into the nation duty free. This wiped out the advantages gained by Hawaii through the 1876 reciprocity agreement. The desire to invest in Hawaiian sugar vanished overnight. Nobody wanted to buy Ewa stock.

Castle & Cooke was already too deep in Ewa to drop out. The firm stretched its credit to the limit, borrowing from banks in Honolulu and San Francisco as well as from individuals. Charles M. Cooke, by then wealthy in his own right, even pledged his personal resources to keep the Ewa project afloat. By the fall of 1891, Castle & Cooke had just about scraped through the bottom of the barrel.

The crowning humiliation came shortly afterward when a Castle & Cooke check for $54 bounced at the Bishop Bank, which had already refused a $5,000 advance, so shaky was the company's financial position.

Although there is no evidence to support it, a legend persists that a few years later, after Castle & Cooke's finances were restored by the eventual success of Ewa Plantation, several of the Castles and Cookes decided the Bank of Bishop should get its comeuppance for having refused to cash that $54 check back in 1891. Charles Cooke, who had pledged his personal finances during the height of the Ewa nightmare and had been Ewa Plantation's first president, gathered together several C & C directors, so the story goes, and marched into the bank, followed by a husky Hawaiian pushing a wheelbarrow.

They tendered a large "pay to cash" check, withdrawing the company's entire account. The money, all in gold coins, was wheeled through the downtown streets to be deposited in the new Bank of Hawaii, which had just opened in December 1897.

The opening of the new bank spelled the end of the banking monopoly in Honolulu, which had been held so long by the Bank of Bishop, and the Cookes were behind the new venture. J. B. Atherton was vice-president of the new bank, Clarence H. Cooke was secretary, and within a year Charles Cooke became president.

The legend notwithstanding, records do show that Castle & Cooke opened the first checking account at Bank of Hawaii. When savings accounts were introduced, four of the first five depositors were Cookes—Charles, George, Alice, and Theodore. The Cooke family has been closely associated with the Bank of Hawaii ever since. Castle & Cooke did not resume business with the Bishop Bank until 1934.

(In 1895, Bishop sold his bank to Samuel M. Damon and moved to California, where he died in 1915.)

At the height of Castle & Cooke's financial difficulties back in 1891, one of the Castle grandsons recalled many years later, Father Castle arose from his sickbed and began to pace back and forth on the lanai of his home whistling. (He had a habit of pacing and whistling that way when he was worried.) Finally, he put on his clothes and hurried downtown to talk to J. B. Atherton. The only solution, he had decided, was to get the needed financing from Claus Spreckels, the California "Sugar King" who had years earlier tried to get control of Hawaii's sugar production. Castle had battled Spreckels for years, but right now, in Castle & Cooke's shaky condition, he was not above swallowing his pride and appealing to Spreckels for help, though he knew Spreckels was sure to drive a hard bargain.

By this time, Spreckels was back in California, and the task fell to Atherton to handle the delicate negotiations. In October 1891, Atherton wrote to his brother-in-law, Charles M. Cooke, president of Ewa Plantation:

> The situation is not pleasant, as you can see, but I won't give up as long as there is a chance to succeed. Baldwin & Alexander [sic] owe us $140,000 or more that must be paid or taken over by Spreckels & Company, if necessity requires. If an assignment has to be made, I shall make it to S & Brothers [Spreckels] and Bishop & Company, who are our principal creditors. The sale of all of our bonds, Ewa and RR [Oahu Railway], would help very much and especially as Spreckels will assume A & B's debt, making over $440,000.

A few weeks later an agreement had been hammered out, and Atherton again wrote to Cooke:

> This has been a tough week and until yesterday I thought there was no hope here, from the attitude of Spreckels; but yesterday, after a long talk with Mr. Claus Spreckels present as well as Mr. [R. P.] Rithet [Castle & Cooke's San Francisco financial consultant], who urged the measure for the benefit of all concerned, [they] consented to buy at par [certain shares of] Haiku, Paia, Hawaiian Sugar Company, Honomu, Inter-Island, (etc.), for a total of $146,000. Of course, this reduces debt and interest and is, so far, good, sorry as I am to lose Haiku and Paia, but the sale had to be made to get any start.

Sacrificing their profitable Maui sugar interests in the Haiku and

Paia plantations—after pouring twenty years of sweat and toil into them—in order to keep their Ewa project afloat looked like sending good money after bad. But the money enabled Ewa to weather the crisis. Construction of the mill and the laying out of the plantation proceeded.

Soon Sam Alexander was able to write to one of the Cookes: "I am rejoiced to learn from Joe Atherton that Castle & Cooke are still on their legs. They have lost business, it is true; but if they can weather this year's crisis, they may be able to regain their old position. It would be a national calamity to have the old firm of Castle & Cooke go under. Castle & Cooke in their days have been public benefactors. More than one owe their start in life to the generous aid afforded by the firm."

Henry Baldwin had become one of the outstanding sugar producers of the islands. To check the security for its loans to Castle & Cooke, the Bank of Bishop had asked him to appraise the Ewa project and estimate how much sugar it could produce when fully developed. Baldwin reported that Ewa was equipping its mill for twice as much sugar as it would ever get. He estimated that with smart farming, Ewa might eventually produce up to five thousand tons of sugar a year, but no more.

For the next few years, it looked as though Baldwin was right. Troubles continued to beset Ewa. The local milling machinery, installed just in time to handle the first harvest in 1892, proved hopelessly inefficient. The mill was designed to operate by a new diffusion process, which required that the cane be sliced before the juice could be extracted. The slicer did not work, and rail cars loaded with cane jammed up outside the mill. At one time a thousand tons of mature cane were burned becuase they could not be processed. "That mill couldn't grind the yolk of an egg," the Ewa manager growled. The first harvest produced a disappointing 2,849 tons of sugar. Two years later, 5,000 tons of sugar were lost because of mishaps at the mill.

Finally, in desperation, Castle & Cooke sent a man to the United States to scout for better mill machinery. In St. Louis he bought from the Fulton Iron Works a nine-roll crusher designed for Louisiana cane. When this machinery was installed at Ewa, it revolutionized cane crushing in Hawaii.

The mill was only one of several innovations in sugar production engineered by Ewa. The plantation contracted for Honolulu's street-sweepings for fertilizer, then it applied saltpeter and dried blood to the soil. This fertilization program eventually grew into one of agriculture's outstanding soil-feeding programs.

Ewa began to surpass the fondest dreams of its promoters. By 1898 it had put Henry Baldwin's prediction to shame; production that year totaled 18,284 tons of sugar, the next year 22,300 tons.

In the years that followed, Ewa's yields were to border on the fantastic. By 1922, production averaged 9.23 tons of sugar per acre. Eventually, one field of 120 acres yielded 18.09 tons of sugar per acre, a world record.. In 1925, Ewa reached an annual production of 50,000 tons.

IN 1896, WILLIAM McKINLEY WAS ELECTED president of the United States, and he leaned toward annexation of the islands. The Spanish-American war two years later convinced Washington that Hawaii was a vital Pacific bastion for security, which had better be taken under America's wing before some other country claimed it.

Congress, by joint resolution, annexed Hawaii on August 12, 1898. At Iolani Palace the Hawaiian standard came down the pole and the American flag went up instead. The few Hawaiians who attended the ceremony watched in bitter silence as the "foreigners" rejoiced. Royalists ignored the ceremonies entirely and gathered at Washington Place, Queen Liliuokalani's private residence, to offer tears and sympathy.

The Territory of Hawaii was established in June 1900, and Sanford Dole, president of the former republic, was appointed the first governor of the new territory.

With annexation the price of sugar began to rise, a boon to all of Hawaii's sugar planters.

Flush with profits from Ewa Plantation, Castle & Cooke was ready to make another plunge in sugar. Northwest of Honolulu, between the Waianae and Koolau mountains, a plain cuts across Oahu. On its northern end, the plantation established in the 1860s by the second Levi Chamberlain had grown into the small but prosperous Halstead Plantation.

After Ewa Plantation had shown what an abundance of water could do for sugar, Ben Dillingham made plans to extend his railroad around the western shore of Oahu from Ewa to the Halstead Plantation at Waialua. Dillingham thought he saw in the Halstead Plantation another Ewa, so he gathered in adjoining lands and proposed a consolidation into one large operation. Again, he turned to Castle & Cooke.

In October of 1898, the Waialua Agricultural Company, Ltd., was organized with capital stock of $3.5 million. At the time, the Halstead Plantation, the core of the enterprise, consisted of only several hundred acres, one small mill, a five-million-gallon-a-day pumping station, and one set of steam plows.

Waialua was no Ewa with flat or rolling fields lying at a low elevation, proven water sources, and land leased from a single estate. Waialua sprawled over rugged terrain at many altitudes; it had a heavier, but by no means dependable, rainfall, and the land ownership was a jumble. Many of Waialua's water rights dated from ancient taro patches, irrigated by the mountain waters ever since the Polynesians settled Oahu. Leases or fee-simple titles had to be negotiated with hundreds of ownerships, covering cane lands, water rights, forest reservations, ranch lands, and lands not suited for cane but necessary for investment protection. Some of the owners or lessees had, in turn, leased to small cane, rice, taro, and pineapple growers.

Castle & Cooke's plantation quilt-makers brought off one fine swap of 118/168th of 2.038 acres for 100/168th of 2.6007 acres. They also arranged, in a single stroke, one 12,000-acre deal. When the patchwork was done, Waialua consisted of 10,000 acres of sugar lands, plus an additional 12,000 acres too high in elevation for growing cane but which later, to the surprise of the founders, would prove ideal for pineapple.

In 1899, the first year a crop was harvested, $758,463 was poured into improvement of the property and equipment taken over from the Halsteads. The 300 acres then in cane produced 1,741 tons of sugar. The next year 1,025 acres produced 5,681 tons, but almost one-third of the crop was lost because the new mill was not completed. By 1900 another $1.5 million had been invested. The plantation was now in debt to Castle & Cooke for more than half a million dollars.

However, cane acreage and sugar output continued to zoom: 2,000 acres yielded 12,000 tons; 2,800 acres bore 17,000 tons; 3,112 acres produced 19,768 tons. Soon annual operating expenses had reached the million-dollar mark, big farming in any league. By 1908, Waialua was ready to declare its first dividend, a conservative 6 percent. After that, dividends averaged 11.5 percent for many years.

The year of the first dividend coincided with completion of a vast, new irrigation project at Waialua. The new plantation had more natural rainfall than Ewa, but it was not enough for the acreage planned. Management attempted to supplement the water requirements from wells, but unlike Ewa, some of Waialua's fields were on high ground, calling for a heavy pumping load. The cost was exorbitant.

In 1900, two engineers, L. G. Kellogg and B. L. Clark, had made a proposition: "Put up $181,000 and we'll build a dam across the Kaukonahua stream to catch the rainwaters from the Koolau range. We can get you enough water to irrigate 4,800 acres by gravity, and it'll save you $140,000 to $160,000 a year in pumping expense."

Waialua stockholders provided $90,000, and Castle & Cooke the rest. The dam created a winding lake seven miles long. The cost had climbed to $300,000 by the time it was completed, but it could impound 2,540 million gallons of water and actually released four times that much annually to the land below. By 1928 the engineering that rerouted the rainfall put Waialua's annual sugar production into the 50,000-ton class along with Ewa. Waialua was to join Ewa as two of the largest, most efficient sugar plantations in Hawaii.

MEANTIME, ON THE ISLAND OF HAWAII four other plantations had been established in the North Kohala district alongside Father Bond's "missionary" plantation. All had had good years, but they also had frequent bad ones when the rain failed to appear. Envying the success of other sugar irrigation projects, Kohala's growers began to wish they, too, had a ditch to bring water from the mountains.

An immediate problem was the intense jealousy among the five plantations. The plantation managers had no love for one another and weren't about to do anything to help their neighbors. They ruled their realms in totalitarian fashion, determined to maintain their independence, and about the only time they saw each other was at church when they exchanged cool greetings. Three managers who cultivated adjoining acreage reportedly did not see or talk to each other for nearly twenty years, other than the Sunday nod.

The managers could not even agree on the time of day. Although it might be 6:00 A.M. by the sun's reckoning, one manager would blow the mill whistle at 5:00 to put his crews to work, while across the road another manager had set 5:30 as the time to begin. Managers even established their own "daylight saving time" on whim. It became so confusing with all the whistle-tooting that the agencies finally called a meeting to establish uniform hours for everyone.

That's why it's remarkable that the famous Kohala Ditch ever got started. But in 1904 promoters obtained a permit from the territorial government to build a ditch from the mountains to the Kohala peninsula. When completed, it would carry water from an area with 200 inches of annual rainfall to lands where rainfall varied from 20 to 80 inches a year.

The Kohala Ditch Company was organized by the Hind family, owners of the Hawi Mill Plantation Co., and M. M. O'Shaughnessy, the engineer who built San Francisco's great Hetch Hetchy dam and aqueduct, was hired to do the job. Seventeen lives were lost in the building of this spectacular ditch system. And as usual the cost estimate was too conservative. The final price tag was almost five times the original capital subscribed.

Before the ditch was constructed, the other sugar plantations in the Kohala area contracted to take stipulated quantities of water based on estimates of ditch flow. When the ditch was finished, the flow, for much of the time, was far lower than expected, and Hawi, which needed the water most of all, was the loser. The ditch produced an average of about 19 million gallons of water a day, but daily flows ranged from a high of 40 million gallons to a low of 7 million gallons.

As a result of mergers over the years, Kohala Sugar Company wound up as the only surviving plantation in the district by 1937. Production the following year exceeded 35,000 tons of sugar. (It had become owner of the Kohala Ditch Co. in 1930.)

J. B. ATHERTON, ASTUTE BUSINESSMAN though he was, was sometimes unable to adjust his rigid ideas sufficiently to get along with people. Specifically, he was unable to get along with some of the second generation of Castles and Cookes.

One of these was James B. Castle, fourth of the Castle sons. Following graduation from Oberlin College, he returned to Honolulu and was assigned to a modest job at Castle & Cooke. He later became a partner in the firm.

J. B. Castle soon exploded with ideas for the development of Hawaii, ideas even more dynamic than the dreams of his father. He was a born promoter. His enthusiasm and visionary ideas annoyed Atherton, with whom he clashed frequently. Feeling that he was being held down unnecessarily by Atherton's authority, he eventually resigned to seek operations in which his ideas would be given free rein.

In subsequent years his activities left their mark on generations to come. He was one of the backers of Ewa Plantation. On the windward side of Oahu, he acquired large acreages and founded the Koolau Agricultural Company, which he hoped would become the biggest sugar plantation on Oahu. The dream never materialized, but in 1917 the huge acreage was bought and developed into the Kaneohe Ranch by his son, Harold K. L. Castle.

Jim Castle built a railroad to connect with B. F. Dillingham's railway beyond Waialua, and he proposed a tunnel under the Koolau Range to extend the line of the Honolulu Rapid Transit Company, which he had helped organize. But it was more than half a century before a tunnel joined the two sides of Oahu.

A hospitable extrovert, Castle built a huge, boxlike mansion projecting over the surf at the Diamond Head end of Waikiki Beach. The structure eventually became the home of the Honolulu Elks' Club.

As with any visionary, some of his projects fell flat. On the Kona coast of the island of Hawaii, where his father had hoped to found industries to support the people, he and his brother, William R. Castle, undertook to rehabilitate plantations under a plan whereby sugar would be grown by small farmers and sold to a central mill. Neither this nor a lumbering operation to produce ties from the hard, native ohia wood for the mainland's Santa Fe railroad proved successful.

At one time he became interested in a Russian sect called the Molakans, who lived in California. Believing that they would make good settlers for Hawaii, he opened up land on Kauai to homesteading and spent $30,000 to bring the group to that island. Unfortunately, the Molakans did not like Kauai, and Castle had to pay their fare back.

But young Castle's successes far outweighed his failures. Perhaps his biggest coup was acquiring a controlling interest in Claus Spreckels' huge Hawaiian Commercial & Sugar Company on Maui. Spreckels had been battling for years for dominance of the Hawaiian sugar industry, and Castle sought to end that threat.

He entered into an agreement with a group of stockbrokers in San Francisco to acquire 51 percent control through purchases of H. C. & S. stock on the open market. A price of $1.9 million was to be paid upon delivery of the shares. The agreement specified a deadline of November 15, 1898. It was Castle's intent to turn over his control of H. C. & S. to a Hawaiian sugar company in return for a part interest in the company.

A story persists that he first approached J. B. Atherton, president of Castle & Cooke. Although there is no evidence to support the tale, he allegedly asked Atherton for a sizable percentage of ownership in C & C and a seat among the officers. Atherton, stiff-necked, conservative, and still highly suspicious of the dynamic young businessman, turned the offer down cold, or so the story goes. If true, Atherton was also turning down an opportunity to make C & C the largest sugar factor in Hawaii.

In any event, it is fact that Castle went to Alexander & Baldwin. He had reached an agreement with A & B even before the H. C. & S. shares were purchased in San Francisco. In return for the H. C. & S. stock, Castle received a 25 percent interest in the A & B partnership. In 1900, following A & B's incorporation, he became first vice-president of the company, keeping the same 25 percent ownership—second in size only to the holdings of Henry P. Baldwin, president. J. B. Castle continued as a senior officer of A & B until his death in 1918.

Although it cannot be verified whether Castle & Cooke had the opportunity to acquire control of H. C. & S., it is recorded that in 1897—a year before the J. B. Castle coup—C & C did lose its profitable agency business for the Haiku and Paia plantations on Maui to Alexander & Baldwin. A & B had opened its own agency in Honolulu in late 1895. (C & C had sold its interests in these two plantations some years earlier in order to survive the Ewa financial drain.)

ANOTHER OF THE SECOND GENERATION who made his mark was Charles Montague Cooke. After returning from Amherst College, he, too, went to work in the Castle & Cooke store. He likewise developed ambitions and in the late 1870s pulled out to become the Cooke of Lewers & Cooke, hardware and building material merchants who became the principal competitors of Castle & Cooke's hardware business. A unique feature in the articles of incorporation of Lewers & Cooke was a clause authorizing the directors to spend part of the company's earnings on philanthropies.

C. M. Cooke soon proved that he was one of those individuals whose Midas touch turned almost any enterprise into gold. He was one of the founders and the first president of Ewa Plantation. He also was a founder of Waialua Agricultural and participated in organizing sugar growing operations at Kahuku, Lihue, and Wailuku, and at least a dozen other businesses.

In 1895, a year after Father Castle's death, Cooke moved to California, establishing his family in Oakland. By 1898 he was back in Hawaii to become president of the new Bank of Hawaii. A year later he took over the presidency of C. Brewer & Co., which had picked up the agency representation for several plantations pioneered by Castle & Cooke. After that, the Cookes were more actively associated with Castle & Cooke competitors than with the business their father had helped to found.

IN 1898, CASTLE & COOKE DECIDED to get rid of its merchandise business. The operation was sold to B. F. Dillingham for $194,000 worth of notes and shares in his new Pacific Hardware Company.

Dating back to the days of the depository, when the partners outfitted sailing vessels and hoped their skippers would return to pay their bills, was an accumulation of promissory notes aggregating $600,000. These were written off as a total loss, and the retail business that had launched the firm of Castle & Cooke forty-seven years earlier came to an end.

Sale of the merchandise business did not, however, signal the end of diversification. When returns from Castle & Cooke's investments in Waialua, Ewa, and other lucrative sources began rolling in, the company had dollars for new investments. One was the Hawaiian Automobile Company, which proposed to revolutionize transportation in Honolulu with a fleet of surreys powered by storage batteries. Unfortunately, the batteries failed with irritating frequency. Though J. B. Atherton personally used a tiller-steered electric in place of his horse and buggy, Castle & Cooke's venture with the horseless carriage was a failure.

After Ewa demonstrated the importance of fertilizing sugar, Castle & Cooke helped launch the Hawaiian Fertilizer Company, organized by Cooke's youngest son, Amos Francis. He, too, had earned his first dollars behind the Castle & Cooke counters, then had cut loose to manage the Pacific Navigation Company, operating ships between Hawaii and the South Seas.

One of the firm's biggest ventures was into the refining of sugar. Refining of the coarse, brown raw sugar had been tried in Honolulu as early as the 1860s by the Honolulu Sugar Refining Company, of which S. N. Castle had been president. The refinery had been short-lived, however, and island planters continued to send their raw sugar to the United States in barrels and kegs. They were growers, not refiners.

In the late 1890s, Castle & Cooke again sensed a rule-or-ruin crisis in the making because of Spreckels' continued pricing tactics. So the company invested $112,500 in a 37.5 percent interest in one of Spreckels' rivals, George W. McNear's California Beet Sugar and Refining Company at Crockett on upper San Francisco Bay. To protect its plantations, C. Brewer & Co. bought a 25 percent interest. This refinery handled Hawaiian sugar from 1898 to 1903.

ON APRIL 7, 1903, J. B. Atherton died at his home, a victim of dengue fever. All business and government in Honolulu closed for the funeral service at Central Union Church where a recitation of his accomplishments was given: he was an early supporter of the YMCA; a trustee of Oahu College and Kawaiahao Seminary; an owner of *The Star*, a Honolulu afternoon newspaper; and a member of thirty-nine organizations.

"One month of last summer witnessed the distribution by him of $35,000 in charity," the *Honolulu Advertiser* reported, "and since his illness, he has lifted the debt of $13,000 of the Hawaiian Board of Missions."

Ben Dillingham characterized Atherton as "a man who carried his religious principles with him into his daily life. It was, with him, no mere garment to put on and off with the occasion."

Chapter 8

Island Fleet

"I AM NOT ONE OF THOSE MISSIONARIES who came around the Horn, brought it with him and has been tooting it ever since." That was one of the favorite self-descriptions of E. D. Tenney, who guided and controlled the fortunes of Castle & Cooke for more than thirty years as manager, president, and finally chairman of the board. Another favorite Tenneyism was the statement that he was the only Castle & Cooke executive who was "neither a preacher, Sunday school teacher nor deacon."

Edward Davies Tenney, a nephew of Angeline and Mary Tenney Castle, was the Horatio Alger prototype, the young man who started by sweeping out the store and rose to the presidency, the man who made it to the top by his own sweat and thoroughly enjoyed the prestige and power that came with his hard-earned position.

Tenney came to the islands from Plainfield, New York, in 1877, but instead of looking up his relatives, he found a job as luna on a plantation near Hilo. When in 1880 he contracted rheumatism while working twelve to fourteen hours a day in the frequent rain of the Hilo area, plantation doctors sent him to Honolùlu for treatment.

After several months there, Tenney asked J. B. Atherton for a job. At the time, there were fourteen on the Castle & Cooke payroll, and the lowliest three were Hawaiians, who did the muscle work. One was quitting, and Atherton offered Tenney the vacancy at $35 a month. Tenney took it and was soon raised to $50. For this he worked from six in the morning, when ships were about to sail, until after midnight. He opened the store in the morning. He operated a two-wheeled hand truck, trundling kegs of nails up the muddy paths from the wharves to the store. He checked the loading of sugar boats and lent a hand with the stevedoring.

Tenney learned sugar handling, ship operation, the hardware business, insurance. He sold washing machines, patent medicines, boilers, and hay. With a flair for getting things done, he rose rapidly, acquiring a junior partnership in 1889. And along the way he became the brother-in-law of George P. Castle, who married Tenney's sister Ida.

In spite of his kinship with the Castle family, Tenney was known as an Atherton man. When the firm was incorporated in 1894, he became corporate secretary and later vice-president. He also became secretary of Ewa Plantation and Waialua Agricultural Company. It was Tenney who found the sugar mill machinery in St. Louis that saved Ewa from becoming a disaster.

When J. B. Atherton died in 1903, George Parmelee Castle was elected to succeed him. But Castle was a reluctant president and agreed to accept the position only on condition that a new position, manager of Castle & Cooke, be created and filled by "a person of proven business ability and judgment." Who else but Ed Tenney? He had been with the company since 1880, knew every phase of the business, and was a smart, aggressive go-getter. Elected manager and first vice-president, he was to be the company's tough-willed boss for the next three decades. He went on to completely remodel the house of Castle & Cooke.

It's hard to picture two men more different than Tenney and his predecessor, J. B. Atherton. Tenney eventually became a one-man oligarchy—bluff, gruff, a dictator of all that happened within his company.

"Tenney was a czar," said a Honolulu businessman who knew him well. "Everybody was afraid of him. He was strict in everything, yet people knew he was fair in what he did."

Tenney liked power. He was not satisfied merely to be a corporation manager—and later president. Hail-fellow-well-met, booming, domineering, he loved to go to directors' meetings and steamroll them with his hearty voice, exuberant personality, and iron will. At one point, he was president of Castle & Cooke, Matson Navigation, Hawaiian Trust, the Hawaiian Sugar Planters' Association, Ewa Plantation, Waialua Plantation, and Kohala Sugar, and a director of a dozen other companies, including Theo. H. Davies & Co., a direct competitor in the sugar factoring business.

Tenney would boss a directors' meeting of Ewa Plantation, then put on his panama hat and walk across the street to a directors' meeting of Hawaiian Trust Company and call the signals there—to much the same group. One friend sought to deny stories that Tenney pounded the table at board meetings. "But he did tap it with a finger or two until it bounced. At that point, you either voted the way he demanded or he adjourned the meeting." Sometimes he tapped with a gold-headed cane.

When Tenney became manager of Castle & Cooke, the company was part owner of and agent for Ewa, Waialua, and Kohala Sugar and agent for Waimea Sugar Mill Company, Fulton Iron Works of St. Louis, Standard Oil Company, Weston's Centrifugals, George F. Black Steam Pumps, E. W. Deming's System of Clarification, and Babcock & Wilcox Company (boilers). In addition to the New England Mutual Life Insurance Company, it represented the Aetna Fire Insurance Company and the Alliance Assurance Company of London.

All pretty mundane, perhaps, compared to the dried codfish, Uncle Tom's Cabin and Dr. Jayne's Celebrated Family Medicines sold by Brothers Castle and Cooke—but certainly more profitable. The company's net income in 1906 was $149,742, despite a shaky sugar business attributed to "political unrest in Cuba." By 1910 profits were $426,646, and the firm owned stocks and bonds valued at $848,500. That same year capital stock was increased from $1 million to $2 million by a 100 percent stock dividend, and Ed Tenney's salary was boosted from $7,000 to $8,000 a year.

Each March, Tenney prepared a written report for the annual stockholders' meeting, going into great detail about the company's operations of the past year. He was supposed to have monthly reports for directors as well, but often they were not ready because of "congestion in the accounting department."

The reports and forecasts were, all in all, cheery. In 1905 the first mention was made of cash Christmas presents for the company's employees. The next year, Tenney was proposing a profit-sharing plan. The company shared its earnings with the community and the world, too. There was $50 for a Leper's Christmas Fund, a donation for the Harvard Medical School of Oriental Diseases in Shanghai, $100 for the YMCA, $1,000 for the "Osaka fire victims," and $500 for "earthquake sufferers in Sicily."

One curious item, $25 for "Diamond Head Charley," was a gift to a man who held forth in a small house on the famous promontory to sight the arrivals of Matson ships and signal the information to those who cared. By that time Castle & Cooke cared—it was Hawaii agent for Captain William Matson's growing fleet of ships that steamed between San Francisco and the islands.

CAPTAIN MATSON, a barrel-chested man with a sea-weathered face, a thatch of black hair, and a heavy mustache, was walking down the street, not far from Honolulu's waterfront, one day in June 1907. He soon encountered one of the Castles—George Parmelee, the reluctant president of Castle & Cooke. Matson said he was scouting for an agent in Honolulu to drum up more business for his fleet of steamships. Would Castle & Cooke be interested? "Why don't you talk it over with Ed Tenney?" Castle suggested.

So the captain turned into the Stangenwald Building on Merchant Street, where Castle & Cooke had its offices. Tenney was at his rolltop desk with its stuffed gooney bird brooding on top. When he recognized his visitor and learned of his mission, he adjusted his pince-nez spectacles and hitched forward in his chair.

Captain Matson had been plugging away at his private saga of achievement for forty years. Born in Sweden in 1849, he went to sea at age ten as "handy boy," was a seaman at fourteen, and at eighteen had his first whiff of the sugar trade while transporting coal by schooner to Claus Spreckels' sugar factory south of San Francisco. With dollars saved and borrowed, Matson bought an interest in a three-master, the *Emma Claudina,* and sailed her to Hilo in 1882.

The *Emma Claudina* carried a 300-ton general cargo to the Big Island and took sugar, molasses, and sperm oil back to the United States. Five years later he was master of the brigantine *Lurline,* in which he had a 25 percent share. Islanders owned most of the rest.

At the time San Francisco was a city of 250,000 people with horse cars, cable cars, and down on the waterfront and out in the harbor, nearly one thousand ships a year—three-quarters of them windjammers. Hawaii was a colorful little country that seemed to hold great promise for an adventurer like Matson, who could speed from San Francisco down the two thousand nautical miles to Hilo in two weeks if he had a northeaster in his sails, or three weeks if the winds were against him. But he wanted larger, faster ships that could carry more cargo at more profit.

In 1891 he bought a wooden bark, the *Harvester,* which carried ten passengers as well as freight. Next he added a steel bark, and then the *Roderick Dhu,* which had a cold storage plant and electric lights. Soon he had a fleet of seven, all windjammers.

But the Age of the Steamship had arrived, and the new vessels were leaving him in their wake. Captain Matson had stuck to sail long enough; it was time to turn to steam. That meant giving up the one-man operation and incorporating. The Matson Navigation Company was organized in 1901. Its first steamship, the *Enterprise,* set off for Hilo in

1902, and she was the most modern ship in the Pacific, powered by oil instead of coal. Captain Matson had gone all out; three more steamships, all oil burners, were added to the fleet.

Matson had always liked Hilo; he'd made money there. Only when his fleet and his plans outgrew Hawaii's second seaport did he decide to make Honolulu his main Pacific terminus. For half of 1907 his *Hilonian* had been putting into Honolulu. But his agent, W. G. Irwin & Company, was also agent for his competitor, Oceanic Steamship, and Matson felt his affairs were getting short shrift.

Castle & Cooke had been in shipping for half a century. The company had been part owner and Honolulu agent for several schooners and barks, an interest it sold in 1901 to buy into the Planters' Line. In 1907, it was still the agent for Planters, handling island sugar and cargoes for a fleet of ten sailing vessels.

Matson believed the islands had to have bigger, faster ships and more of them, operating on regular and dependable schedules with better service all around—and he proposed to supply that service.

After Ed Tenney heard Matson's proposal that C & C become his agent, the outspoken manager bellowed, "No! Why in hell should we?" Captain Matson bellowed right back, emphasizing where he stood in the shipping business and where he intended to go—"and, by God, it isn't to hell either, Mr. Tenney!"

Later that day the captain was astonished when Ed Tenney hurried down to the waterfront to proclaim that Castle & Cooke would indeed like to serve as his agent. It seems the usually weak-voiced George Castle had howled when he heard of Tenney's curt turndown and had done some rare bellowing of his own, "You find Matson and make a deal with him before he gets together with one of the other agencies. And don't waste any time doing it!"

Ed Tenney and Captain Matson shook hands, and the deal was closed. What was to become a fifty-six-year association with Castle & Cooke—and for many of those years an immensely profitable one—began without the scratch of a pen.

That first year Castle & Cooke hustled enough freight for the Matson ships' homeward trips to double the steamship company's profits. For Matson, the net gain for the last six months of 1907 was $23,000. For Castle & Cooke, commissions totaled $2,529. Reviewing the year, Tenney noted with a straight face that there had been "a gradual decrease in the business of the sailing vessels; consequently it is well that we have secured the agency for his [Matson's] line of steamers, if we wish to continue a factor in the shipping business of these Islands."

Castle & Cooke divested itself of its 731 shares in Planters' Line in a swap for 429 shares in Matson, and it invested $100,000 cash in Matson stock to be used in the construction of a new steamer. From then on, Matson and Castle & Cooke became virtually synonymous in the islands. By 1913, Castle & Cooke's commissions from Matson passenger and freight business were almost ten times what they had been from all shipping sources a decade previously. By 1916, C & C, while employing only 27 people in its main office, supervised an average of 334 persons hired by steamship operators to hustle freight, clerk, and otherwise serve Matson vessels at the Honolulu wharves.

To insure a supply of oil for his ships, Matson bought several wells near Santa Maria, California, and built a four-inch pipeline to a shipping terminal at Gaviota. Later he laid another line from the rich Coalinga Field to Monterey Bay. Outfitting several sailing ships and a steamer as tankers, he pioneered the carrying of bulk oil to Hawaii, Alaska, and the Pacific Northwest. In 1910, Matson founded the Honolulu Oil Company, which drilled wells on leases in California. Castle & Cooke invested $140,000 in the new oil company as a friendly gesture to the captain. By 1960, this "friendly gesture" was paying Castle & Cooke $400,000 a year in dividends, and when Honolulu Oil was liquidated in 1962, C & C's shares were worth $23,274,638.

"BOAT DAY"—the arrival of a passenger ship—was a gala event in Honolulu. At the blast of the Hawaiian Electric Company's whistle, Tenney invariably grabbed for his panama, and the entire office staff of Castle & Cooke, along with much of Honolulu, hurried to the dock to bid the newcomers welcome. Flower leis, bought for twenty-five cents from picturesque vendors, were heaped upon the shoulders of arriving passengers, and the Royal Hawaiian band played lively music while hula girls danced.

In the afternoon the whole process was reversed when the ship left for a new port. Streamers and confetti were added for departures, and the band played "Aloha Oe," a haunting melody that unfailingly produced streams of tears, on both deck and dock.

Captain Matson's first *Lurline* had been a brigantine costing $32,000. His second *Lurline* was a freighter with room for fifty-one passengers. But in the captain's mind were plans for a true passenger ship, one that would have eleven bathrooms and carry 146 passengers. When manager Tenney told the Castle & Cooke directors of the captain's dream, they voted to invest another $100,000 in Matson. C. Brewer & Co. and Alexander & Baldwin also came in on the deal. The captain's dream was the *Wilhelmina* (named for Tenney's daughter). She entered the island run in 1910. Then came the *Manoa*, followed by the first *Matsonia*, half again as large as the *Manoa*. In 1917 came the *Maui*, at a cost of $1,650,560. She was powered by the biggest geared turbine ever installed in an American ship up to that time and was equipped with gyro pilot as well as compass.

All the Matson ships made money. Castle & Cooke hustled business in the islands, and the captain pounded the pavements in San Francisco. Matson was everywhere on the waterfront with his handsome buggy and fast-stepping horse. A natty dresser, he was a familiar sight in well-tailored suit, satin tie, stickpin, seal ring, buttonhole carnation, and flowing mustache. He could take a sailor's skin off in seaman's language, then turn around and deliver a solid, articulate address to the San Francisco Chamber of Commerce, of which he was president.

The glittering *Maui* was the last of the Matson ships to be bid *aloha* by the line's founder. Captain Matson died in 1917.

He was succeeded in the presidency (at $250 a month) by the man who had never asked for a written agreement, E. D. Tenney. Ever since becoming Matson's Hawaii agency, Castle & Cooke had been buying more and more stock in the steamship company. Three of the other Big Five companies bought, too, and acted as agents for Matson on the other islands—Alexander & Baldwin on Maui; C. Brewer & Co. on the Big Island, and Amfac and Alexander & Baldwin on Kauai. But Castle & Cooke was recognized as Matson's first of kin in Hawaii.

In 1914 the Panama Canal opened—a boon for ocean travel from Hawaii to the East Coast. Prior to World War I, occasional automobiles and electric trolleys were traveling the streets of Honolulu, and horses no longer whinnied in terror at their appearance. Auto races had become a regular event at Kapiolani Park, as were polo matches and sulky races. Honolulu boasted an amateur symphony orchestra, and the Bishop Museum had opened. The city's buildings had been numbered, letter carrier service had begun, and the city elected its first mayor.

The Moana Hotel, still standing among the skyscrapers of today's Waikiki, was a popular beach resort. In downtown Honolulu the Alexander Young Hotel's roof garden attracted the dancing set, while a popular hotel for weekends was the Haleiwa, a "destination point" for Dillingham's railroad on the north shore of Oahu. It was operated by the Kimball family, who later became famous as owners of the Halekulani Hotel in Waikiki.

When America entered the war, Hawaii's citizens worked diligently, as people in the States did, sending their sons to become soldiers, supporting Liberty bond sales, and planting "Food Will Win the War" gardens.

The price of sugar was high. Ewa Plantation's profits in 1916 were $1,754,769, and Waialua was close behind with $1,497,754. Castle & Cooke's profits that year jumped to $950,882, compared with $414,928 the year before, an achievement that prompted management to give all C & C employees an extra month's pay. Even the lowly plantation worker received a whopping 53 percent bonus—a generosity urged by president Tenney in recognition of the sharp increase in living costs. The 1916 gross income included $210,000 in Matson dividends, $119,805 in sugar agency commissions, $93,500 in shipping commissions, $14,000 in insurance proceeds, and the rest in other stock and bond income.

A number of German ships, which had taken refuge in Honolulu harbor since 1914, were seized when the United States entered the war. So was one of the Big Five companies, Hackfeld & Company, which was to become American Factors. But all in all Hawaii was a long way from the war zone, and life was relatively normal.

The islands did, however, suffer one severe shock. Just prior to America's entry into the war, the American Hawaiian Steamship Company moved its fleet of freighters, which had carried a substantial share of Hawaii's sugar, to the Atlantic Coast in pursuit of more profitable business generated by the war. Matson Navigation jumped at the chance to supply the islands with all their transportation needs. When the U. S. Shipping Board commandeered Matson's *Maui, Matsonia,* and *Wilhelmina* for military duty to France, Tenney kept a bridge of ships operating between Hawaii and San Francisco by collecting all the wooden ships and German vessels he could get his hands on.

With the end of the war, Matson added two 14,000-ton freighters, the *Manulani* and the *Manukai,* the largest cargo carriers in the Pacific. Tenney announced that, with completion of new freighters then on order, Matson would be able to carry all of Hawaii's sugar and canned pineapple cargo. By 1920 nearly a million tons of freight a year moved over the Honolulu waterfront, and 75 percent of it arrived or left in Matson bottoms. Four years later Matson carried 95 percent of the 1,689,000 tons handled by the agency. By 1925, Matson had sixteen freighters in operation.

Little wonder that Castle & Cooke directors in 1923 authorized Tenney to buy Matson shares when available at prices he considered advisable. He lost no time in communicating this authorization to his other self, president Tenney of Matson.

OVER THE YEARS, Castle & Cooke had concentrated most of its attention on developing industry within the islands. The sole exception had been its pioneering of the California and Hawaiian Sugar Refining Company at Crockett, California, in 1905. To free themselves once and for all from Claus Spreckels, Castle & Cooke and nearly all the other Hawaii plantations and agencies outside the Spreckels orbit organized the Sugar Factors Company, Ltd., to buy, sell, transport, and arrange for refining of Hawaiian sugars. The group reopened the old McNear refinery at Crockett and set up C and H to refine and sell island sugar in the States. C and H, established as a cooperative owned by Hawaii's sugar companies, has been in operation ever since.

Before the war Ed Tenney had decided to take Castle & Cooke further afield. Within a few months, the company acquired a miscellaneous assortment of stocks and bonds, including shares in the Bank of California, Pennsylvania Railroad, California Telephone & Light, Poulsen Wireless, Santa Cruz Portland Cement, Sterling Oil & Development, and many others. None of the holdings was large, but the list was impressive when Tenney talked with bankers.

In October 1916, Ed Tenney had become president of Castle & Cooke—in name as well as fact—when George Castle had voluntarily stepped down from the presidency.

As president, Castle had presided at directors' meetings for thirteen years, but a study of the minutes indicates he seldom opened his mouth—Tenney did practically all the talking.

Castle wore rimless glasses and a neat, short-cropped beard and mustache. His habitual attire was a white suit accompanied by white canvas sneakers, which he purchased by the case. "He was like a sparrow," said an associate.

Like many missionary children, he was often frugal in small things but generous in matters of philanthropy. He was stuffy by some people's standards, and his innate primness often showed. Once, after returning from a steamer visit to Maui, he reported, wide-eyed, to manager Tenney, "I saw people being intimate right out on the deck!"

"George," Tenney retorted, "people have been hanky-panking since Adam and Eve, and I don't think there's a damn thing we can do about it!"

Castle had indeed been a reluctant president, but if nothing else, he did make one major contribution: he snapped Ed Tenney into action with Captain Matson. In the eventual fortunes of Castle & Cooke, that was a momentous contribution.

But business was not for him. He was happiest when working on his beloved projects in education, church, and general philanthropy. The words on a plaque installed in Kawaiahao Church after his death in 1932 summarized the man: "He Went Around Doing Good."

Chapter 9

One-Man Rule

IT WAS 1924, and Castle & Cooke had a brand-new headquarters building. It was an imposing five-story structure complete with stately columns, located at Merchant and Bishop streets in the heart of Honolulu's financial district. The site and structure cost a magnificent $868,000.

Everyone was proud of the new headquarters. Those tall, granite columns had a sturdy, substantial look—the proper countenance for a firm as solid as Castle & Cooke. Just how solid the company had become in the almost thirty years since it was incorporated was described by president Tenney at the annual stockholders' meeting on March 6, 1924. He began, "I am pleased to report that the past year has been a prosperous one." That had become a familiar opening line. Of course, some years had been more prosperous than others, but there had never been a loss, and dividends had been generous.

The 1923 profit was $618,888, from which $393,400 was paid in dividends. Since incorporation in 1894, Castle & Cooke had made a profit of $12,308,550 and had paid $6,299,400 in dividends. That worked out to 1,049.9 percent on the original capital of $600,000, or an average yearly dividend of 36.2 percent over a period of twenty-nine years. There had never been a cash dividend lower than the first one, which totaled $48,000. Payments to stockholders had been as high as $615,000 in 1920.

Castle & Cooke's success was partly due to the individual successes of the companies in which it had sizable investments. American Factors (C & C bought into this firm when it was "Americanized" during World War I) earned $1,142,885 in 1923. Theo. H. Davies & Co. (Tenney sat on the board) had a profit of $517,487. Matson's profit was $1,069,712. Honolulu Oil earned $1,697,988, and Honolulu Iron Works $382,800. In sugar, Ewa Plantation, as usual, was a big money-maker with $1,378,653, while Waialua ran its usual second place with $1,129,413. Kohala Sugar was running weak at $44,683— it never was in a league with Ewa or Waialua.

These and other stock and bond investments continued to bring in the biggest chunk of C & C gross income in 1923, amounting to $643,808. Agency commissions for sugar totaled $133,755; for shipping, $176,911. Insurance brought in $41,763, and assorted incomes another $55,000. This added up to a total of $1,051,251. Operating expenses were only slightly in excess of $200,000, and taxes and bonuses were lumped at $173,000.

The Castles, the Athertons, and Ed Tenney continued to have a tight hold on Castle & Cooke stock. Together, their holdings accounted for almost 90 percent of the shares outstanding. George P. Castle controlled 7,671 shares, compared with 972 on the day of incorporation in 1894. The S. N. Castle Estate represented 14,765 shares; it had begun with 2,038. The J. B. Atherton Estate, whose namesake had started with an equal 2,038 shares, now held the biggest block of stock—16,737 shares. Tenney now owned 3,571 shares; he'd started with 500. These increases in shareholdings during the twenty-nine years since incorporation were due primarily to stock dividends.

On the same day Tenney reviewed the 1923 figures, he said he had come to the conclusion that his reports were too revealing and that he was divulging too much confidential information for the company's good. W. R. Castle moved that the president be "authorized and directed to prepare his annual report for distribution to the shareholders in such form as he may consider for the best interests of the company." The motion was carried unanimously.

Tenney's one-man rule of Castle & Cooke was so complete that he did not even divulge much information to his own directors. This finally caused some ill feelings among members of the Castle family.

"Ed was as arbitrary as anyone could be but none of us really objected since he knew more about the business than all the rest of us put together," recalled Castle's grandson, Harold, who sat on the C & C board for fifty years. "He managed to keep it that way. At board meetings, he had everything cut and dried. He told us exactly how he wanted us to vote, and most of us didn't know what we were even voting on. The minutes could just as well have been written beforehand . . . ."

At last Harold protested. "Here I was, going to board meetings representing the Castle Estate, of which I was president. I represented 25 percent of the firm's stock, and things were happening without any of us knowing about it.

"So I went to Tenney and told him, 'I don't like the fact that when I'm questioned by the Castle family about our affairs, I can't answer intelligently. We don't necessarily want more power in Castle & Cooke affairs but we want some information about what's going on. What we'd like is an executive committee to consult with you before the directors meeting so we would at least know what we're voting on.' "

Tenney agreed to Harold's proposal and appointed a committee. He still ran the show, but the family had some forewarning—at times—of what he was up to. "At least we began to cast our votes with some semblance of knowledge," Harold said. "Tenney tried to live up to his agreement—but he persisted in making off-the-cuff deals, sometimes remembering to tell the directors a month or so later when it was too late to check him."

On the other hand, president Tenney believed in full disclosure to directors and stockholders on a vast variety of business minutiae, including the plumbing problems in the new headquarters. At the 1926 annual meeting, shareholders were informed that "there were a number of lavatories and urinals either cracked or badly crazed." A settlement of $441.60 had been arranged, but it unfortunately did not include the installation of new equipment. Solemnly, Tenney reported further, "During the past year we have experienced considerable trouble with the toilets in the ladies' restrooms but have solved the difficulty by installing Kotex vending machines in each of the rooms. These machines were purchased at $27.50 each, but will pay for themselves in a very short time."

BEING PRESIDENT of both Castle & Cooke and Matson kept a man busy, but for a man like Ed Tenney it was rewarding. He reveled in the power and prestige—and the multitude of fringe benefits that came to the boss of a big steamship company, such as taking his own limousine and chauffeur along when he made a trip to San Francisco. He also frequently took his daughter Wilhelmina, who in 1940 became the first woman director of Castle & Cooke, serving on the board until her death in 1951.

Wilhelmina was slight of frame but strong of will, and like her father she was always ready to tangle with anyone who disagreed with her. Although raised as an Episcopalian, she got into an argument with the bishop—and lost. She promptly became a devout Catholic and eventually willed the bulk of her estate to the Catholic church. Yet Tenney

Hall, on the grounds of St. Andrew's Church in Honolulu, remains as a monument to the Episcopal faith of her father and mother. She loved flowers, and her orchid collection was famous. She also loved the arts and contributed thousands of dollars to the Honolulu Symphony and the Honolulu Academy of Arts.

On Matson trips Wilhelmina and her father often sat at the captain's table, where they had a standing order for fresh strawberries when in season. Once there were none aboard, and a bystander who witnessed the dressing down Tenney gave the steward said it was nothing less than horrendous. Old-timers still cringe over the times when the old man's Lincoln was dented as it was hoisted from the ship's hold. It never seemed to happen to anybody else's car.

But whenever Tenney returned to Honolulu, he never failed to bring cargoes of fresh fruit for Castle & Cooke employees. Apples, peaches, apricots, grapes—all the fruits that were almost unknown in the islands—were distributed, an entire case per person.

His "good mornings" about the office were bustling affairs, with rough stories straight off the docks to twit the more solemn of his "missionary" associates, and he was forever pinching the behinds of the company's secretaries. But he also kept track of all his staff and their problems. "And how is your mother's arthritis?" he would ask a secretary.

Tenney usually wore a light gray suit and a straw hat in Honolulu. On the mainland he would switch to a derby, and when he crossed the nation by rail, he wore white gloves so he wouldn't get his hands sooty. He often arranged lavish dinner parties in the railroad diners.

Tenney's big home on Honolulu's Pensacola Street was entered through a porte cochere, and the surrounding gardens contained orchid houses, flowering shrubbery, spreading shade trees, and a tennis court. Honolulu's wealthy lived in style in those days, and it was not uncommon to have four or five full-time yardmen manicuring the grass. Inside the mansion, an Oriental cook might be preparing dinner for the evening's guests—fruit cup (in the summertime, it could be fresh mangoes and lychees), soup, perhaps a fish course, a rib roast, and dessert. Dinner was served by maids dressed in kimonos, who glided softly over the polished floors in their silent white *tabis*.

The Tenneys had a reputation for being good hosts. "He was a kind man . . . a thoughtful man who liked to do nice things for people," said a Honolulu woman who had often been a guest in the Tenney home. "At their dinner parties he would usually greet each lady with a purple Cattleya orchid from his own garden."

The casual and colorful Hawaiian clothes so in evidence in modern Hawaii were not worn in the days when the Tenneys entertained. Women did wear *holokus*, a formal version of the *muumuu*, when they attended Hawaiian parties, but men wore white trousers and white shirts open at the neck.

The time of the Tenneys was the time of the "at home" and the weekend house party. Each Wednesday afternoon women who lived in the Nuuanu region served tea and cakes to all who visited; Monday was the day for open house in the Waikiki area; Tuesday might include the Tenneys' home on Pensacola. Socialites could visit their friends around town with ease under this zoning system. A woman wore a hat and white gloves when she "came to call," and she left two calling cards in a silver plate when she departed.

Honolulu's business leaders, as they prospered, acquired beach sites on the other side of the island, where they built what they called "country places." These were usually board and batten structures with numerous bedrooms and baths, big kitchens and multiplace dining tables.

The Tenneys' weekend house, known as "Kaiahulu," was located at Mokuleia, at the far northern end of Oahu, and the best way to travel there was aboard "Dillingham's Folly." Servants were always there so guests could be relaxed and carefree—bathing, playing tennis, or lounging lazily. The dinner table was set with Haviland, and there were peacocks in the garden.

In the evenings there were quantities of good food and drink and entertainment—frequently with audience participation, Hawaiian style. Sometimes their parties took the form of a *luau,* a Hawaiian feast that included *kalua* pig, baked in an underground rock oven. The more common *poi* supper included all the native dishes except the pig. Among foods served were *laulaus,* a kind of Hawaiian grab-bag consisting of a pouch of ti leaves which has been stuffed with *luau,* a vegetable resembling chopped spinach, plus morsels of butterfish and pork, the whole being steamed. Sometimes the menu included chicken *luau,* poultry cooked with thick coconut milk and spinach. Always included were *lomi* salmon, salted raw fish combined with chopped tomatoes and green onions, baked sweet potatoes, and a coconut pudding called *haupia.* Sometimes there were small dishes with bits of smoky beef, seaweed, and a small shellfish called *opihi.*

If the Tenneys' guests included mainlanders, they were probably less than enthusiastic about *poi,* a slightly sour tannish-gray paste made from taro root. It's eaten with one or two fingers and is a running accompaniment to the rest of the foods, which are also eaten with the fingers if the dining is authentically Hawaiian.

There were Hawaiian songs, usually accompanied by a ukulele and followed by an assortment of hula dancing by both men and women. It was impromptu, relaxed, and "Hawaiian casual." Tenney later deeded his Mokuleia property to Castle & Cooke for the use of its employees. It is still a favorite vacation spot for scores of employees, and many come with their families from the mainland to enjoy its Old Hawaiian atmosphere.

BY 1925, THE MATSON ORGANIZATION was rapidly expanding its passenger business. Ed Tenney decided the company should offer luxury both afloat and ashore, having been persuaded by William P. Roth, Matson's general manager in San Francisco. Roth was a good-looking island stockbroker who had done well by marrying Captain Matson's daughter, Lurline. He also had demonstrated that he knew how to run a steamship line.

Roth loved luxury, and he figured there were a lot of well-heeled people in the world who shared his enjoyment of the good life. He talked to Tenney about developing a livelier tourist industry for Hawaii by building a truly luxurious passenger liner and an equally luxurious resort hotel in Hawaii. Tenney was enthusiastic.

"The siren call of the Islands is a call that cannot be denied," read an early Hawaii Tourist Bureau advertisement. "Turquoise blue of summer skies . . . green-clad mountain slopes . . . imperial jades of undulating ocean . . . the glories of Hawaii Nei beckon to the traveler from afar." In the winter, according to the Tenney-Roth plan, Matson would haul America's rich to tropical seas; in summer, it would haul schoolteachers and the short-term vacation crowd.

Tenney authorized construction of the *Malolo,* to be the finest passenger ship ever seen in the Pacific. The $7.5 million contract was let in 1925, and the accommodations—for 650 people—were to be deluxe. The ship would make a round trip between San Francisco and Honolulu every fourteen days.

Next the entrepreneurs started talking about a place for their guests to stay. The Young Hotel and the Blaisdell in downtown Honolulu offered little glamor. At Waikiki there was the twenty-four-year-old Moana and the nearby Seaside Hotel, neither with any great style. These properties were controlled by the Territorial Hotel Company, headed by Conrad C. von Hamm, who was at the time talking about enlarging the Moana.

Discussions began, and the result was an amalgamation of forces by von Hamm, Tenney, and Roth. President Tenney of Matson and president Tenney of Castle & Cooke became president Tenney of

Territorial Hotel Company—and almost half of the directors came from Castle & Cooke.

A beautiful palm grove in Waikiki was the site selected for the new $2 million hotel. A fifty-year lease was negotiated for the site, and six hundred acres of the Waialae Ranch, four miles away on the far side of Diamond Head, were leased for a golf course.

The hotel was to be called the Royal Hawaiian, "reviving memories of the old hostelry of that name" that had once existed on the edge of downtown Honolulu, according to the news release. By October 1925, when Warren & Wetmore, well-known hotel designers, had completed the plans, the estimated cost had increased to $3.5 million. R. T. Stevens, a landscape architect of national reputation, was engaged to fill twelve acres with tropical foliage. Seth Raynor was chosen to design the eighteen-hole golf course at Waialae. And N. W. Ayer advertising agency was hired to spread the word of Hawaii's—and Matson's—charms throughout America and around the world.

By now, Tenney was so involved in the problems of tourism, aship and ashore, that he resigned as manager of Castle & Cooke (but continued, of course, as president). He selected Frank Atherton, grandson of Amos Cooke and younger son of J. B., to succeed him as manager.

The site chosen for the lavish new hotel was an ancient gathering place of Hawaiian royalty, a legendary watering place fed by several springs. Old Hawaiians warned the New Yorkers that it was no place to put up a heavy structure. But the architects, experienced with Manhattan's rock foundation, said they could anchor the six-story building and make it solid. The Hawaiians had their laugh when the nearly completed Royal began sinking into the marsh. Matson sent a frantic call to Admiral R. R. Harris, a retired naval engineer, who managed to save the quagmired hotel with additional, and expensive, bulwarks. The Royal was completed and ready for business in sixteen months.

C & C executives devoted many hours of their time to overseeing the construction of the new hotel, but the company got no remuneration for services rendered. Manager Atherton reported to his stockholders, "The Matson Navigation Company has taken the position that we should be satisfied to wait for added compensation which should accrue to the firm by increased business when the *Malolo* is in service." He had been given the word by Matson and Castle & Cooke president Tenney.

The Royal Hawaiian Hotel has been described as Moorish in style, but at that time it was called Spanish. Why Spanish in Polynesia? "It was the time of Rudolph Valentino," one of the architects later explained. "Valentino was always playing sheik in North Africa or wearing gaucho boots in Spain. He was very romantic—the idol of millions of women. America was very Spanish in that period—Spanish shawls draped over pianos and around women's shoulders. Spanish style houses and buildings were everyplace." So the Royal was Spanish.

It was more than that—it was international in decor. There was a Persian Room for dining and a theater-ballroom decorated with barges floating down the Nile. The gallery was French, the rugs were from Czechoslovakia, and there were Italian cherubs in the frescoes.

The manager, Arthur Benaglia, was a native of Milan who had come to Honolulu after service with Canadian Pacific's famed hotel chain. He soon built up a staff of 300. There were 60 people in the kitchen (even the ice cream maker had three assistants), 95 waiters, 40 room boys, 20 bellboys, 10 elevator operators, 5 telephone operators, 2 doormen, 2 pages, and 8 Chinese lobby boys, dressed in "Cathayan costumes," to haul the steamer trunks and other luggage. Benaglia equipped his hotel with 38,624 dishes, 28,284 glasses, 20,292 knives, forks, and spoons, 22,573 towels, 30,988 sheets, blankets, and bedspreads, and 25 cages of canaries.

The great day of the Royal's opening arrived on February 1, 1927, and twelve hundred people were invited for the ceremonies and a black-tie dinner. Festivities got under way with a concert by the Royal Hawaiian band. Dinner began at 7:30 P.M. with a menu of "Coupe Czarine, Jordan Almonds, Celery Hearts, Mixed Olives, Green Turtle Soup Kamehameha, Supreme of Mullet Albert, Medallions of Sweet Breads Wilhelmina, Mousse of Foie Gras Princesse, Squab-Chicken Casserole Mascotte, Salade Lurline, Royal Hawaiian Givrée, Gourmandise, and Moka."

Dinner was followed by an hour-long pageant, arranged and directed by Princess Kawananakoa (who could have been Hawaii's queen if the monarchy had survived). The pageant—"colorful and semi-barbaric," said the press—depicted the arrival of King Kamehameha the Great on Oahu and included a fleet of fifteen canoes carrying fierce warriors, oarsmen, and kahili bearers. As the king stepped ashore, he was greeted by five beautiful princesses, each representing a major Hawaiian island, and sat upon a throne to enjoy a program of Polynesian dance and chants. Then everyone flocked to the ballroom for dancing.

By now, the Royal Hawaiian represented a $4 million investment (three-fourths of it Matson money) and was, in the words of the *Honolulu Star-Bulletin*, "the finest resort hostelry in America." To celebrate the occasion, the *Bulletin* published an eighty-page special edition, filled with detailed descriptions of the elegance of it all.

"The Coconut Grove lanai is gay with Chinese lanterns and

brightly painted furniture," the paper reported, "and afternoon tea and Hawaiian selections are featured from 4 to 5:30 each day . . . . Tea dansants ($1) are to be a Saturday afternoon feature and dinners will be $2.50, including cover charge for dancing . . . . The gardens are a wilderness of flowers and evergreen beauty with 40 varieties of plants. The tree ferns were imported from the Volcano House" on the island of Hawaii.

The reporters gave a thorough tour of a typical bedroom. "Sea green walls and deeper green rugs—suggestive of leaves . . . drapes and lampshades in soft apricot . . . and the pictures are quaint old-fashioned flowers in gay shades . . . . The beds have jade green and coral bedspreads . . . . The pincushions are jade green, covered with lace and honeydew silk ribbon to match the lampshades . . . and the pillows are stuffed with pure white goose feathers."

"Long gone are the days of a primitive people untouched by civilization," the *Bulletin* intoned editorially as it hailed Hawaii's new "recreation era." The Royal became known as the "Pink Palace of the Pacific."

Unfortunately, the *Malolo*, the luxury ship that would bring the wealthy to fill the Royal, had not coordinated with the hotel's grand opening very well. She didn't reach Honolulu until almost ten months later.

Launched in 1926 at the Cramp Yards in Philadelphia, she was, as manager Roth said, "a ship of superb characteristics." But on her trial run she ran into another ship, a collision that sent her back to the yards for repairs costing $500,000. When she finally put to sea, she developed a tendency to roll, a difficulty that caused jeering passengers to nickname her the "Rollolo." She gave her owners constant headaches, but roll or not, for the next two decades—part of the time under her new name, the *Matsonia*—the ship made transportation history in the Pacific.

With opening of the Royal, Castle & Cooke found itself in the travel business as well as the shipping business. The company opened a travel agency, and its officers added to their other duties the chore of seeing that the hotel operated efficiently.

In the long run the Royal was a financial flop, and Castle & Cooke lost every cent it invested. In glamor, however, it was great. In the first five years of operation, the Royal registered fourteen thousand guests, including "monarchs, princes, royalty of all descriptions—even our own American royalty . . . Mary and Doug," said the newspaper.

That meant Mary Pickford and Douglas Fairbanks, husband-and-wife film stars and perennial favorites with movie-goers of that era.

Mary and Doug, in fact, were on a trip around the world and writing a ten-part syndicated series about the sights they'd seen. "Of all the places Douglas and I visited on our trip around the world," wrote Mary, "Honolulu is the most beautiful and alluring."

The publicity in the nation's press worked wonders, and all sorts of notables came to check the truth of the statement. Mrs. Lammot Du Pont of Wilmington spent the entire summer of 1931 at the Royal. Guests from overseas included Annie, Viscountess Cowdray, and her granddaughters, the Honorable Nancy and the Honorable Joan Pearson of London.

There was a constant stream of wealthy honeymooners at the Royal. Nelson Rockefeller and his first wife honeymooned there; so did Henry Ford II and his first wife. Al Jolson and Ruby Keeler came to finish an interrupted honeymoon. Newlyweds Mr. and Mrs. J. Paul Butler brought with them their ultramarine Rolls Royce roadster, and Henry H. Rogers, Jr., shipped over his Hispano Suiza phaeton, complete with silver disc wheels.

But not all the guests were wealthy. Groups of Shriners found reasons for staying at the Royal, as did the nation's politicians. Thousands of pictures were taken of the guests and sent back promptly to mainland newspapers. The photos showed women with cloche hats, pleated skirts, and bulky handbags, and men in coats, ties, and straw hats. Modesty still prevailed in beach dress, although a few males were emerging on the sands "topless."

Passengers arriving in Honolulu were greeted with the following bit of news, as headlined in a local newspaper:

DIVING BOYS ON WATERFRONT TO BE 'GENTLEMEN'

Promise to Wear
More Clothes, Not
Sass Passengers
Or Ships Officers

SUDDENLY, THE MATSON ENTERPRISE discovered it had lively competition for the tourist passenger to Hawaii. At the end of World War I, a group of Los Angeles capitalists had bought three old German liners from the Alien Property Custodian, renamed them the *City of Honolulu,* the *City of Los Angeles*, and the *Calawai*, and launched a new steamship line to the islands. At first Matson ignored the upstart—not only Lassco (as the Los Angeles Steamship Company was known) but Los Angeles harbor and all of Southern California as well. After all, Matson had the Hawaii freight under control, thanks to Castle & Cooke.

Then came the rude awakening. Lassco had teamed with Honolulu's Dillingham interests to develop freight business in Hawaii and was edging into Matson's private province. Worse yet, Lassco, with its inexpensive old steamers and lower rates, poured tourists into Hawaii by the thousands. But instead of dropping them in Honolulu and letting them find their own way about, Lassco made port in the neighbor islands, conducting impressive sightseeing tours. To meet the competition, Matson and Castle & Cooke bought into Inter-Island Steam Navigation Company, which organized Inter-Island Airways (later to become Hawaiian Airlines) and constructed the Kona Inn on the warm Kona coast of the Big Island.

Just as Lassco was becoming a menace to Matson, the *City of Honolulu* burned and sank in Honolulu harbor. Good news for Matson? No!

"Damn it, damn it, damn it," Tenney erupted. "Why did that have to happen?" He was anticipating what Lassco might do with its insurance money, and his hunch meant trouble. With the insurance, Lassco could finance a new ship, one well able to compete with Matson for the luxury trade. So Matson dug down for $4,900,000, bought the Los Angeles Steamship Company, sold its nine old ships, and added Los Angeles as a regular port of call for its own ships.

Meanwhile, Matson had absorbed three steamers of Oceanic Steamship Company, the line organized in 1885 by Claus Spreckels for the run between San Francisco and Australia via Honolulu. In the early 1930s, Matson built two government-aided luxury liners, the *Mariposa* and the *Monterey*. A third luxury vessel, the *Lurline*, was built with Matson funds for the Hawaiian run. With the *Malolo/Matsonia* and the *Lurline* operating on the California-Honolulu route, and the *Mariposa* and the *Monterey* through the South Seas, Matson was truly entrenched.

Landlubber Ed Tenney had pyramided Matson, and Castle & Cooke as well, into the most potent steamship system in the Pacific.

ON DECEMBER 6, 1930, Ed Tenney, age seventy-two, completed fifty years of service to Castle & Cooke, and it was a sentimental occasion in the Honolulu headquarters. Wires of congratulations came from the mainland, and friends dropped by to extend best wishes. At noon the officers and employees assembled in the small board room to present a special picture album of Castle & Cooke's people and places, and a spokesman from the freight department told the old gentleman how much he meant to all the employees.

Tenney had a gift for the employees, too. He presented the company with a large seascape by Lionel Walden, long famous in Hawaii for his ocean scenes. For thirty-five years the painting hung over the company vault. Considering how amply Tenney had stuffed that vault with sound securities, it might have been more appropriate to have had his portrait hanging over the company strongbox.

By that time Tenney had become chairman of the boards of Castle & Cooke and Matson, having relinquished the presidency of C & C to Frank Atherton. Bill Roth had become president of Matson. For the next few years, Tenney spent most of his time in his apartment at the Mark Hopkins Hotel in San Francisco, where he could watch—somewhat dimly—his beloved Matson ships come and go. In recent years Tenney had undergone repeated cataract operations, but his vision was becoming increasingly impaired.

On April 29, 1934, he went for a Sunday afternoon ride in San Francisco with his sister, Ida, the widow of George Castle. After dinner they returned to his suite, and as they sat talking, he suffered a heart attack. He was dead when a doctor reached his side.

His death, at seventy-five, was the top story in Honolulu's morning paper, complete with a two-column picture of the old tycoon leaning on his sturdy cane. "He was a clean fighter but a relentless one," wrote the editor. "He was true to his ideals and to his beliefs—and always to his friends."

"Edward Davies Tenney . . . his was a peerless leadership," said the resolution passed by the board of Castle & Cooke.

Tenney had surrounded himself with young men of character, force, self-confidence, and energy. His reasoning processes were direct and based on a powerful understanding of the human equation. He could command silence and respect at any board meeting, and five minutes later be swapping salty stories with a stevedore on the docks or a laborer on the curbstone.

The Tenney estate, which was estimated to be $2.5 million, consisted largely of Castle & Cooke, Honolulu Oil, and Matson Navigation stocks. It was left to his son, Vernon, and his daughter, Wilhelmina.

LESS THAN TWO YEARS AFTER Ed Tenney's death, Frank Atherton submitted his resignation as president and manager of Castle & Cooke. He had regarded himself as an interim president, and now he wanted more time for travel and for his religious, civic, and welfare interests. He had been in business thirty-nine years, half of the time with C & C, and it was time to relax. On December 31, 1935, he became chairman of the board.

In his quiet, thoughtful way Frank Atherton had been a good president. Ed Tenney was a hard act to follow; compared to his flamboyancy, the Atherton style was lackluster. Like his father, J. B., Frank was retiring and ascetic. He had a lean face, topped with a thatch of white hair—the face of a man of peace, an idealist. Unlike Tenney, he had no wish to dominate anybody. He regarded himself as a trustee for the public, and his business and private lives were geared that way.

As manager, president, and later board chairman, Atherton contributed substantial character to the company. Any executive with a position on the board of directors had unusual opportunities to build up his personal fortune. Due to Atherton's injunctions, however, this was "out" so far as Castle & Cooke executives were concerned. The company might make informed, calculated plunges—and did—but the men who worked for the firm were to engage in no speculating. They made their money in and through Castle & Cooke, and all their energies went directly to Castle & Cooke.

Atherton, like his father, had been physically frail ever since an illness at Wesleyan University. For a long time, he was too weak to work. He did fill a number of positions at the Bank of Hawaii but had to retire in his thirties to preserve his health. He made an effort at body building by wielding Indian clubs. He also played golf, made small bets, and, between strokes, would stretch out on the green fairways to enjoy the soft, balmy breezes, the passing clouds, and the splendor of the Hawaiian landscape.

After four years of Indian clubs, he felt strong enough to return to work. He joined Castle & Cooke, and Tenney put him at a desk next to his. Tenney's deliberate expletives and waterfront jokes frequently made Atherton blush, but Tenney liked the man and started preparing him for the presidency.

Atherton saved a third of his salary, gave a third of it away, and lived on the remaining third. His first item of personal business on the first of every month was to draw and expend what he called his "trustee account"—a fund from which he advanced money to deserving individuals and institutions of all types. Dozens of young men and women owed their opportunities for a college education to Frank Atherton's assistance. And his Christmas list was a thing of wonder. Little churches, struggling schools, people he had encountered and wished to remember in a practical way—they numbered more than fifty. Every year a small school in Kentucky received a check from a mysterious man named Atherton who lived on an island far out in the Pacific.

While he found happiness in his generosity, Atherton was businesslike about it. If the sum advanced was a loan, he took a note. Though he never pressed for payment, the notes were filed methodically in his office safe, and when he died in 1945, they had grown into a pile nearly two feet high.

Another of his habits was collecting string and wrapping paper until they choked his desk. Often chiding himself about this, he would attribute it to his early missionary training, which insisted that nothing be destroyed that might serve a useful purpose.

Women employees at Castle & Cooke received two American Beauty roses twice a week. And every Thursday a box of Whitman Sampler chocolates arrived with the compliments of Frank's brother, Charles, who had been treasurer during the early part of Frank's regime.

Charles Atherton had some charming idiosyncrasies. Because his doctor thought it would help his high blood pressure, he would walk at least part way between the office and his home in the Manoa Valley district of Honolulu. On these trips he would carry a large sack of bread, dropping a trail of crumbs for a retinue of appreciative mynah birds and sparrows following in his wake. When he rode the Manoa tram car, he would insist on alighting and helping each lady get on or off, thus throwing the car completely off schedule. He habitually wore a white suit with a high military-looking collar. When seeing friends off on one of the ships, he was often mistaken for a steward and would be asked by passengers to carry baggage aboard. He would oblige them, then with a grave nod of thanks, accept a tip.

Frank Atherton worked hard in the community, too. He was president of the *Honolulu Star-Bulletin,* a vice-president of five corporations, and manager of the J. B. Atherton Estate.

One of his hobbies was hybridizing hibiscus, and he created hundreds of new varieties. He also cultivated orchids, importing plants and seeds from many parts of the world. The collection finally became so large it required the full-time attention of an orchid specialist. Atherton was also a stamp collector. He specialized in rare Hawaiian issues and assembled the most complete Hawaiian collection in the world, which he eventually presented to the Honolulu Academy of Arts.

ED TENNEY WAS THE FIRST chief executive in Castle & Cooke's history to serve more than fifty years with the company. Alexander G. Budge was the second. When Frank Atherton decided to move up to chairman of the board at the end of 1935, Budge was his choice for successor. Budge went on to serve as president for twenty-four years and chairman of the board for eleven more. His selection marked the first time that a non–family member had ever become head of a major Hawaii company.

Alex Budge, born in Grand Forks, North Dakota, on December 4, 1891, joined Castle & Cooke in 1920 as an assistant secretary. He had graduated as a mechanical engineer from Stanford University in

1912 and had become a sales engineer with the San Francisco firm of Charles C. Moore & Co. In 1916, his company sent him to Hawaii to sell boilers to the sugar plantations.

"I was the greenest piece of merchandise ever to arrive in the Islands," he recalls. "I was the least experienced person in the firm, and the only reason I was sent was because the others refused to go. In fact, my boss was advised to give me a round trip ticket."

Selling boilers in Hawaii in those days required zeal and perseverance. "Cracking plantation managers was a real job," Budge says. "Since they didn't trust each other, they weren't about to do business with a young sprout who knew nothing about sugar. I got tossed out of Oahu Sugar Company time after time. I would catch the morning train out to the mill, get turned down, buy a handful of bananas for lunch and catch the afternoon train back.

"The North Kohala District on the Big Island wasn't anything better. Here were five plantations, and each manager detested the other four. A salesman who called on one of the managers first was certain to be berated by the others for having overlooked their importance by not calling on them first."

His office in Honolulu wasn't the fanciest either. "It was in a loft used by the Boy Scouts for their meetings. I had the only sink in the building so the Scouts used to come in to wash their bean pots while I was trying to write alibis to the home office for not selling more equipment."

When America entered World War I, Budge left Hawaii to serve as an ordnance captain in France. After the war, he returned to the Moore company and to Hawaii. He prooooooo ved to be a capable boiler salesman as well as engineer, and it wasn't long before his capabilities came to the attention of Castle & Cooke, who represented Charles C. Moore & Co. in Hawaii. He was hired in 1920.

Budge's first major assignment at Castle & Cooke was to supervise the engineering and related work involved in the electrification of the pump systems at C & C's sugar plantations. When work began two years later on the new corporate headquarters building, he was named by president Ed Tenney to supervise construction. As Budge, whose red hair earned him the nickname of "Pinky," recalls, he had more grief from the "sidewalk superintendents" than from the job itself. "There were heated arguments most of the time."

When the company occupied the new building in 1924, Budge inadvertently incurred Tenney's wrath when he moved the president's furniture. "Tenney was an inveterate cigarette smoker but with great effort, he gave them up in 1916. When we were moving, I transferred all the things in his old desk to his new one. There was a box of cigarettes full of worm holes so I threw it away. Going through his new desk, he called me in and asked me if I had seen his cigarettes. I told him I had thrown them out. 'Goddamn it to hell, Budge, I would rather have them than anything in the whole damned office. That box contained the cigarettes I quit on.' ''

Budge, it turned out, was one of the very few men at C & C who ever dared to answer back to the boss. Tenney would frequently burst into uncontrolled anger at people, and it would spell permanent hard luck for any of them if he found out they were afraid of him. Budge wasn't. Tenney would stamp out of his office madder than ever, his cane thumping on the floor. But he would be back in an hour, with the thunderstorm spent and never any ill feelings.

Budge became corporate secretary in 1924 and vice-president and secretary in 1932. He had been vice-president and assistant manager of Castle & Cooke prior to his election as president in 1935.

Chapter 10

The Fruit of Kings

WHEN ALEXANDER G. BUDGE STEPPED UP to the presidency of Castle
& Cooke, the company was recovering rapidly from the effects of the
Great Depression. In fact, the directors had just voted to increase the
company's stock to $10 million through an 80 percent stock dividend. A
significant contribution to its profits that year (1935) had come from its
21 percent ownership in Hawaiian Pineapple Company, acquired three
years earlier.

Castle & Cooke's investment in Hawaiian Pineapple was the result
of a 1932 reorganization to save Jim Dole's depression-plagued firm
from going bankrupt and to keep controlling ownership in island hands.
By 1935, Dole was chairman of the board—but in name only. Former
Castle & Cooke executives were running the pineapple company, and
several others from Castle & Cooke also sat on its board, representing
both C & C interests and those of Waialua Agricultural Company, of
which C & C was part owner and for which it served as agent. Waialua
owned 37 percent of Hawaiian Pineapple, also as the result of the 1932
reorganization.

Castle & Cooke's investment in pineapple was beginning to prove
most valuable. Hawaiian Pineapple was able to resume dividend
payments in 1935, and these provided a substantial contribution to
C & C profits—a total of approximately $62,000 from payments
on C & C's direct 21.3 percent investment as well as from the company's share of payments to Waialua. In addition, the Hawaiian Pineapple reorganization agreement provided C & C with 5 percent of the
pineapple company's profits (almost $67,000) and an agency fee of

$50,000. Added to all that, Castle & Cooke also handled all the insurance and shipping business of the pineapple company.

The 5 percent cut from Hawaiian Pineapple's profits was suspended at the end of 1935, but C & C's share in dividends more than made up the difference, exceeding $1 million by 1938. It was turning out to be a most profitable venture—far more so than had been thought possible when Castle & Cooke flatly rejected Jim Dole's invitation to invest in his new company in 1901.

THE ORIGIN OF PINEAPPLE is uncertain. It was discovered by Christopher Columbus on his second trip to America, and Marco Polo reported seeing the fruit on his journeys to the Far East. Captain Cook found pineapple in Hawaii when he "discovered" the islands in 1778, indicating the Polynesians had brought it with them when they arrived.

Pineapple, with its spiky-leafed crown, has been called the "King of Fruits." In past history it has also been known as the "Fruit of Kings" because in Europe, during the sixteenth and seventeenth centuries, pineapple could be grown only in hothouses, and only royalty could afford to enjoy its exotic flavor. In time the pineapple became a symbol of hospitality and appeared as a decorative motif, especially on European-designed silver and china. It even emerged, carved in wood, atop bed posts.

At the time of the California gold rush, wild-growing Hawaiian pineapples had become well established, and many thousands were gathered and transported to San Francisco, where they were sold at fantastic prices. The fruit was small but delicious, provided it hadn't spoiled in the holds of the sailing ships. Unfortunately, spoilage was heavy, so the business didn't look promising enough for Brothers Castle and Cooke or their contemporaries to get involved.

The foundation for the present industry in Hawaii was laid by Captain John Kidwell, a former nurseryman who arrived in the islands in 1882 from San Francisco. Kidwell imported a dozen pineapple plants from Florida in 1885 and the following year brought in a thousand more from Jamaica.

After pineapple culture had become a small hothouse business in England, France, and especially in the Azores, the British took some plants back to the West Indies to try to grow them out-of-doors. The varieties that returned to the Caribbean had undergone quite a change. The one that became most popular was the Smooth Cayenne, hard to ship but delicious to eat. This was the type that Kidwell brought to Hawaii. It grew even more lustily than it had in the hothouses of Europe or the gardens of the West Indies.

Kidwell experimented with shipping fresh pineapple to the mainland but, as in gold rush days, spoilage was still a major problem. He decided the only way to market the fruit was to can it. John Emmeluth, a plumber friend, undertook to find a way and, by trial and error the two finally succeeded. The first shipment to San Francisco was bought for speculation by Jacob Blumlein, a wholesale grocer.

Kidwell and Emmeluth leased 140 acres of land at Apokaa, near Pearl Harbor, and by 1892 had 100,000 plants growing. With a few Honolulu backers, Kidwell organized the Hawaiian Fruit & Packing Company. The Apokaa pineapple acreage lay alongside the new Ewa sugar plantation, and Ewa's management wanted that adjoining land that was being "wasted" on pineapple. Ewa persuaded Kidwell to switch to sugar. Kidwell sold his little cannery, founded the Apokaa Sugar Company, ripped out his pineapple plants, put in cane—and went broke. Ewa picked up the land.

The next champion of pineapple was Byron O. Clark. At Kidwell's abandoned Apokaa project, he found a pile of pineapple plants alongside the road. He loaded them into his wagon, took them home to Wahiawa on Oahu's high central plain and set them out in long rows. This was something new in pineapple culture. Previously the plants had been set out in beds and cultivated by hand. Clark also demonstrated that pineapples would grow on higher ground and thrive with less moisture. Before, they had been considered suitable only for the same land that sugar men wanted.

Clark opened a small cannery and had minor marketing success, as did others at Wahiawa. The homesteaders demonstrated they could grow pineapples in Hawaii better than they were grown anywhere else, but nobody really knew how to market them profitably.

JAMES DRUMMOND DOLE showed them how. In 1899, Dole had come to Hawaii fresh out of Harvard to seek his fortune. He was a distant cousin of Sanford Dole, president of the former Republic of Hawaii and about to become the first governor of the new territory. Young Dole had nothing particular in mind when he arrived in the islands. He once mused that he thought he would grow tobacco, make his fortune, and spend the rest of his life swinging in a hammock, smoking black cigars. But by 1901 he had decided on pineapple.

Dole took over a sixty-acre homestead on the Wahiawa plateau, eighteen miles north of Honolulu, and grew vegetables and pineapples. When the latter flourished, he organized the Hawaiian Pineapple Company. Albert Judd (the missionary doctor's grandson) was president for the first three years, and Dole was manager. Dole was a man of ideas, great ambition, and tremendous energy that made up for his lack of financial assets, which he later said consisted only of "a name, two horses, a harrow and a wagon," plus sixty acres and several hundred plants.

Whereas other pineapple pioneers had been merely ignored, Dole and his plans for revolutionizing the world's taste for canned pineapple were greeted with jeers by sugar-minded Hawaii. The *Honolulu Advertiser* printed an editorial deprecating the whole idea: "If pineapple paid, the vacant lots near town would be covered with them."

Dole tried to raise capital but got little support. Castle & Cooke, for one, said no. Dole wanted $20,000 for incorporation and initial equipment, but it was soon evident he was not going to get much help from island businessmen. Back in Boston, he raised $14,000, which he used to buy a boiler, an engine, a pineapple sizer, and a slicer. He also managed to interest Joe Hunt, a California food packer, and, through him, Samuel Sussman and Jacob Blumlein, who in turn brought in others.

Blumlein and Sussman were able merchandisers and financiers, as well as experienced food packers. (Sussman later became the "S" in the famous S & W food brand.) With Hunt (later to found Hunt Foods) as sales agent, Dole's company found itself with $50,000 and ready for business.

Dole's 1903 pack was 1,893 cases, a quantity that can be packed in fifteen minutes in today's Honolulu cannery. The following year, he packed 8,810 cases and the third year hit 25,000.

The early-day pineapple center, Wahiawa, was separated from Honolulu by deep gulches, and the roads were terrible. Freight wagons bogged down, and teamsters quit. When Dillingham laid rails between Wahiawa and Honolulu in 1907, Dole moved his cannery to the city, where labor and water were plentiful. He then persuaded American Can Company to build a plant next to his cannery so that he could save the freight costs of shipping preformed cans from the mainland.

But a bottleneck to large-scale production soon appeared. Cannery equipment was still operated by hand and could process only two to three fruit a minute. If Dole's cannery was to avoid being engulfed by pineapples, a faster way had to be found to prepare the fruit. Dole hired Henry Ginaca, a young mechanical draftsman from the Honolulu Iron Works. By 1911 he had created a machine that made possible the mass production of canned pineapple. The Ginaca machine could size, peel, core, and cut the ends from the fruit and deliver perfect hollowed cylinders to the packing tables at speeds of 80 to 100 pineapples per minute. The cylinders were then cut into slices for canning.

In 1907, when financial depression hit the mainland, Dole's company had 108,000 cases packed and enough fruit in the field to fill 225,000 more. There was a glut of pineapple on the market. But Dole proved himself a smart promoter. He organized other pineapple growers into an association, which placed advertisements in United States magazines. This was one of the first nationwide consumer advertising campaigns in America, and it sought to introduce this strange and delicious fruit to housewives, few of whom had ever seen it. "It Cuts With a Spoon—Like a Peach," one of the advertisements explained.

James B. Castle had purchased some shares in Dole's company, sold them soon afterward, and later bought stock in the Wahiawa Consolidated Pineapple Company, a Dole competitor. Because of family connections, Castle & Cooke reluctantly agreed to advance funds to liquidate debts of Wahiawa Consolidated and to help harvest and pack its 1908 crop.

"What the final outcome of this business will be, it is hard to say," manager E. D. Tenney reported to his stockholders, "but, eliminating the hot air of its promoters, I am inclined to think we are safe in making these advances." But by midsummer, Castle & Cooke had $120,000 tied up in advances. There were 30,000 cases of the previous year's pack still unsold, with twice that amount yet to be packed. By October, the company was into pineapple to the extent of $203,000. It took several years for Castle & Cooke to extricate itself from this venture, and Tenney and company were pretty sour on pineapple.

But the young industry continued to grow. Between 1907 and 1909, Waialua Agricultural Company leased 3,000 acres of land not suitable for sugar to Dole's Hawaiian Pineapple Company and other pineapple operators. By 1913, when planters had more than 6,000 acres of Waialua's lands in pineapple, the sugar company began to wonder if it shouldn't go into the business directly. But it did nothing.

By 1916, Jim Dole had leased 3,676 acres from Waialua. The California Fruit Canners' Association, which had absorbed the Hawaiian Preserving Company (and would later become part of California Packing Corporation and then Del Monte), had 4,315 acres of Waialua land in pineapple.

Dole, although he was not yet using his name as a brand, was fast becoming king of the pineapple industry. Needing more land on which to grow fruit, he bargained with Waialua in 1922 for 12,000 acres of their non-sugar land on a seventeen-year prepaid lease with the right of renewal. For the lease—and $1,250,000 in cash—Dole would give Waialua one-third ownership of his Hawaiian Pineapple Company. Waialua accepted.

Castle & Cooke was Waialua's dominant stockholder, with 20 percent, and also its agent. That meant Ed Tenney and associates now had an indirect interest in pineapple. In only a matter of months, Tenney was reporting to his board that Hawaiian Pineapple had agreed to place all its insurance with Castle & Cooke for a fifteen-year period, to be followed by all of Dole's freight business for a similar period. Hawaiian Pineapple was then shipping 790,000 cases of product a year, and this volume was to multiply rapidly.

WITH THE CASH RECEIVED from Waialua Agricultural Company, Dole promptly went out and purchased the island of Lanai, sixty miles from Honolulu, for $1.1 million. He had visited the 90,400-acre island several times previously and was convinced it could be converted into an ideal site for a second plantation for his Hawaiian Pineapple Company. He visualized a plantation of at least 10,000 acres in size, perhaps even as much as 15,000 acres—the largest in Hawaii.

For years, Lanai had been a forlorn, almost barren cattle-sheep-and-goat ranch. Lying in the lee of Maui's mountains, it received little rainfall from the trade winds. Industrious Mormons in 1854 had attempted to establish a Polynesian "City of Joseph" there, but it was difficult. Isolation was almost total, and with little water the land was hard to cultivate. Even clever Walter Murray Gibson, the man who later became King Kalakaua's cohort and chief adviser, had not solved the problems, so the Mormons finally gave up the island.

After Gibson died in San Francisco in 1888, his daughter inherited his Lanai lands and tried growing cane but failed. Then Charles Gay and the Lanai Company ranched until 1917, when they sold out to Frank and Harry Baldwin, who continued a cattle operation. In 1922 the Baldwins had a long-desired opportunity to purchase Ulupalakua Ranch on Maui, and word reached Dole that they'd sell their island for $1.1 million. Dole leaped at the offer.

A lot of people wondered if he knew what he was doing. "People thought Lanai was good for cattle raising and nothing else," Dole admitted years later. "But we found soil there that tested well. Climate, altitude, rainfall and natural drainage were about what we wanted. On the other hand, there were no harbors, no roads, no towns, no labor, no food or water supply, no population, and much of the good soil was densely covered with enormous cactus. Most folks think cactus and deserts go together. Maybe that's why Lanai was overlooked so long."

Getting rid of the five-foot cactus was a difficult job. Finally the problem was solved by hitching heavy cable chains to tractors and dragging the cactuses down to earth, where they rotted.

"Dry Dock" Smith—who got his nickname because of his Pearl Harbor dry docks—was hired to build a harbor where tugs and barges could load pineapples for the sixty-mile trip to the Honolulu cannery. Twenty miles of roads were laid down, and water was brought across a mountain from the windward side to a reservoir near Lanai City—a new town with houses for plantation workers, stores, schools, a hospital, a library, a bank, social halls, gymnasium, movie house, warehouses, and repair shops. And 15,000 acres of pineapples were planted.

If anyone had doubts about Dole's ability to grow pineapples on Lanai, they changed their minds when the first crop was harvested in 1926. The fruit was among the best grown in Hawaii. Dole was soon canning 35 percent of all of Hawaii's pineapples. Seven other companies packed the balance.

Pineapple plantation managers were every bit as autocratic as their counterparts in the sugar industry. None was more colorful than H. Blomfield-Brown, an Australian who became the first superintendent on Lanai. It has been some forty years since he retired, yet the name of this storybook character continues to roll off the tongues of old-timers who knew him.

"Lanai City is immaculate," reported Riley Allen, then editor of the *Honolulu Star-Bulletin,* after he had visited the island. When Allen asked "Brownie" how he kept everything so tidy, he replied, "By keeping at it." And he did. Tidiness was an obsession with the man, and woe to the child who threw a gum wrapper or other scrap on the ground. If a family didn't keep its yard manicured, the manager dispatched a cleanup crew to do the job, then sent a bill for services rendered.

"Brownie" was also personally immaculate. He often wore a pith helmet, a white bush jacket, and high leather boots that glistened in the sun, despite the fact that red dust covered the island. He maintained a supply of boots—polished constantly by his servants—and he changed them several times a day.

Today Lanai City is famous for its Norfolk pines, introduced by the late George Munro, one of Hawaii's outstanding naturalists. Blomfield-Brown's home, now a social club, is almost hidden by the tall, graceful trees, but when "Brownie" lived there, not a shrub impaired the view. The manager kept a spyglass on his front porch, and he would scan the fields to check on the laborers. If they weren't moving fast enough to suit him, they soon heard about it.

Aussie expressions frequently showed up in his correspondence with Dole officials in Honolulu. "And a jolly good cheerio," he once ended a letter to the company president. Another letter recounted the details of a particularly rough trip home to Lanai by interisland steamer:

"It was so rough coming home that I arrived without my upper set of teeth. This is the second time this sad occurrence has happened to me between here and Honolulu. By Gad, I was ill!"

JIM DOLE SOON BECAME one of Honolulu's leading businessmen. He made several trips to the mainland each year, and when he returned reporters were waiting to record his every word about how he found business conditions, what the marketing prospects were for pineapple, and so on. He was usually a front-page story, but would soon become a world figure, thanks to something called the Dole Derby.

In 1927, Charles Lindbergh made aviation history by flying across the Atlantic. The *Honolulu Star-Bulletin* immediately suggested there should be an airplane race from California to Honolulu—it would make aviation history in the Pacific. When discussion turned to the prize money, Dole was approached. Realizing that such publicity could benefit his pineapple business, Dole accepted the invitation and offered $25,000 as first prize and $10,000 as second.

However, tragedy dogged the race from the start, and by the time it was all over, ten lives had been lost. Before the race even began, planes were wrecked and people killed as pilots prepared for the flight. Two men died when their plane crashed on the way to the take-off site in Oakland. Next day a plane dropped into San Francisco Bay, but the occupants were able to swim to safety. Yet another entrant managed to jump when his engine failed, but his parachute never opened.

More tragedy followed, as the race finally got underway in August 1927. Two planes crashed on takeoff, two more turned back with engine trouble, and two crashed at sea, killing five people including a pretty Michigan schoolteacher who had simply come along for the ride. Two more flyers lost their lives in the search for those who had gone down at sea.

Only two planes arrived in Honolulu, the *Woolaroc* and the *Aloha,* which was the lone Hawaiian entry. Dole, Hawaii's Governor Wallace R. Farrington, and hundreds of people were at Wheeler Field to greet the winners. But the celebration was a sober affair, considering the tragic loss of life. The race had already lost a good deal of its punch anyway. Two months earlier army lieutenants Lester Maitland and Albert F. Hegenberger had made the trans-Pacific flight, followed by Ernie Smith and Emory B. Bronte, who landed in an algarroba tree on Molokai.

The Dole Derby gave Jim Dole publicity, but not the kind he wanted. An ill-planned "stunt" was the gist of the complaints. The nation's press began asking questions about the rules that governed the race. By modern safety standards, the regulations had indeed been casual, and Art Goebel, the grand prize winner, admitted plugging a leak in his gas tank with a wad of chewing gum. But the rules were made by the proper federal authorities, not by Jim Dole. He had nothing to say about how the race was run; he just provided the prizes. Nevertheless, he took the brunt of much of the criticism.

But a few months later, at a National Geographic Society banquet in Washington, William P. MacCracken, assistant secretary of commerce for aeronautics, said: ''These are the daring deeds of heroism that some have seen fit to call 'stunts' in aviation. I declare that it is to such fliers as these—and to such 'stunts'—that aviation owes its progress.''

AT THE CASTLE & COOKE ANNUAL MEETING in 1931, president Atherton reported that the company's earnings for the previous year were $840,370, down $120,372 from the year before. He noted that, considering ''the general economic depression that has ruled the world,'' the showing was fairly satisfactory, and he hoped prosperity was just around President Hoover's corner. But it wasn't. When the Christmas bonus of one month's salary was given at the end of 1931, it was accompanied by a warning that it probably would not be repeated next year. In April 1932, salaries and pensions were cut.

Generally, the depression was less severe in Hawaii than on the mainland. Castle & Cooke, for example, never missed a dividend. But soon the officers and directors were to know genuine financial concern. The cause was Waialua Agricultural Company's one-third ownership of Hawaiian Pineapple Company, acquired in the 1922 lease agreement. Jim Dole was in serious trouble and before it was over, he would lose the giant complex he had started with a mule and a plow in 1901.

In retrospect, Dole's problems seem to have been caused by bad timing. Millions of pineapples, including those from the new Lanai plantation, had been canned for the American housewife. In 1931, Dole had borrowed $5 million to finance even bigger plant facilities, floating debentures due in five years. He also owed the banks $3.5 million.

Within a year, the depression had struck, and housewives had stopped buying pineapple. In fact, the entire mainland fruit market was dead. Dole had millions of cans of pineapple that nobody wanted, and on his two plantations 230 million plants were flourishing, each one promising to bear a new pineapple within the next eighteen months.

Dole had recently perfected new methods of manufacturing a better pineapple juice, and he was hopeful that this new canned beverage would come to his company's rescue. Unfortunately, time and money for promotion were lacking. Meanwhile, he had lost his traditional market dominance for his solid-pack pineapple due to a reluctance to cut prices. When he finally did trim them, it was too late.

Mainland banks were growing uneasy about Dole's predicament. As word got around, other mainland interests, including General Foods, began eyeing the distressed company, thinking they might pick it up cheap. The idea of outsiders' purchasing Hawaiian Pineapple sent shivers up the spines of local business leaders, who prided themselves in the home ownership of practically every island industry.

At a board meeting in late 1932, Dole admitted his financial position was "very threatening." Hawaiian Pineapple had lost $5.4 million in the first nine months of that year. A committee that included three Castle & Cooke executives was appointed to figure out a way to get Hawaiian Pineapple "through the existing depression . . . and to find where the money can be raised."

The salvage plan called for organization of a new company to take over Hawaiian Pineapple's assets and debts, and issue $1.5 million of convertible preferred stock to be offered to stockholders of the old company on a pro rata basis. Waialua agreed to take its one-third share of $500,000 and, together with Castle & Cooke, to underwrite the remaining $1 million. But not enough stockholders wanted the new shares. Castle & Cooke wound up with a 21 percent ownership and Waialua with 37 percent. Together, they owned more than half of the reorganized company.

The reorganization was approved on December 29, 1932. Jim Dole, at fifty-six, was moved "upstairs" to be chairman of the board, and Castle & Cooke executives took over the management of the new Hawaiian Pineapple Company. Under its new management, combined with generally improved U.S. business conditions, Hawaiian Pineapple soon reversed its downward trend. By 1934 sales were strong, and the new juice product was doing especially well. Prohibition had just been repealed, and pineapple juice was being promoted as a great little mixer with gin.

By 1936, the $8.5 million debt of Hawaiian Pineapple had been turned into a $2 million credit balance. Two years later, when sugar was being produced at a loss, Waialua Agricultural Company's share in Hawaiian Pineapple's dividends was $1.1 million. Castle & Cooke, of course, also profited, both from its 21 percent interest in Hawaiian Pineapple and its 22.6 percent interest in Waialua.

At the time Dole became chairman of Hawaiian Pineapple in 1932, there were accusations that he had been removed from the presidency at Ed Tenney's instructions because of a disagreement with Matson over pineapple freight rates to the East Coast. Isthmian Lines had offered a rate of $9 per ton for shipping pineapple to New York, while Matson was charging $14 per ton because of transshipment at San Francisco for the voyage through the Panama Canal. Dole discussed the problem with Matson and reported to his board in early 1931 that Matson was proposing $11 per ton to New York. Still, this would cost Hawaiian Pineapple Company almost $200,000 more a year.

According to the minutes of that meeting, Hawaiian Pineapple's board "unanimously voted that the freight rate matter be left in the hands of management with full power to act . . . with the understanding, however, that the Matson Navigation Company is to participate in the agreement if such participation can be arranged without too great a sacrifice." Dole decided the sacrifice was too great and did business with Isthmian.

Immediately after becoming chairman, Dole was sent on a "well-earned rest," a vacation that took him across the mainland and into Canada. He kept waiting for "the call" that would summon him back to Hawaii to lend his services, but it didn't come. More and more, he became embittered—and with some cause. Upon his return in the spring of 1933, he wrote, "I found myself first without desk room and then installed among the boxes and labels in the storeroom where I received friends of the company who could find me. Here I was almost completely ignored . . . ."

In sadness he noted all that he had achieved for the company—and Hawaii—and asked why "I have been discredited by my own people." And, he added, "it may be emphatically asked why our company should deliberately try to discredit me when it is continuing to use and capitalize the trade and public confidence in my name."

He had a point. By now, the name Dole was being stamped on the end of every can of pineapple, and it had been introduced as a brand name on the new and highly successful pineapple juice. Previously, the company's pineapple had been packed under such names as Ukulele, Aloha, and Hawaiian Club. Now, at a time when they were ignoring him, Dole's successors were featuring his name on their product.

The charges went on and on for years. Finally, in 1948, it was recommended that "it would be to the best interests of all concerned if Mr. Dole were to sever his relationship with the organization as an executive officer." Mr. Dole severed it, although he continued to receive a sizeable remuneration from the company. He moved to San Francisco, where he established a food machinery company and became a pineapple consultant. He died in Honolulu in 1958 at the age of eighty.

Chapter 11

Richards' Revolt

UNTIL A SHORT TIME BEFORE HIS DEATH in 1974, at the age of eighty, Atherton Richards was a familiar sight at Honolulu's Pacific Club. He would roar into the parking lot in his blue Chevrolet convertible, the breeze rumpling his thinning hair. Although palsied by Parkinson's disease, he was a peppery man to the end—still a fighter, still feisty.

In recent years he had been embroiled with his fellow trustees who managed the affairs of the Bishop Estate. It was Atherton against the rest. A few years earlier he had opposed the choice of a site for the state of Hawaii's new capitol building. Out of his own pocket he financed a series of double-page newspaper ads explaining why a different location was more desirable. Many agreed that the location he advocated was, indeed, preferable to the place where the structure stands today, but his solo strategy got him nowhere.

It was typical. Atherton Richards, a man of keen intellect and imagination, was an individualist and a maverick. All his life he was a loner, a stance that got him into deep trouble with Castle & Cooke and eventually lost him his job.

When Hawaiian Pineapple was reorganized in 1932, Atherton Richards, great-grandson of Amos Cooke, grandson of J. B. Atherton, and nephew of Frank Atherton, had been transferred from his position as treasurer of Castle & Cooke to take over the presidency of the ailing pineapple company. He had left a financial advisory partnership in New York to join C & C in 1925.

In his new position, Richards soon got Hawaiian Pineapple turned around and into a profit position. As far as the public was concerned, all was peaceful on the pineapple front.

But actually a conflict was growing between Richards, who wanted to run his own show, and the top people at Castle & Cooke, who had put him in his job. And power blocs were developing out of the stock ownership of the Castle and Atherton families.

All of this came to light on a July morning in 1940 when the 170 C & C stockholders received large, white envelopes in the mail. Therein was a sixteen-page "memorandum" from one who was a director of Castle & Cooke, a scion of one of its founding families, and head of the islands' largest business concern—Atherton Richards. He announced that a fight was on for control of Castle & Cooke, a fight that was going to be conducted, not in the quiet of the agency's board room, but out on the sidewalk.

The immediate occasion for appeal to stockholders was what Richards described as "the sequence of events and the 'rush tactics' which seemingly have been employed to 'blitzkreig' and confuse a still undisclosed group of Castle & Cooke stockholders—the aim being to establish a one- or two-man control of the affairs of Castle & Cooke under the device of a voting trust or irrevocable proxy." The proposed voting trust would have included Atherton, Budge, Harold Castle, and Richards himself. Richards charged that his uncle, board chairman Frank Atherton, president Alex Budge, and senior vice-president Harold Castle were seeking means "by which they could, if they desired, perpetuate themselves for 10 years, come what may." Further particularizing, he claimed "intrusion or harassment by the executive 'group' of Castle & Cooke" in the business of the pineapple company.

Because the influence of Castle & Cooke reached into so many sectors of the Hawaiian economy, the progress of the row was watched with the greatest interest by everyone, and newspaper "play" was heavy. Also, it was a first-rate fight among the giants, the first time the curtain had been pulled aside to reveal the inner workings of the highly organized Hawaiian business hierarchy.

People who had knowledge of island affairs began to think back. Those with long memories went back to 1925, when Richards, a brilliant, cocksure youth, first started to work at Castle & Cooke. They recalled that he had been regarded as headstrong, willful, and likely to get in a lot of people's hair. But they also recalled that his keenness had been conceded and his abilities given magnificent scope when Jim Dole's pineapple empire was reorganized.

There had been growing rumors of sharp differences of opinion over "business philosophies"—meaning, in C & C's view, how well

Hawaiian Pineapple's president worked with the company's directors; in Richards' view, how much his directors were representing pineapple company interest and how much Castle & Cooke's interest.

It developed that Richards had submitted a memorandum to his Uncle Frank in which he requested the "probable removal" of Alex Budge as C & C president. He also urged that two other top executives also go.

The showdown was, perhaps, an inevitable clash of personalities, but what immediately precipitated it was the dissolution, in December 1938, of the S. N. Castle Estate, which held 27.5 percent of Castle & Cooke's capital stock. Its breakup (for tax purposes) and the scattering of its assets among seventy-five stockholders left the J. B. Atherton Estate, with its 31 percent control, in a particularly powerful position in the agency.

In addition, it came out that Atherton Richards had been instrumental in inducing the Atherton Estate to add to its holdings in Hawaiian Trust Company, which voted another 10 percent of Castle & Cooke stock as trustee and held proxies and powers of attorney for 18 percent more. This additional leverage would have had nothing to oppose it but widely scattered holdings, and it was these holdings that the management was trying to pull together by an appeal for proxies.

To Richards' public blast, Atherton, Budge, and Castle replied with one of their own. Their printed letter, mailed to C & C stockholders and widely read by the public, pointed out that their solicitation of irrevocable proxies—by then reduced from ten to five years—was defensive rather than aggressive. The solicitation, they said, was intended to protect against the strong possibility that Atherton Richards might seek to gain control of Castle & Cooke.

Their letter added that it was Richards who had successfully argued against dissolution of the J. B. Atherton Estate, which initially had planned to follow the action taken by the S. N. Castle Estate. It also pointed to Richards' role in the Atherton Estate's recent increased investment in Hawaiian Trust Company and concluded:

> We believe that the motivating force behind Mr. Richards' action in connection with the foregoing transactions was directed toward his attaining virtual control of the affairs of Castle & Cooke . . . . We believe that the facts herein set forth, coupled with the dictatorial and arbitrary attitude he has displayed in your Company's affairs, clearly indicate his ambitions . . . .
>
> A majority of the stock of the pineapple company is owned by Castle & Cooke and Waialua Agricultural Company, for which

your Company acts as agent and in which your Company is the largest stockholder. Under the circumstances your Company and its management have a very real and substantial responsibility for the pineapple company and its success . . . . Mr. Richards has undoubted qualifications as an executive, yet experience has shown that his value is greatly restricted by an unwillingness to cooperate with others, even his associates.

A stern letter to the rebellious Richards from Harold Castle was also distributed to stockholders. It included in its observations:

You went to work first for Castle & Cooke in 1925, at the instigation and upon the request of Mr. F. C. Atherton. At that time, Mr. E. D. Tenney was the head of the firm and he took the position that it was a mistake to bring you in; that your temperament in dealing with others was characterized by selfishness rather than by cooperation; that, in addition, you were not a good sportsman; that no good would come of this association and that trouble would be definitely in store for the future. In deference, however, to the wishes of Mr. Atherton, and in recognition of the large holding of the Atherton Estate, Mr. Tenney acquiesced and you entered the firm . . . .

It apparently was not long before these anticipated difficulties began to arise and, because of your constant conflict with the management and other executives, as well as outsiders, it was felt by the officials of Castle & Cooke that you could not continue with the firm . . . . In the pineapple company it seems you carried on in the same manner . . . .

Atherton, you are a forceful and dominating character; your determination, backed by large stockholders, could go a long way . . . . I have often said that you are almost a genius, or at least a financial one—a term somewhat vague, but to a layman like myself I imagine that it implies an unusually highly developed mentality, not always accompanied by good balance and stability. I picture a stagecoach of the old days, careening along a narrow road hanging on the side of some ragged cliff, with yourself in the driver's seat directing its progress and pointing the way; but if I were a passenger, I would want some steady old-timer holding the reins, with his foot on the brake and being mighty sure that the wheels stayed on the ground.

When the pineapple company's stockholders convened August 29,

1940, everyone thought Atherton Richards would be tossed out on his ear, but at the last minute Uncle Frank forgave all and in sorrow rather than anger urged that the Castle & Cooke rebel be given one more chance as chief of the world's largest pineapple company.

Atherton told the stockholders' meeting:

> As many of you know, there has been considerable criticism on the part of many stockholders as to the attitude and utterances of your president [Richards] . . . . These criticisms of your president are not merely due to emotional reactions, but to two main reasons: One is a lack of confidence in his fairness and judgment on many occasions. This has been due to a lack of complete frankness in his disclosures on some matters to the board of directors . . . . I speak as one who at times has felt this situation acutely . . . .
>
> I feel that the personal attitude of your president toward some of the directors and many businessmen, both here and on the mainland, has been such as to arouse antagonism and ill feelings . . . and I believe it has caused unfavorable reaction against the company . . . . This whole situation has been clearly and at some length presented to the president.
>
> He has admitted before many of us that he has made real mistakes in the past, which he deeply regrets; that he realizes the gravity of this situation and has assured us he will do everything in his power to show and maintain a different attitude in the future.
>
> He has promised to cooperate fully with the board of directors and will devote his best efforts to carrying out the policies as determined by the board . . . . We are all human and everybody is liable to make mistakes . . . .

Richards was to be given one more chance.

"Richards raised so much hell when he learned he was to be ousted," Harold Castle recalled in later years, "that Frank Atherton—gentle soul that he was—couldn't take it. He didn't have the temperament to handle his nephew. Richards caused him such great agony he caved in to family pressures." Budge, apprised in advance that Atherton would probably give in to pleas of Richards and his supporters, declined to serve on the pineapple company's board.

But the truce didn't last long. Richards remained in office only until the spring of 1941, when new differences arose. He simply could not adjust to a position subordinate to the board, so on April 28, 1941, the insurgent president was fired.

THIRTY YEARS LATER Richards was still convinced he was right in challenging Castle & Cooke management. "It was not my intention to question the integrity of Frank Atherton or Harold Castle," he said. "But their business judgment and prudence in allying themselves with Budge's voting trust idea was certainly open to question."

Budge in later years said, "Richards might have gotten me ousted if he had not made the mistake of injecting Mr. Atherton and Mr. Castle into the picture. Had he gone after me alone, things might have turned out differently."

In the end the Atherton Richards dethroning demonstrated the new power of career men in Castle & Cooke's management: Budge was boss of Castle & Cooke. Thus, family management made way for newcomers who had gained their positions on merit and ability. After the removal of Richards, not one top executive in Castle & Cooke traced his blood line back to S. N. Castle or Amos Cooke.

"The change was long overdue," Harold Castle observed.

*The name **Lurline** has been famous throughout the history of Matson Navigation Company, which Castle & Cooke represented as Hawaii agent from 1907–63. In 1887, Captain William Matson became part owner of a brigantine that was to be his first **Lurline** (left). His second **Lurline** (below) was an oil-powered freighter with accommodations for fifty-one passengers. She entered the Hawaii service in the 1900s.*

*Many members of Hawaii's Oriental community, originally im-
ported to work in the sugarcane fields, became wealthy as merchants in Honolulu. Chun Afong built this mansion (above) in
1857 for his growing family, which eventually numbered sixteen
children. The house on the opposite page was the last home of
Mrs. S. N. (Mary) Castle (shown on the rear seat of the carriage
with her parasol). The house was built in 1900 near an ancient
Hawaiian place of refuge overlooking Manoa Valley; it com-
manded a panoramic view from the mountains to the sea.*

Sugarcane at Ewa Plantation Company was hauled in mule-drawn carts along portable tracks to the main rail line that led to the plantation's mill.

Cane farming at Ewa was large-scale agriculture. The fields were prepared for planting by huge plows, drawn by two enormous steam-powered tractors. Ewa became one of the most productive sugar plantations in Hawaii.

Construction of the Wahiawa reservoir dam in 1900–04 assured a steady supply of water for Waialua Agricultural Company's cane fields. The plantation continues today as Waialua Sugar Company.

Waialua's mill and rail yard are shown as they appeared in 1920. Trucks now do the cane hauling.

Joseph Ballard Atherton became the first president of Castle & Cooke following incorporation in 1894. He had been a partner since 1862 and had married one of the Cookes' daughters, Julie, in 1865. He died in 1903.

George Parmelee Castle became the "reluctant" president of Castle & Cooke following the death of J.B. Atherton. But business was not for him, and he resigned in 1916 to devote full time to philanthropy.

Edward Davies Tenney, one of C&C's most flamboyant leaders, guided and controlled the company's fortunes for more than thirty years until his death in 1934. For many years, he also ruled Matson Navigation Company.

Above: James Bicknell Castle, fourth of the Castle sons, was a dynamic young man, who left Castle & Cooke to enter ambitious business ventures elsewhere. He became a senior executive of Alexander & Baldwin in 1900.

Above right: William Richards Castle, S. N.'s second son, became an attorney. He participated in several of his brother James' business efforts, and the two were instrumental in the organization of Ewa Plantation.

Right center: Charles Montague Cooke, second of the Cooke sons, also left C&C to pursue his own ambitions. He became the Cooke in Lewers & Cooke, was president of the Bank of Hawaii and later of C. Brewer & Co., Ltd.

Bottom: Benjamin F. Dillingham, once a sailor stranded in Honolulu in 1865, organized Hawaii's first railroad in 1888 with the backing of S. N. Castle. The railroad led to the development of Ewa and Waialua.

It's so different

No more like ordinary Pineapple than a Baldwin apple is like a raw turnip

James Drummond Dole came to Hawaii in 1899 to seek his fortune. By 1901, he had decided on pineapple. Eight years later he was advertising his product nationwide. Below, he examines one of his early crops.

This was a typical packing table scene at Jim Dole's pineapple cannery in 1919.

These Ginaca machines, developed in 1911, revolutionized pineapple canning.

This was a typical pineapple harvesting scene before mechanization in 1946.

The island of Lanai became Dole's second plantation.

The Woolaroc, piloted by Art Goebel, was the winner of the ill-fated Dole Derby in 1927. Only one other plane completed the historic flight.

The Royal Hawaiian Hotel, the famous "Pink Palace" of Waikiki, was opened in 1927. As Matson's agent, C&C supervised its construction and management.

In the early days (above), Waikiki's lone hotel was the Moana, built in 1900. In 1946 (far left), the Royal and the Moana still dominated the shoreline.

Child movie star Shirley Temple, shown with Jim Dole, visited Hawaiian Pineapple Company's cannery in Honolulu during a 1935 trip to Hawaii. Dole was keenly alert to the value of publicity for his pineapple products.

"Boat Day" was a festive occasion on the Honolulu waterfront during the heyday of Matson's tourist business before World War II. Arriving passengers were greeted with flower leis and hula dancers, accompanied by the Royal Hawaiian Band. Departing vessels were adorned with countless streamers of brightly-colored confetti, and the haunting notes of "Aloha Oe" invariably produced a tear or two as the ship edged away from the dock.

Herbert Hoover, then secretary of commerce, later president of the United States, attended the 1926 christening of Matson's luxury liner, the Malolo. Also present were Wilhelmina Tenney (left), daughter of E. D. Tenney; Mrs. William (Lurline) Roth, daughter of Captain Matson; and the Roth daughters, Lurline and Berenice.

The Chinatown fire of 1900, which was deliberately started in order to "burn out" bubonic plague, raced out of control and destroyed most of that area on the edge of downtown Honolulu. Castle & Cooke's offices (far right) escaped damage.

In 1905, Castle & Cooke moved its headquarters to the Stangenwald Building, still standing on Merchant Street across from present headquarters.

In 1911, Castle & Cooke moved down the street to larger quarters in this building, since demolished, at the corner of Merchant and Fort.

In 1924, C&C moved into its own handsome new building at Merchant and Bishop.

Frank C. Atherton, chairman   *Alexander G. Budge, president*

*Atherton, Budge, and Richards were involved in the 1940
"public" fight for control of Castle & Cooke. Richards eventually lost. Years later, White also lost his job.*

Atherton Richards, boss at Dole   *Henry A. White, Richards' successor*

Adjustment
1941-1948

Chapter 12

Fateful Sunday

THE HAOLE RULERS OF HAWAII had large staffs of Oriental extraction to wait upon them, and their maids usually wore kimonos and tabis.

"That all ended December 7, 1941—after the Japanese attack on Pearl Harbor," says the widow of a Hawaii business executive and a friend of the Tenneys, Athertons, and Budges. "I remember on December 8—when all of us were in a state of shock not knowing what would happen next—our maids came to us and said the Cookes' maids were just going to wear plain American dresses from now on and could they also? Nobody wanted to be 'Japanese' after December 7."

If people in the forty-eight states were stunned by Japan's Sunday assault on their principal Pacific bastion, it was nothing compared to the numbing shock that overtook the people of Honolulu as they saw much of the U.S. fleet, hundreds of planes, and navy, army, and marine installations destroyed on the very edge of their city. By noon a large part of the Pacific fleet was aflame, sunk, or out of commission, and airfields, barracks, planes, and hangars were in blazing shambles. More than two thousand servicemen and civilians were dead, and hospitals were filled with the burned and wounded.

Pearl Harbor was a terrible defeat. There were no observation planes in the air. Battleships were moored side by side without protection. Planes at Hickam, Wheeler, and Bellows fields were parked wing to wing, and few ever got off the ground. Most of the army's anti-aircraft guns were without shells, which were stored miles away, and more than a third of the fleet's officers were on weekend leave. An inexperienced army lieutenant even brushed aside early radar warnings of the attack.

Almost unbelievable confusion followed, but it was not the civilian population that was confused. The man who was chief of the FBI in Hawaii in 1941 later remarked, "Nowhere under the sun could there have been a more intelligent response to the needs of the hour than was given by the population of these Islands."

While bombs and torpedoes were still falling, hundreds of civilian doctors and nurses rushed to Pearl Harbor and other high-casualty areas. Within an hour the community blood bank was supplying 1,200 units of plasma, and hundreds of people of every race lined up to give more blood. Civilians immediately began guarding vital installations, and thousands more manned evacuation centers and feeding stations, or volunteered for any job to which they might be assigned.

The impact of the war on Hawaii's industry and agriculture was instant, and Castle & Cooke with its varied business interests was in the middle of everything.

Press accounts, carried widely in mainland newspapers, described how Japanese plantation workers hacked large arrows in the green cane fields to direct Japanese bombers to their targets, but these reports were pure fabrication. Although Castle & Cooke's Ewa and Waialua plantations, adjacent to major U.S. military installations, were not hacked by Japanese workers, they were hacked repeatedly by the U.S. military. At Waialua more than a thousand acres of cane were ripped out to make military bases from which to hit the enemy. At Ewa, where the mill was riddled by enemy gunfire, hundreds of additional acres of crops were bulldozed for airstrips, barracks, and ammunition dumps. More than a million dollars' worth of cane was plowed under on Oahu within a day or so.

"By nightfall of December 7," recalls John Midkiff, then Waialua's manager, "troops had moved into my yard, dug a huge hole and filled it with enough explosives to blow up the island. No one seemed to know why, then or after the war. Let's say there was a little 'confusion.' Our bulldozers, crawler cranes and trucks were taken out of the fields to build airfields. I was ordered to supply as many as 500 men a day from my work force to help build defense installations. One truck driver, missing for weeks, finally showed up with the simple explanation that 'the army put me to work.' "

In the first hectic weeks there was little appreciation on the part of military authorities of the long-range need for sugar, pineapple, and shipping. One officer issued orders to blow up the big Wahiawa reservoir that supplied water for Waialua's sugarcane. He was afraid enemy planes might see starlight reflected on the water and get a "fix" on nearby Wheeler Field. The easily discernible Pacific shoreline was within a few miles, and nothing could camouflage the ocean, but the officer insisted he was right. "Before they could blow up the dam," says Midkiff, "we got to a higher authority who recognized the utter stupidity of the order. It was halted just in time."

The military also requisitioned most of the canned fruit that Hawaiian Pineapple and other companies produced. The cannery was blacked out completely and during the peak season ran day and night.

Company plantations on Oahu were in the middle of major military activity, and chunks of acreage were converted to potatoes and other vegetables that could help feed the military and local population. At Waialua, cane fields near the ocean were converted to potato fields in order that the military could have a clear field of fire in case the Japanese swarmed ashore on the beaches, as was first feared.

Equipment and manpower were commandeered, cutting the labor force drastically; barge shipments from Lanai were so delayed that a considerable tonnage of fruit rotted in the fields.

OVERNIGHT, KEY CASTLE & COOKE PEOPLE found themselves in wartime jobs. President Budge, caught on the Pacific Coast on December 7, wangled a flight to the islands just in time to be drafted for the military governor's staff. He was placed in charge of controls for materials and for allocation of shipping space for essential civilian supplies.

The December 7 attack caught Castle & Cooke short of cash. Budge asked George Montgomery, head of C & C's San Francisco office, to call on the Wells Fargo Bank & Union Trust Company to see if Castle & Cooke's credit was good for a million dollars. The bank's president replied, "Back in 1906, when we couldn't get through the earthquake and fire debris to open our vaults, Castle & Cooke never worried about their deposits. I guess we don't need to worry about their credit today."

Although work forces were slashed in half, sugar plantations managed to stay close to normal production levels. Ewa and Waialua dropped only a few thousand tons between 1941 and 1945, while Kohala actually showed a slight increase.

Fortunately, by close scheduling of incoming ships plus highly efficient stevedoring, enough vessels became available to carry some crops to mainland markets. Matson carried heavy loads of military cargo and lost fifteen of its ships to enemy action. Castle & Cooke

Terminals, operating around the clock, earned the reputation of being the most efficient wartime cargo handlers in the nation.

All of this wearying war activity was conducted under strict military control. Shortly before noon of December 7, territorial governor Joseph B. Poindexter, under pressure from Washington, ceded his authority to a military governor. Martial law was declared by midafternoon, and islanders began living under the most rigid blackout and curfew ever imposed on U.S. citizens. From dusk to dawn they were confined to their homes; schools were taken over without warning; the vital protective writ of habeas corpus was suspended; and civil courts were closed. Military courts alone decided the guilt of anyone picked up for alleged infringements of rules and regulations, some of which were even made retroactive. Few were ever found innocent by the provost judges, and before regulations were softened, islanders paid nearly $3 million for such "crimes" as a speck of light showing through a blackout curtain. Another "sentence" was a mandatory order to give a pint to the blood bank. There was no appeal.

J. Garner Anthony, the territorial attorney general, challenged the legality of military rule as early as May 1942, but it was not until February 1946 that the U.S. Supreme Court repudiated the army's actions and held that martial law was unconstitutional—that the people of Hawaii could not be denied their rights under the Constitution. Although they had been denied such rights for years, not a single dollar of the illegal fine money was ever returned, and no apology was made to the civilian populace. Litigation such as Anthony's, plus public opinion and improvement in the military situation, brought a relaxation of martial law by mid-war, but curfews and other restrictions continued for many months.

THERE WERE 158,000 PERSONS of Japanese ancestry in Hawaii when the war began, and like the Cookes' maids, they did everything possible to shed any ties with the land of their ancestors. In Pacific Coast states all those of Japanese ancestry were rounded up and sent off to barren detention camps, but in Hawaii there was no serious move for such mass confinement. Only a relative handful of Japanese who were believed to be sympathetic toward Japan's expansion plans were detained. This faith in the Japanese population at large was entirely justified, for no case of sabotage was ever reported in Hawaii.

For islanders of Asiatic background, the war was indeed the final test of their Americanism. The army placed Americans of Japanese ancestry (AJAs) in their own combat unit, made up primarily of men called in the first four drafts before the war. This became the 100th

Infantry Battalion. After training in Africa, this outfit went into action at Salerno in September 1943 and fought with distinction. In 1944, 2,800 AJA volunteers from Hawaii joined mainland AJAs to form the 442nd Regimental Combat Team, and this unit absorbed the remnants of the 100th as its first battalion.

The combined forces came out of the war as the most decorated ground unit of its size in U.S. history. Altogether these soldiers received more than six thousand decorations in 225 days of fighting. Over 80 percent of Hawaii's war casualties were borne by persons of Japanese blood, although they and their kin made up only one-third of Hawaii's population. These soldiers, like those of Chinese, Filipino, and Korean extraction, may have gone into uniforms as Asiatics, but they came back thoroughly American.

While the Japanese-American soldiers were in Europe, upheaval occurred in their hometowns. Thousands of lonesome American soldiers and sailors who were passing through Hawaii gave AJA girls a great rush, treating them exactly like their girl friends back home. When the Japanese-American soldiers returned, they found a totally Americanized womanhood awaiting them.

More and more, Hawaii became the staging area for America's push in the Pacific, and by 1944 the military population on the tiny island of Oahu was just under 500,000—a figure higher than the civilian population. By now, in addition to pineapple, Hawaiian Pineapple Company was turning out ten tons of candy a day for U.S. soldiers and sailors.

Hotel Street, Honolulu's "sin lane," was jammed as bored men in uniform sought entertainment. Nearby River Street, lined with bordellos, had servicemen lined up for blocks awaiting their brief moments with the likes of Mamie Stover.

The Royal Hawaiian Hotel was taken over by the military as a rest home for battle-tired navy men, as were many other buildings. Downtown streets and public transportation were packed, and so were churches as each Sunday men and women in the military beseeched care and courage from their Maker.

And then suddenly it was all over. V-J day came on August 14, 1945, and the city where it all began went on a delirious binge.

Chapter 13

Soul Searching

THE HAWAII THAT EMERGED from World War II was a transformed paradise. It was so different from the Hawaii of song and story, the Hawaii of Samuel Castle and Amos Cooke, that many *kamaainas* talked of migrating to new paradises. Few did, however, because the war left utopias few and far between, and with all its faults, Hawaii was still one of the best paradises in the world. In fact, Hawaii looked so good to thousands of servicemen and war workers that they chose to stay in the islands. Hawaii's civilian population soared above the half-million mark for the first time, then fell off in 1949, when the armed services cut back their installations and thirty thousand civilians returned to the mainland.

After cleanup crews removed hundreds of miles of barbed wire from beaches and cleared mountains of military rubbish, Hawaii looked pretty much the same as in prewar days. Cloud-shrouded, jungle-covered peaks still dominated the luxuriant landscape; coconut palms swayed, beaches called to the suntan seeker, and the aloha spirit bounced back in full force.

But beneath the surface significant social and economic changes were brewing. Revolt against the maladjustments of the old Hawaii had been churning for years; so, likewise, had reforms to correct these maladjustments. Both were in limbo for "the duration," but after V-J

Day pressure for evolution came swiftly. A long upheaval was beginning, one that would change the relationship of management to labor, of
Caucasians to Orientals, of the "haves" to the "have-nots."

Several factors contributed to this upheaval, any one of them a
sufficient topic for a volume. Sketched briefly, as they affected the
house that Castle and Cooke founded, these factors included: the
deeply-felt urge for statehood; a passion for self-analysis that has
been called "the missionary spirit cropping out in the third and fourth
generations"; the search for peaceful processes to replace strife in
industry; super-mechanization on the plantations; and the anxious
hunt for livelihoods to maintain a mainland standard of living for the
growing island population.

Admission into the Union as a full-fledged state was already a
Hawaiian dream when the republic was annexed by the United States in
1898. Thereafter every delegate sent to Congress by Hawaii introduced
a statehood bill in Congress, but statehood was still only a rosy dream
nearly fifty years later. Not until 1935, when delegate Samuel W. King
persuaded the House of Representatives to send a subcommittee to
Hawaii to study the situation, had statehood been taken seriously in
Washington. By that time it was a deadly serious matter in the islands.

The Jones-Costigan Act had arbitrarily classed Hawaii's sugar
crop (with that of Cuba and other offshore foreign producers) in the
quota that limited the tonnage of white sugar that could be shipped
to the mainland. This discrimination won over many islanders who
hitherto had opposed statehood on the grounds that the Asiatic bloc
would dominate politics and public affairs. But now it was obvious
that if Hawaii had had two senators and a representative (by 1962
two representatives) who could bargain in Congress to protect
the islands' interests, the discrimination in the sugar act might have
been headed off.

There were other fields in which the islanders felt they needed more
representation in Washington during the 1930s, too. The army and
navy, as they converted Hawaii into a Pacific bastion, might encroach
more and more on civilian rights—a fear that proved well-founded when
war broke out. Also Hawaii's people were paying more federal taxes
than the citizens of several states, and without statehood this was
taxation without representation. Finally, air transportation had brought
Honolulu closer in hours to Washington than it was to Hilo in Father
Castle's day.

The territorial legislature put the question to the people in a pleb-
iscite in 1940—"Do you favor statehood for Hawaii?" Despite a lingering concern among the haoles that the Orientals would run everything

if Hawaii became a state, the vote was yes by two to one. Yet many influential islanders were still doubtful. Some were for statehood publicly, but against it privately. (Castle & Cooke was in favor of statehood, both publicly and privately.) This divided opinion confused investigating subcommittees, sent year after year from Washington as guests of the territory. Hawaii's legislature dutifully voted money to pay the expenses of investigating congressmen, though the frequency of these junkets became a stock Hawaiian joke.

All investigators reported approximately as Senator Cordon of Oregon did in 1948, when he wrote that "Hawaii has met the requirements of statehood . . . . As a state it could more effectively manage its own affairs and contribute to the welfare of the nation . . . . The United States, by granting statehood to Hawaii at this juncture in history, could demonstrate to the world that it means what it says and practices what it urges when advocating true democracy for all peoples." But no approval would come from Congress for another eleven years.

LONG BEFORE THE WAR FROZE HAWAII into its paternalistic status quo, Castle & Cooke's Alex Budge took the position, as did heads of several other important island companies, that Hawaii would have to qualify for statehood by keeping in step with mainland thinking.

An outburst of hostile articles and books hit U.S. news stands and bookstores just prior to the war and during the war years, criticizing Hawaii in general and the Big Five specifically for feudal practices, monopolies, and exploitation of the people by the scions of entrenched wealth. The published criticisms and exposures gave Hawaii a bad press, undermined the statehood cause, and provided material for union organizers who played upon the hate-your-boss theme.

Many men in high government positions accepted the accusations without question. Secretary of the Interior Harold Ickes, whose department ruled Hawaii, was asked what he meant when he excoriated the Big Five. He replied, "Oh, you know, the five big families that control everything in the Islands." Islanders knew of no five families who dominated Hawaii. Many of them could not even name the five factoring companies that were generally regarded as the ogres. An opinion poll showed people thought the Big Five included the Dillinghams, the Bishop Estate, and the Hawaiian Electric Company, among others.

Gradually it dawned on the agencies and other important concerns that the long-established it's-none-of-the-public's-business policy had yielded sour fruit. Islanders traveling on the mainland were amazed to find their homeland, which the Hawaii Visitors Bureau and Matson advertisements portrayed so glamorously, was not only misunderstood but in many cases thoroughly disliked by many people who knew nothing about it.

The epidemic of criticism threw the islanders into a spell of self-survey. It is doubtful if any other American community ever looked at itself as objectively as the islanders did during the first years following the war. Heads of fifteen companies, including all the Big Five, raised a jackpot to employ the firm of Ivy Lee & T. J. Ross, New York public relations counselors, to make a study of Hawaii's industry and social structure, and tell the islanders what they should do. Completed in 1946, the study made drastic recommendations, but for more than a year it was kept secret in the files of the fifteen sponsors. Finally Budge and several colleagues induced the committee to do something about the skeletons that Ross had found in Hawaii's closets.

Ross recommended that the leading island companies divest themselves of their stock interests in rivals and foster some real competition. Such divestment had already been completed by Castle & Cooke, which years before had participated in the organization of many companies and accumulated either stock interests or memberships on many directorates.

When Budge became C & C president, he found himself on some forty boards. "Whenever someone wanted to do business with one of those outfits and had to contact me—and then ran into me on some of the other boards—it naturally made him sore that I always turned up," says Budge. "I didn't blame him. So I got out of the director game." When he finished his spree of resignations, Budge's list of directorships was reduced to seven, limited to those businesses in which Castle & Cooke had a large financial stake. Other officers of Castle & Cooke followed the same course.

Simultaneously Castle & Cooke disposed of holdings in agencies that were its competitors. Out went the interest in American Factors and Theo. H. Davies. Sold also were holdings in Inter-Island Steam Navigation, Hawaiian Air Lines, Pacific Chemical & Fertilizer, and Honolulu Iron Works. Matson followed suit by selling its interests in American Factors and Inter-Island Steam Navigation.

Several big estates had been broken up and distributed among the heirs. The three largest Honolulu trust companies thus gained powerful voices in many businesses by reason of the stocks they administered for the heirs. The younger generation of Castles, Cookes, Athertons, and other old island families struck out for themselves as individuals and competitors.

The Ross survey not only recommended that the Big Five and

others set their houses in order but advised them to staff themselves with capable spokesmen to explain their policies and activities to employees, stockholders, and the public. Many did this, luring the best industrial and public relations talent they could from the mainland.

In the field of industrial relations, Budge was convinced that the perquisite system had to be converted to pay for the working man. Castle & Cooke "was, without question, the leader in Hawaii in changing over from the old system," says a retired C & C executive.

The Hawaiian plantation system of perquisites had grown with the beginning of labor importation into the islands. To make plantation life more attractive, the companies had built and maintained entire villages, with free quarters for the bachelors and cottages for the married men, plus hospitals, recreation facilities, schools, and stores. All were considered part of the wages paid to plantation employees.

While this paternalistic system had been necessary at one time, Budge was convinced it was inequitable. He reasoned that the worker with a large family and a free cottage received a larger reward for the same job than did the single man living in a barracks. He had long been determined to toss the perquisite system out the window.

Castle & Cooke, Ewa, Waialua, Kohala, and Hawaiian Pineapple Company also began issuing popular-style stockholder and employee reports, which were dramatized with charts and cartoons, and took the mystery out of at least one Big Five operation. The pineapple company launched an educational program that became a model not only for other Hawaiian companies but for mainland companies as well.

Late in 1946, the pineapple company asked a professor of sociology at the University of Hawaii to organize some of his advanced students into opinion poll teams and send them into the homes of the company's workers to find out what they thought about their company. The returns were little short of astonishing. Many employees thought the president personally owned the company instead of its 5,830 stockholders. Many rated Hawaiian Pineapple as one of the Big Five, and few had any idea where the company's money came from or how it was spent.

"No wonder these people fall for the hate-the-boss propaganda of the unions," said the president. "If they don't understand the company they work for, how can they believe in us?"

The pineapple company's industrial and public relations staffs set to work to dramatize the company's story in terms that every worker could understand. The dramatizers were teams of employees themselves, chosen from the lower supervisory ranks and specially trained to talk with their fellow workers as equals.

In one dramatized story, entitled *It's Not All in the Paycheck*, a blown-up pay envelope mounted on a display board was opened in front of twenty or thirty workers by a fellow employee, who told what he found there over and above the paycheck covered in the union wage contract. As he took out the retirement insurance plan, the sick-pay card, the two-week-vacation-with-pay chart, the recreation program schedule, the group life insurance policy, the medical and hospital care certificate, and other items, he explained how much the company invested in each of these features, a total of more than $750,000. The moral was that the company could do this only because it made money, which it could do only if workers worked.

Other skits dramatized various aspects of Hawaiian Pineapple's operations. One analyzed the annual reports, showing where the pineapple dollar came from and what happened to it. It pointed up the fact that the 5,100 year-round employees, augmented by 3,000 more during the summer, garnered seven times as much out of the pineapple dollar as the stockholders who had put up the capital.

Hawaiian industry as a whole undertook to lift the veil of secrecy from its operations. This was done through another organization recommended by the Ross report, the Hawaiian Economic Foundation. Its purpose was to make surveys, assemble facts, and explain Hawaiian industry generally.

The first report, published in 1948, threw an entirely new light on the popular idea of who owned what in Hawaii. The study revealed that control of the islands' assets no longer was lodged in the Big Five. Instead, more than 1,000 corporations owned Hawaii's business. Of these, 20 had assets of $10 million or more, and 83 had assets ranging from $1 million to $10 million. The total assets of the 831 corporations that made financial figures available to the foundation were valued at $902,974,000 and were owned by 34,225 stockholders, nearly all islanders.

The foundation dug out illuminating facts about the relative size of the factoring companies. The largest of the group (based on 1946 financial data) was American Factors, with resources of $32 million and owned by 2,169 stockholders, most of them islanders. Next came Alexander & Baldwin with assets of $24 million and 813 stockholders. Third was Castle & Cooke with resources of $20 million and a list of stockholders that had increased from 24 in 1927 to 926. C. Brewer & Co.'s $17 million was fourth, and Theo. H. Davies & Co., with $12 million, was fifth. Together the group had assets of $105 million.

The octopus of interlocking ownerships proved to have been shorn of most of its tentacles. Only A & B held stock in another factoring company—a 7½ percent interest in American Factors. Much of the

stock held by the Big Five was in the sugar companies they had financed
and for which they still served as agents.

AN INTERESTING SIDELIGHT to the report was the number of Chinese-
Americans and Japanese-Americans who had become large property
owners. During the war, a million or more soldiers, sailors, and airmen,
plus thousands of civilian workers, had recklessly tossed dollars around
for food, souvenirs, entertainment, and services, leaving behind the
fattest jackpot the islanders had ever shared. By economic alchemy,
most of these squandered dollars became new Hawaiian capital as they
slipped through the fingers of merchants, waitresses, party girls, laun-
drymen, and others into the vaults of banks. On December 7, 1941,
Hawaii's bank deposits totaled a quarter of a billion dollars. Shortly
after the war ended, deposits had tripled.

This new wealth produced its share of astonishing changes. Much
of it found its way into hands of astute third- and fourth-generation
Chinese-Americans, who had the foresight to buy Honolulu property
early in the war when timid haoles were selling. The Chinese operate
through an island device known as a *hui*, a Hawaiian word meaning a
group or syndicate. Bankers in Hawaii speak of this as "friendship
capital." Over a telephone, a live-wire hui promoter sometimes raises
up to half a million dollars in an hour (with nothing on paper), permitting
him to snatch up a new business quickly.

This system was illustrated shortly after the war when a valuable
piece of land near Waikiki came up for sale in the settlement of an estate.
Much of Oahu's fee-simple land is as precious as land on Manhattan
Island, and this particular parcel was much needed for a modern hotel
and apartment development. Castle & Cooke's management considered buying the land and making necessary improvements, partly
as an investment and partly to meet an urgent need for housing, but
when the bids were opened, it was found that a Chinese hui had
acquired the property.

The Japanese-Americans have a device for raising friendship capital called *tanomoshi*. Each month ten to thirty members put one
hundred dollars apiece into a pot, which is then awarded to one of the
group, on the basis of bidding or drawing lots, to enable him to start a
small business. All members, including those who have drawn the pot
previously, continue to make monthly payments until each one has had
a chance at the *tanomoshi* dollars. At the end no money remains, and
all loans have been repaid. This system set up hundreds of Japanese in
little businesses, just as the huis plunged many Chinese into more
spectacular deals.

The rise of scores of thriving new concerns exploded the idea that nobody could go into business in Hawaii in competition with the Big Five's favorites. When S. H. Kress opened a big store in the heart of Honolulu and Sears Roebuck built a large modern retail mart, the word was whispered about that the Big Five had done everything in their power to keep these lusty competitors out of the islands. It made a good story, but Kress and Sears spoiled it by buying advertising space in the Honolulu newspapers to say it wasn't so.

The coming of the mainland chain merchants did much to crack the monopoly picture. If people did not want to buy from stores that were owned in Hawaii, they could go down the street and buy from those that sent their profits to the mainland.

Studies of property holdings in the late 1940s also revealed facts about who owned the Big Five. To use the subject of this history as an example, the largest single holding in Castle & Cooke stock, with 7.6 percent, was that of the Juliette M. Atherton Trust, set up for charitable purposes. (The J. B. Atherton Trust, with its 31 percent holding, had been dissolved in 1942.) The Frank C. Atherton Trust owned 7 percent. Other private estates owned from 2 to 4 percent of the stock, and the active officers of the company held about 5 percent. Although Hawaiian Trust Company, acting under power of attorney for various trusts and individual stockholders, voted 35 percent of Castle & Cooke's stock and had representatives on the Castle & Cooke board, these studies, generally speaking, revealed that centralized control by a few key men no longer existed and that postwar Hawaii's industries belonged to thousands of investors.

Chapter 14

The Labor Wars

WORLD WAR II INTERRUPTED the Great Labor Movement that was picking up momentum in Hawaii in the late 1930s. Only ten years earlier Ed Tenney had sat talking with Jim Dole about the problems of labor: "Years ago I sat behind this desk and imported labor for the plantations—so many head for Ewa, so many for Kohala. How in the hell can I be expected to let these damned labor fellows come in and tell me what to do?"

"So many head"—like so many head of cattle. Those three words tellingly expressed the lingering plantation attitude toward imported labor. The Chinese, Japanese, and Filipinos were uneducated and willing to do stoop labor for long hours and little money. *Give them a roof, keep them healthy, keep them busy*—that was the philosophy.

The importation of labor began with the Master and Servant Law, enacted by the Hawaiian kingdom in 1850, and its very name indicates the relationship that existed between employer and employee in the beginning plantation days and continued into the twentieth century. So how could plantation owners possibly understand the union "agitators" who started poking around in their affairs after Franklin Roosevelt became president and government started "injecting"?

Employers were spared further agitation for the four years that followed Pearl Harbor, yet new working conditions were developing in Hawaii during those war years that added momentum to the labor movement once peace was restored. Something happened that convinced the rank and file that, without union organization, they had little chance of really improving their standard of living.

When war came, men and women of Hawaii were frozen solidly into their jobs unless military authorities decided they were needed elsewhere. Meanwhile, thousands of civilians came from the mainland to build shops, air bases, and highways, for which they were paid high mainland wages, plus bonuses for working in the war zone. Islanders were paid less than mainlanders, yet they were denied the right to strike; if they refused to work, they were subject to heavy fines and even jail sentences. Before long, the "locals" learned that mainland workers who belonged to construction unions had someone to fight for their rights. Unorganized, the islanders had no one to look out for them. They did a slow burn that got hotter every month.

Immediately after V-J Day, the International Longshoremen's and Warehousemen's Union (ILWU), moved on the islands in force with an experienced staff and ample financing. The territorial legislature, prodded by the ILWU, passed a "Little Wagner Act," imposing the same type of control over agricultural labor as that laid down by the Labor Relations Act. Jack Hall, a quick-witted and rough-and-ready young organizer, set up the nucleus of the ILWU organization with a smart staff of organizers including haoles, Japanese, and Filipinos.

Union leaders expanded the ILWU to absorb workers of fifty-seven different companies in twelve kinds of business—cane and pineapple plantation workers, sugar mill and cannery employees, cooks, clerks, laundry workers, guards, drivers, and engineers. Anyone who worked for wages was welcomed into the longshoremen's fold.

In their plantation-organizing campaign in the late 1940s, union spokesmen harped on the racial issue and paternalism, and flayed the perquisite system. To the organizers' surprise, when they opened negotiations with the pineapple companies, the employers agreed. Hawaiian Pineapple Company had already taken steps to discontinue perquisites. It transferred hundreds of company-owned homes to a newly created nonprofit housing authority, from which employees rented houses for cash. The company offered a pay boost averaging fifteen cents an hour in lieu of perquisites and agreed to sign contracts with any labor organization the employees elected as their bargaining agent.

The ILWU next turned its organizing teams on the sugar workers. When plantation managements proposed abolition of perquisites, the union leaders, sensing trouble with the rank and file, accused employers of running out on their responsibilities, but the managers stood pat. On this issue—as well as higher wages and a union shop—a strike of 28,000 workers on thirty-three sugar plantations was called late in 1946.

STRIKES WERE NOT NEW to Hawaii's sugar industry. The first work stoppage of any consequence occurred in 1904 at Ewa Plantation. Five years later employees at both Ewa and Waialua went on strike. All of these stoppages had been short-lived because management had issued an ultimatum to return to work or vacate the employees' free living quarters. In 1920, however, employees went on strike at six Oahu plantations in a walkout that lasted many months and cost the planters an estimated $12 million. Two years later employees of twenty-three plantations went on strike for eight months.

But the 1946 sugar strike was different. Now the employees were members of the powerful ILWU. The strike lasted seventy-nine days, during which mills were idle, irrigation ditches dried, and cane withered. This strike was one of the most disastrous in Hawaii's history, costing workers $8.25 million in lost wages. On Ewa Plantation, dependent entirely on irrigation, the crop loss ran to $3 million. At Waialua, twenty miles away, also under irrigation, rains saved the cane and losses were less. It was the same all over the islands; much irrigated cane dried and lost its sugar-bearing juice (windward-side plantations came off better). This "solidarity" strike, which destroyed $20 million worth of potential sugar, proved the vulnerability of the industry.

In the settlement, workers made substantial gains, but in one sense the increase was a delusion. Living costs and taxes went up, and with perquisites abolished, a new window appeared alongside the pay window. Laborers now drew their new wages at one window (less income tax deductions), then walked to the other where, in addition to their store bills, they now paid rent, medical fees, and union dues. En route home they grumbled that take-home pay seemed to buy less than before.

How these social quakes jolted the sugar industry is revealed by payrolls of the three Castle & Cooke plantations. At Ewa the amount laid out for annual wages and salaries (about 35 percent of the plantation's total operating cost) almost doubled to $3.25 million. At Waialua it soared over the $3 million mark; at Kohala wages climbed to $2.26 million.

FLUSHED WITH VICTORY, ILWU leaders started talking of social as well as industrial revolution for the islands, flexing political muscle through an organization called the Political Action Committee (PAC). They adjusted quickly to the local political modus operandi.

In Hawaii the candidate with the best hula show traditionally had the edge at the polls, so the ILWU employed big-time hula troops to campaign for its candidates. The PAC started demanding that Hawaii's big estates be broken up into small plots for sale to private owners. It called for a fair-practice act forbidding employers to favor one race over another, for extension of minimum wage and hour laws, for larger unemployment compensation, and for legislation guaranteeing year-round employment.

It was good bait for the voters. In 1947 the PAC helped elect fifteen Democratic legislators to the lower house of the territorial legislature. The Republicans had an equal number, resulting in a deadlocking tie. After the customary flower show, singing, and hula dances at the opening of the legislature, ILWU leaders took seats behind the fifteen Democrats to see that they voted right, and for three weeks they stymied the organization of the House of Representatives. Finally, under pressure of mass indignation meetings of irate citizens, one Democrat revolted and the lower house was able to organize for work.

Though the ILWU-PAC temporarily lost its force in the legislature, its officers still called the shots on the industrial front. The islands, unable to support themselves and dependent upon shipping for everything, were at their mercy.

"We hesitate to use the strength we have," explained Jack Hall. "We have to argue with our own people—who have years of accumulated grievances to settle—to be patient. Hawaii has been a pretty feudal territory. It's not so long ago that everyone was afraid to speak. Now no one is afraid of anyone else. The greatest change of all is the change of attitude. But the employers are determined to have another showdown with us."

Actually, many suspected the ILWU was spoiling for a showdown. They had become so accustomed to victory that it seemed almost impossible that they could know defeat. Yet it happened, after the union turned thumbs down on an across-the-board wage raise offered by the pineapple industry early in 1947, just as the canneries were getting ready for the big summer harvest.

ILWU leaders stalled, neither accepting nor rejecting the offer, keeping employers anxious until $60 million worth of pineapples were ripening under the tropical sun. Then, with the harvest so far advanced that it had to be picked and canned immediately, the union struck for a whopping 50 percent pay boost.

By this time the pendulum of public opinion had started its backswing. Hundreds of people volunteered to go into the fields to pick pineapples, and hundreds of employees, ignoring the jibes of pickets, went to work in the canneries. Within a matter of hours, ILWU leaders admitted they had lost the strike. Four days later they signed a contract for less than the employers offered before the workers were called out.

Taking stock, both the ILWU and management recognized that the 1947 pineapple workers' walkout was an abortive strike that settled nothing permanently. The real showdown was yet to come. Hawaii lapsed into an industrial cold war that might turn hot anytime the ILWU leaders felt strong enough to crack the solid employer front, as represented by the Hawaii Employers' Council. Both sides recognized the bottlenecks to the islands' economy—the waterfront, the truck drivers, the Matson lifeline of ships, the sugar and the pineapple industries— where the union might put the squeeze on the livelihood of half a million people and wrest by force whatever its leaders wanted.

The squeeze play came at midnight on April 30, 1949, in what, considering all its ramifications, was one of the most remarkable and interesting industrial conflicts in American history. The strike lasted more than six months, during which the ILWU "threw the book" at Hawaii, and the community resorted to every device at its command, not to win the strike but simply to survive it.

The bottleneck chosen by the ILWU hierarchy—Harry Bridges and Louis Goldblatt from the mainland, Jack Hall for the islands—was the Honolulu waterfront. By calling out two thousand longshoremen, the ILWU cut off Hawaii's source of supplies completely. Neither sugar nor pineapple could go to market; no supplies, food, clothing, or medicine could come from the mainland by sea.

ILWU leaders demanded parity with Pacific Coast waterfront wages (a raise of thirty-two cents an hour) or arbitration, which meant that an outside party would decide what employers had to pay, regardless of what the islands' economy could afford. Though arbitration meant the end of collective bargaining, "parity" and "arbitration" were smart issues, particularly when islanders were trying to convince the rest of the country that they had climbed to a mainland standard of living and were therefore qualified for statehood.

There was another side to the parity story. As wages in Hawaii trebled in a decade, both employers and unions had built up a parity among island industries. The waterfront workers were already the highest paid; pineapple was next, then sugar. A thirty-two-cent increase for two thousand longshoremen would mean pressure for a similar pattern of increases for pineapple and sugar workers, whose contracts came up next.

As the strike dragged on, dramatic and unexpected episodes ensued. Housewives organized a "broom brigade" and picketed ILWU headquarters on the Matson dock for three months. Small businessmen, with stocks of needed supplies tied up, organized an independent stevedoring concern, Hawaiian Stevedores, Ltd., to unload ships. The "society cops," a wartime hangover of emergency police, again walked the outlying beats, enabling the Honolulu police force to concentrate on maintaining waterfront peace.

Violence flared only once, when the ILWU "generals" drew the police to one wharf by a feint while their main task force attacked another with crowbars, baseball bats, and clubs, injuring six independent longshoremen.

On the plantations workers stayed on the job, contributing a slice of their wages to the strike fund. Mountains of sugar piled up in warehouses, plantation gymnasiums, and tennis courts. As the multimillion pineapple harvest ripened, the canneries ran out of tin for cans. Matson ships tied to the docks were full of tin that nobody could unload. Dairies and poultry farms ran out of feed. Consignees turned to the courts, which ordered the sheriff's men to get the tin and feed unloaded.

Scores of small businessmen closed their doors, either broke or out of supplies. The "splinter fleet," barges towed by tugs, came into existence, running urgently needed supplies to the islands. On the mainland, canneries packing fruit cocktail and salad, which by regulation must include pineapple, were out of pineapple but surfeited with other fruits.

To save the fruit cocktail situation, two pineapple canneries undertook to slip tug-drawn pineapple barges, like the rumrunners of Prohibition days, into small West Coast ports; but the ILWU flew a token picket force to the mainland to picket the hot cargo. One barge successfully unloaded at Tillamook, Oregon. Another, dispatched by Hawaiian Pineapple Company, tried to unload at the AFL-controlled port of Tacoma but was stymied. It hunted aimlessly for a beachhead, finally making port at The Dalles, Oregon, where an ILWU defense battalion from Portland drove off the local police and citizenry attempting to unload the craft, wrecked the port equipment, and dumped part of the cargo into the Columbia River.

The turning point in the strike came as public wrath crystallized against the community squeeze. The governor's fact-finding commission recommended a fourteen-cent raise, which employers grudgingly accepted and the ILWU bitterly rejected.

The governor appealed to President Truman to invoke the emergency provisions of the Taft-Hartley law. When he refused, a hastily assembled legislature passed emergency bills authorizing the governor to seize the stevedoring companies and operate them, thus putting the territory in the stevedoring business. Cargoes moved over the docks in increasing tonnages. The ILWU appealed to the courts and lost. Then the legislature passed a permanent "Little Taft-Hartley Act" with more teeth than the big one.

The battlefront shifted to the mainland. Matson tried to load ships in Pacific Coast harbors, but the militant ILWU prevented this. Matson, losing three-quarters of a million dollars a month, became a war casualty, weak from the loss of revenue. There were other war casualties, among them the Pacific seafaring unions, whose men were "on the beach" by reason of a strike in which they had nothing to gain.

Pressures for settlement built up on the ILWU leadership. The employers' front cracked. One of the agency companies tried to settle the strike behind the back of the employers' front.

Quick in shifting strategy, the adroit ILWU leadership forced the negotiations out of Hawaii to Washington, where Harry Bridges verbally skinned Hawaii employers before a congressional committee. The scene then shifted to New York, before federal mediator Cyrus Ching. The New York meeting was little more than a sounding board for Bridges. Before the employers recovered their balance, the nimble ILWU chiefs shifted the scene again, to San Francisco and then back to Honolulu, where Bridges suddenly abandoned his major demands for arbitration and mainland parity, and settled for a fourteen-cent raise, plus a seven-cent bonus the following March. Thus ended the 179-day strike, the longest and costliest in Hawaii's history.

THE CONTENDERS AND THE COMMUNITY at large took stock of losses and gains. Both sides, punch-drunk and exhausted, had settled for what neither side wanted, to gain two years of peace—time in which to build up for the next show of strength.

Although the ILWU lost its major demands, it ended the strike with greater rank-and-file solidarity than it had at the start, but the union was broke and soon signed a new sugar contract tying wages to the price of sugar. Nevertheless Big Five and Hawaiian Sugar Planters' Association (HSPA) solidarity was only a memory, and management, outsmarted at nearly every turn, held a new respect for ILWU leadership.

The costly strike, resulting in losses estimated at $100 million, clarified some other points, too. One was that an aroused community could protect itself from one of the tightest and toughest unions in the country. At strike's end the Isthmian Line and chartered Matson ships were delivering a nearly normal cargo of supplies to Hawaii and territorial longshoremen were unloading them.

On the Pacific Coast no "hot" cargo from Hawaii could be moved over ILWU-controlled docks, but cargoes moved smoothly over Gulf and Atlantic docks, despite union threats. Thus Hawaii's economic ties, linked for almost a century to the Pacific Coast, moved back to the Atlantic, where they had been in the early days of Samuel Castle and Amos Cooke.

There have been many labor disputes in Hawaii since the 1949 waterfront strike, including major ones in the sugar and pineapple industries. Yet the public has never since been quite so incensed. For many years now, Hawaii's agricultural workers have been the highest paid in the world, and partly because of that, the thirty-three sugar plantations affected by the 1946 strike are now sixteen. In 1950, Hawaii had nine pineapple companies; today there are three.

Yet there have been pluses all around in the gains of labor. The semifeudal system is no more. An individual is his own boss, and a person of any ethnic background can ascend to positions once reserved only for Caucasians. The whole of Hawaii, too, has prospered with more money in more pockets.

Following Pearl Harbor, life in Hawaii was quickly transformed to a wartime status. Waialua's sugar mill (above) was fenced with barbed wire and camouflaged with paint. Key installations were sandbagged and guarded, and the Royal Hawaiian Hotel (right) was converted into a navy rest center.

Increased mechanization of sugar and pineapple was industry's answer to the higher labor costs that accompanied unionization in Hawaii following World War II. Giant cane-hauling trucks replaced the sugar plantation railroads, and modern harvesting rigs appeared in the pineapple fields.

Following World War II, Castle & Cooke and other Hawaii firms launched programs to explain their operations to their employees. Hawaiian Pineapple Company's program included a dramatization entitled It's Not All in the Paycheck. Specially trained supervisors explained to their fellow workers about the various fringe benefits paid by the company in addition to the regular wages.

Expansion
1948-1976

Chapter 15

The Budge Era

NOBODY CALLS ALEX BUDGE "PINKY" ANYMORE. He is now in his eighties, and his hair has long since turned from red to a creamy white. Formerly a widower, he has remarried and lives in Santa Rosa, north of San Francisco, when he isn't traveling, fishing, or duck hunting in the Pacific Northwest. He finds the climate of the Bay Area agreeable, and three of his four children live nearby. But as advisory director, he is still the patriarch of Castle & Cooke.

A. G. Budge is the venerable gentleman whose knowledge of Hawaii and Castle & Cooke spans more than six decades. He is one of the few left who remembers Ed Tenney and George Parmelee Castle, the Atherton brothers, Jim Dole, and Captain Matson. He still attends quarterly board meetings, makes a point of being on hand for company parties, and keeps in touch with the business of Castle & Cooke through frequent calls at the company's San Francisco office.

Budge is the one who realized that it was time to bring new blood into the management of the family-dominated company and to set up an informal system of recruiting talent. While other companies still hired easygoing friends and relatives, Budge was employing promising main-landers, some of whom rose to senior management levels in the company and some to leadership of other Hawaii corporations who could lure away Budge's young talent. You didn't have to be a main-lander to succeed. Budge also picked "local boys" and long-time employees who had no ties of family or comradeship. He was a leader in bringing persons of Asian ancestry into management, too; Castle & Cooke was, in 1966, the first of the Big Five companies to name an Oriental to a vice-presidency.

Industrial relations and public relations departments, the Hawaii Employers Council—Budge pioneered them all.

His twenty-four-year tenure as president of Castle & Cooke was the longest in the company's history. How did his business contemporaries view his presidency in retrospect? One executive commented that, despite his innovations, he was more of a conservator than a builder. An attorney, long associated with the company, said, "Alex was a coalescing influence—the one man who could bring all those rugged individuals together. He brought into the company a whole group of the ablest people I've ever known."

The late Frederick Simpich, Jr., a mainland recruit who became a senior C & C executive and director before his retirement, knew him well and observed him keenly. A few years before Simpich's death in 1975, he recalled: " 'Coalescing influence' expressed it very well. You must remember the tremendous chasm that existed when Budge took over the presidency in 1935. He had on his hands a family company operating through the trust companies. Then there was the jealousy of Atherton Richards, who had wanted to be president. Budge had people looking at him awfully hard from all directions. He was basically a salesman, yet he never wanted to cause violent dissent. I remember he used to tell me, 'Don't try to be a dead hero.' I think it was Jim Dole who said the key to good management is the intelligent anticipation of agitation, and that's sort of what Budge practiced. He was a marvelous guy for his time. Alex Budge was extremely loyal to his friends. He would build friendship and, at the same time, confidence in what he had to say. For a man with the stereotyped redhead's temper, he could discipline himself magnificently."

Budge's loyalty to his friends was tested when a high officer of one of Hawaii's major companies was sent to prison. Budge called on him once a week.

IN THE LATE 1940s AND EARLY 1950s, C & C talked a lot about diversifying. Hawaiian Pineapple Company had suffered severe losses in a 1952 strike on Lanai, and Budge saw this as a clear demonstration that the firm was too dependent on sugar and pineapple.

How do you diversify in an island chain whose drawbacks are limited acreage of good soil, no minerals, few forests, distant markets, and cost disadvantages, and whose chief resources are a lot of rain and sunshine? "How about the ocean?" asked Bill Bush, then company treasurer, who saw an opportunity in Hawaiian Tuna Packers, a small Honolulu concern that needed growth money.

Tuna Packers, as it was called, was being developed by the late Alan S. Davis, a former Castle & Cooke executive vice-president who had joined C & C in 1936, after many years with Hawaiian Trust Company. Davis, who never really got along with Budge, resigned in 1946 to devote his time to personal business, including Tuna Packers. While with Hawaiian Trust, Davis had handled the affairs of Chris Holmes, an heir to the Fleischmann yeast fortune who was living in Hawaii. More or less as a hobby, Holmes. had bought control of the small tuna company, which was supplied by local fishermen. During the war the navy interned the fishing vessels, but with war's end tuna from the waters surrounding Hawaii found its way to the cannery again. Despite fluctuations in the catch, it was a rich fishery that no one else was tapping.

Shortly after the war Holmes died and left his Tuna Packers stock to Davis. Knowing that Davis needed capital to keep going and expand, Castle & Cooke in 1948 provided funds by purchasing 41 percent of the stock, and a few years later increased ownership to 97 percent by acquiring Davis's stock. Nervous about having such a large portion of his assets tied up in one small company, he was glad to sell.

Diversification also involved an interest in macadamia nuts, which Budge had long enjoyed. Their flavor was superb. Furthermore, they were a product that could be sold by the ounce rather than the ton and at a high price, offering an excellent way to beat the rapidly rising shipping costs between Hawaii and the mainland. Budge asked Simpich to investigate the idea and later to nursemaid it into commercial production.

The macadamia nut is a native of Queensland, Australia. It is named for Dr. John Macadam, onetime secretary of the Philosophical Society of Victoria, who was the first person to call attention to the nut's edible qualities. The first macadamia trees were introduced to Hawaii in the late 1880s as handsome ornamentals, with the nuts as a by-product for the few households that bothered to crack their extremely tough shells and roast them. The first commercial production of the nuts for snack food began in Hawaii in 1916.

Castle & Cooke became the third commercial macadamia nut producer in Hawaii when it organized the Royal Hawaiian Macadamia Nut Company in 1948. The company purchased 3,000 acres of jungle covering an ancient lava bed ten miles outside Hilo, on the island of Hawaii. With the aid of heavy equipment and dynamite, the first 1,100 acres were cleared, and an 80,000-tree orchard was planted—at that time the largest in Hawaii.

Macadamia nuts may be delicious to eat, but the economics of the business left Castle & Cooke with an unpleasant aftertaste. It requires a long-term investment before any profits come into sight. There is a five- to seven-year wait before the trees produce their first nuts, and another eight to ten years before they reach peak production—not exactly an exciting return-on-investment.

By 1956 a small commercial crop had been harvested and successfully test-marketed in New York gourmet shops. As production slowly expanded, distribution was extended to fine food outlets in most metropolitan areas of the country. But it was not until 1964 that Royal Hawaiian turned its first modest profit. The venture contributed a prestige item to the line of Castle & Cooke's food products, but looking ahead, the company's management recognized that more of the land peculiarly suited to the macadamia's demands was needed to reach high production volume. By 1973, Castle & Cooke had no more of that kind of land. C. Brewer & Co. did, so the nut orchard and processing plant were sold to Brewer, with Castle & Cooke continuing to market the nuts under a contractual agreement.

THE COMPANY'S DIFFICULTY in acquiring suitable land for its nut venture pointed up the fact that through the years it had ignored numerous opportunities to own real estate, except indirectly through the agricultural enterprises in which it had an investment. The Castles and Cookes had never benefited from the generous land grants parceled out by Hawaiian royalty. In later years Harold Castle had vehemently opposed real estate purchases by the company, always on the grounds that the price was too high. Budge did not feel it was worth fighting about. In the immediate postwar years, all the company owned directly on Oahu was five and one-half acres (although its affiliated companies owned 155,000 acres).

It was only later—in 1958, when Helemano Company, Ltd., was merged into Castle & Cooke, and in 1961 through the Dole merger— that C & C became the substantial Hawaiian landowner it is today. Helemano was a holding company organized in 1948 to take over all of the assets of Waialua Agricultural Company other than the mill equipment and 200 acres of land around the mill. These assets included Waialua's interest in Hawaiian Pineapple Company and 27,000 acres of land, which produced substantial annual rental payments.

The establishment of Helemano was a defensive move to counteract union bargaining tactics. Union negotiators for Waialua's sugar workers had been basing their demands on Waialua's total profits from both its sugar and non-sugar sources. The intention was to have the plantation's profits come solely from sugar so that labor negotiations would be based only on its sugar activities. For each old share of Waialua, stockholders received one share of Helemano and one of new Waialua.

Thus Castle & Cooke received the same 24.6 percent interest in Helemano that it then held in Waialua, and it was appointed as agent. Helemano netted more than a million dollars in its first year from land rentals and dividends on its Hawaiian Pineapple and other investments.

A continuing story—and one in which A. G. Budge was a constant stimulus—was the mechanization of Hawaii's sugar and pineapple industries. It started before World War II when plantation workers left the fields for more lucrative jobs in defense work. When the ILWU moved in afterward to impose the highest agricultural wages in the world, the two industries had to cut down the labor ingredient of their costs if they were to survive. That really gave a spur to mechanization.

Purchasing new equipment kindled Castle & Cooke's interest in the plantation equipment business. The firm organized Hawaiian Equipment Company in 1946 and later purchased another enterprise, which held the International Harvester franchise for the islands. The venture flourished.

Old methods were being modernized in every sector of the company under the drive of Budge's recruits. Cost controls, systems analyses, budgeting, data processing, steady inflows of production information—all the tools of modern business were now employed within the Castle & Cooke organization.

When Budge joined the company in 1920, there had not been so much as a budget, let alone analytical tools such as return-on-investment. "Tenney," Budge recalls, "would ask a plantation manager what he thought he wanted to spend and then would say, 'Well, I guess that's about right.' It was a hell of a way of doing business, but that's the way we operated."

In 1970, A. G. Budge, the boy from Grand Forks, North Dakota, who came to Hawaii to sell boilers, retired. He had been an employee of Castle & Cooke for fifty years—twenty-four of those years as president.

Chapter 16

Heirs Apparent

THE PRESIDENTS OF CASTLE & COOKE have always selected their successors. Alex Budge indicated Malcolm MacNaughton was the man he wanted when he named him executive vice-president in 1957. As often happens in large corporations filled with ambitious men, another vice-president was competing for the same job. He was Fred Simpich, Jr.

The contest between these two able and personable men had been public knowledge for a long time. Honolulu is small enough, especially its business circles, to know the goings-on, the pressures, the wire-pullings within its major companies. The cocktail circuit and the card tables in the clubs, year in and year out, buzz with whispered fact and fancy.

Newspaper financial writers kept a constant eye on C & C's Merchant Street headquarters and wrote stories conjecturing on the heir apparent. People in the office speculated, and Simpich and Mac-Naughton "camps" developed within the organization.

Is this good or bad for a company? Apparently the good outweighs the bad when such competition develops, for the contest of talents is encouraged in many American corporations. Supposedly each contender will try to outdo his rival with creative ideas and fiscal brilliance and thereby win the presidential nod. In theory the company should become stronger in the process and a better investment for stockholders.

To all appearances, Simpich and MacNaughton offered a good match. Both were in their forties; MacNaughton was born in 1910, and Simpich in 1911. MacNaughton had the edge in education, having attended Reed College in his hometown of Portland, Oregon, and later

Stanford University, where he earned an M.B.A. from the graduate school of business. Simpich, born in New Franklin, Missouri, went to New Mexico Military Institute and the University of Pennsylvania, but received no degree. Both men were good-looking, dressed well, and had a certain swinging style. They were polished in the amenities and possessed good minds, leavened by wit and humor. And they were ambitious.

Initially the two entered a business world that was still fighting a major depression. Simpich's first job was as a clerk with the American Automobile Association in Washington, D.C.; MacNaughton started as a statistician for North American Investment in San Francisco. Although both men have been listed as "Budge boys," Simpich was actually hired during the presidency of Frank Atherton, and Mac-Naughton was employed by the late George Montgomery, vice-president in Castle & Cooke's San Francisco office who acted as a "spotter" for Budge.

Montgomery first became aware of MacNaughton when the latter was playing golf at Stanford. "Malcolm could have become one of the great amateur golfers in our country," said Montgomery. "He used to beat Lawson Little at Stanford. But he decided to be a businessman . . . and he obviously had talent. After North American Investment, he was associated with E. F. Hutton and later a security salesman for Kaiser & Co. Finally I hired him and he started in purchasing. I knew his dad— E. B., who, at age 70, was chairman of the board of the First National Bank of Oregon, president of Reed College and president of the Oregonian Publishing Co., one of the biggest newspapers in the Pacific Northwest. He was a darned good Sunday painter, too. He was a leading citizen of the Northwest."

WHEN WORLD WAR II ENDED, MacNaughton was transferred to Honolulu, and he and Simpich were soon getting the good assignments. Besides the macadamia project, Fred was setting up an operations analysis system, studying better ways of handling Matson cargo, implementing test plantings of pineapple in the Kohala region, and wondering if paper could be made profitably from bagasse, a cane fiber residue. He was the company's "idea man."

Meanwhile Malcolm was getting Hawaiian Equipment into running order and then switched to Tuna Packers. Although his territory involved financial savvy more than ideas, he too could come up with smart new answers to cobwebbed problems.

The two men were simultaneously elected vice-presidents in April 1953. Then Budge announced in December 1955 that, at the board's request, he would stay on as president beyond his normal retirement date in 1956. This gave Simpich and MacNaughton more time to prove themselves.

MacNaughton's first major proposal concerned fish. In 1956, Castle & Cooke exchanged its ownership in Hawaiian Tuna Packers for a 12 percent interest in the venerable Columbia River Packers Association (CRPA) in Astoria, Oregon, producers of Bumble Bee seafood. The Oregon firm needed additional tuna supplies, and Tuna Packers needed a better-known label and wider marketing facilities to move its Hawaiian product on the mainland. It was a good deal for both sides.

Soon after Castle & Cooke's debut as a mainland investor, James Miller, vice-president of Blyth & Co. in Portland, Oregon, made an overture to Alex Budge for liquidation of C & C. Miller had recently completed a highly profitable transaction by consolidating several large Northwest forest holdings and selling them to Georgia-Pacific, and he figured C & C might be ripe for something similar. Miller proposed that Castle & Cooke liquidate by selling out to Blyth. He assured Budge that the firm's holdings could be sold for cash substantially in excess of stated book value or current market value.

Budge decided he owed it to his stockholders to give the proposal serious study. After talking it over with Harold Castle and Ralph Morton, president of Hawaiian Trust, he directed his treasurer, Bill Bush, to examine the proposal and make a detailed appraisal of the company's assets.

Exact values were difficult to determine in view of the varied interests in Honolulu Oil, Matson, and other properties; but the more Bush, a sharp-eyed Scot, checked, the less he liked the idea, and he started expressing opinions to Budge in his Kirriemuir brogue. Bush's work was conducted in strictest secrecy, for the Miller proposal was known only to Budge, Castle, Morton, and himself.

"I never heard of the deal until the very last minute," a slightly abashed MacNaughton admitted. He was understandably surprised, because Budge had already told him that he would be named executive vice-president within a few weeks.

The contest was at last decided, and MacNaughton was headed for the presidency.

It was MacNaughton's fiscal sense that tipped the scales. "But Malcolm had his faults, too," Budge recalled in a 1970 interview. "He was quick—fast—in everything he did—sometimes too quick . . . and he was apt to give offense for that reason. But he'd matured a lot—and was still slowing down when we made him executive vice-president."

George Montgomery concurred: "Malcolm has a very fast

mind . . . and he used to make horseback decisions. But 25 years of experience have made him first study the facts. He can admit making a mistake.''

MacNaughton and Montgomery were once sharing the speakers' table at a Chamber of Commerce luncheon in Honolulu. As Chamber president, Malcolm was sentimentally explaining to the audience that Montgomery had given him his first job.

"The experience was rewarding but the pay was lousy," said MacNaughton, at which time Montgomery stood up and smilingly observed, "It has always been Castle & Cooke's policy to pay people what they are worth.''

And what happened to the Miller proposal? "When I was finally clued in and given a chance to check over Bill Bush's analysis, I was as cold to the idea as Bill was,'' says MacNaughton. "Later on, I was invited to take part in a meeting with top Blyth officers in San Francisco.''

As the sessions developed, it became apparent that Miller was the only Blyth man with any enthusiasm for the deal. He stated his case and concluded, ''I can't see Castle & Cooke going any place as a corporation. You can make quite a deal right now by getting a higher price than the quoted value of your assets.''

The presentation was received coolly by both sides. Blyth's top men decided against making Miller's tentative offer firm, indicating the decision was based, in part, on the questionable values given to Honolulu Oil and Matson.

At the time, Honolulu Oil was quoted at $58 per share with very few sales. Matson shares had been quoted at $26 in 1955 with no sales in either 1956 or 1957. No one really knew what they were worth, and this, it turned out, was fortunate for Castle & Cooke. Within a few years the firm was able to sell its Honolulu Oil for $100 a share and its Matson stock for $65.

When Blyth broke off the discussion, MacNaughton and Bush were particularly delighted and immediately began making plans to get the firm into such shape that it would never again be vulnerable. They were going to change from an investment company to an operating company. "We were convinced the firm *could* 'go some place' and we were determined to see that it would,'' says MacNaughton. "We believed we could do far better for our stockholders by staying together than by liquidating.''

CASTLE & COOKE HAD BEEN IN BUSINESS for more than a hundred years, yet its participation in other companies was, for the most part, that of a minority stockholder. In 1957, for example, the company's only wholly owned operations of consequence were Castle & Cooke Terminals, Hawaiian Equipment Company, and Kohala Sugar Company (the latter just a fraction short of 100 percent). It owned only 34 percent of Waialua, 27 percent of Ewa, 15 percent of Hawaiian Pineapple Company, 14 percent of Matson, and 12 percent of Columbia River Packers.

One of MacNaughton's first proposals was that C & C buy more stock in Columbia River Packers. In 1958 it increased its ownership from 12 percent to 30 percent. A year later it found it could buy more stock from Transamerica Corp., which had been ordered by a federal court to get rid of either its industrial operations or its bank properties. Several Pacific Northwest stockholders then decided they were willing to sell a sufficient number of their Columbia shares to give Castle & Cooke a 49 percent interest, and that's when MacNaughton insisted on 51 percent. He got it—and more. A deal was made for C & C to buy enough shares to give the company a 60 percent controlling interest.

As the result of another MacNaughton proposal, Helemano Company, the holding firm organized ten years earlier to take over the bulk of Waialua's non-sugar assets, was merged into Castle & Cooke in 1958. Helemano's assets included the one-third ownership of Hawaiian Pineapple Company that had previously belonged to Waialua. Upon merger, C & C's ownership in the pineapple company jumped from 15 percent to 49 percent. Castle & Cooke began purchasing Hawaiian Pineapple shares on the open market; by the end of 1959 it had controlling interest—52 percent.

MEANWHILE, THE PINEAPPLE COMPANY had once again been given a new president—the upshot of another bitter controversy over management of the business, which had come to a head two years earlier.

When Atherton Richards was fired at Hawaiian Pineapple, it was chiefly because he resisted what he considered "meddling" by the entrenched powers at C & C. Henry White, originally one of the entrenched, had been his replacement. Now it was White who was unhappy with "meddling" and with people who did not, in his opinion, understand the business of marketing pineapple. Tensions between White and the pineapple company board (heavily populated with Castle & Cooke men) increased month by month, and soon Alex Budge was suffering through his third major shake-up at the pineapple company.

White was a local boy, born in Honolulu in 1897, a year before Hawaii was annexed by the United States. Son of an Irish mother and a schoolteacher father, who died when Henry was nine, White had come up the hard way. To support a family of two sons and three daughters, his mother had spent her meager means for cows to start a small dairy. Young Henry helped her with the milking and peddled the dairy products before and after school.

He worked hard and took side jobs of all sorts. While in high school, he opened and swept out offices. After class he handled shipping claims and sometimes, on payday, carried trays of coins to the wharves to pay the stevedores. In the early evening he reported to the Honolulu Gas Company for two hours of duty as a troubleshooter, and he ended the day as ticket taker at the Popular Theatre. By the time he was sixteen and a sophomore at Punahou, White concluded that classes were interfering with his jobs, so he quit school to work full time for Hawaiian Electric.

After a stint with the Second Regiment at Fort Shafter, Hawaii, during World War I, followed by more odd jobs in Honolulu, White decided to seek his fortune in San Francisco in 1921. But after six weeks of unsuccessful job hunting, he welcomed a cablegram offering him a bookkeeping post with Castle & Cooke.

When Atherton Richards went to Hawaiian Pineapple as president following the pineapple firm's reorganization in late 1932, White was chosen to replace him as treasurer of Castle & Cooke. He was also elected to the Castle & Cooke board at that time. At the same time he served as treasurer of Hawaiian Pineapple and sat on its board of directors. Two years later White became a vice-president of the pineapple company, and in 1937 he was elected executive vice-president of Castle & Cooke. He resigned his C & C executive positions when he became president of Hawaiian Pineapple.

In the years after Richards left office in 1941, Henry White brought the Hawaiian Pineapple Company a long way. At the beginning he had to get the company through the desperate war years. After the war, production and sales increased considerably, and finances were strengthened; marketing procedures were revamped, and canning techniques improved. The company adjusted well to the labor revolution, being an up-front leader in public and industrial relations.

In 1950, White convinced his directors Hawaiian Pineapple needed more acreage for its Wahiawa plantation. He arranged the purchase of the John Ii Estate for $10 million, with the aid of a low-interest loan, to add approximately 15,000 acres of land in central Oahu, of which half was suitable for intensive agriculture.

In earnings there had been good and lean years, including a $1,634,000 loss in 1952, the year of a prolonged strike on Lanai. But despite generally good showings, there were board members who were unhappy with the way Henry ran the company. Like his predecessor, he liked to run his own show, and that created frictions.

In 1955 he built a can manufacturing plant because he could not obtain cans at a low enough price from American Can Company. But then he turned around and sold Hawaiian Pineapple's paper box making facilities to Weyerhaeuser for $2 million. The two moves seemed inconsistent to some directors. White replied that the box plant was aging, and he did not have enough cash for both a box and a can factory. Such major decisions, of course, required board approval, and it was given—but grudgingly by some directors.

The truth was that Henry White had long run the company independently, acting more or less autonomously in setting its course in major investments or divestments.

THE NAME DOLE by now was the best known in pineapple and dominated the marketplace. Without benefit of a preliminary market test, White decided the name was so famous that it would have magic pulling power on other products, too—peaches, pears, string beans, and other fruits and vegetables. The company should break away from dependence on a single product, he argued, if it ever expected to achieve economic stability.

White was even talking about moving Hawaiian Pineapple's headquarters to the mainland. But first he started looking up and down the Pacific Coast for cannery acquisitions. He already had the Barron-Gray cannery in San Jose, California, which had been purchased in 1948 as a place to pack Dole fruit cocktail, a large user of pineapple tidbits.

Despite the success of Barron-Gray, a number of Hawaiian Pineapple's directors were lukewarm to White's program, yet they went along with a proposal to increase the company's authorized capital stock so that shares could be available for the acquisition of mainland properties.

Many canneries were checked, and finally, in 1955, White bought two—Paulus Bros. in Salem, Oregon, one of the biggest canneries in the Pacific Northwest, and F. M. Ball & Co. in Oakland, a packer of fruits and vegetables.

Hawaiian Pineapple paid $1,537,000 in stock for the Salem company and $3,412,500 in stock and cash for the Oakland plant. Soon a stream of string beans, pears, peaches, tomato juice, and catsup came out of cannery cookers, destined for the familiar red, white, and blue label emblazoned with the name Dole. And there were plans for Dole berries, cherries, asparagus—a full line.

But the American housewife didn't buy. For years she had reached loyally for the name when it was wrapped around a can of golden pineapple, but she was unimpressed when she saw it on other fruits or vegetables. Libby, Del Monte, S & W, and others had maintained high quality products on U.S. grocery shelves for years. They were entrenched—as they deserved to be—and to lure the buying public away from their products would require millions of dollars for advertising and promotion. Dole was used to spending millions in promoting pineapple, but the board was not about to approve additional millions for a venture that held no guarantee of success.

Even if the board had approved the expenditure, it would not have solved another potential problem. Competitors with a profit safeguard in their broad lines of established products could afford to cut their prices on pineapple, thereby hitting Hawaiian Pineapple where it hurt. White would have to meet their prices whenever they felt like cutting them, and that would cut the pineapple company's profits.

It soon did. From profits of $5.3 million in 1950 and $3.1 million in 1953 (following the 1952 loss), Hawaiian Pineapple's earnings had eroded to $1.4 million for the fiscal year ended May 31, 1957.

So began the final disenchantment between the board and Henry White. Alex Budge, on behalf of the directors, told White to cut his expenditures and ease up. But, Budge said later, "Henry insisted he was right and wouldn't back away from his position."

At one point in the running confrontation, White suggested to Budge that "since Castle & Cooke is so damned unhappy with the way Pine is being run, why don't you sell out?" White even looked around for a prospective buyer, but nothing came of it.

"No one on the Pine board was a marketing man or understood our problems," said White in retrospect. "They were too conservative in their thinking. They wanted to keep the status quo. They wanted to be guaranteed a profit on every deal and were disappointed if results were not immediate. They were too much under the influence of certain Castle & Cooke executives. It wasn't a good setup."

Budge had a different view: "We had to keep a checkrein on Henry. He had a lot of ideas we couldn't gamble on. We had only so many dollars available. We tried to reason with him but he wouldn't take our advice. He seemed to resent any board action if it went counter to his thinking. The situation was becoming intolerable. We could hardly agree on anything." One thing they did agree on was calling in John Forbes, a San Francisco CPA and business counselor, to review Hawaiian Pineapple's operations and plans. Forbes, after several weeks of probing, reported to Budge that White was "spending money recklessly in several directions." The pineapple company's president denied the accusations vehemently, charging that he was "being treated shabbily" by the board.

By now it was late 1957, and White was totally at odds with most of the directors. Furthermore, the price of Hawaiian Pineapple's stock had dropped to seven dollars a share, less than half of what it had been a year earlier. The board decided that the only thing to do was move White upstairs to a chairmanship (an empty seat since Jim Dole bowed out) and put in a new president. White got his walking papers, and it was Budge who had to deliver them. "It was pure hell to go through," Budge recalls, "for Henry and I had been closely associated and personal friends for so many years."

White admitted, "It came as a shock, even though I'd been thinking about resigning because of harassment by certain board members . . . . I had no quarrel with the decision. If you can't agree, someone has to go. But Io did object to the cavalier manner in which the news was given me."

A few days after Christmas, Henry White bade farewell to an auditorium filled with officers, technicians, secretaries, and handymen in the Dole offices in Honolulu. He explained, as one often does in such cases, that he had long been wanting to "ease up," so he was leaving the presidency. Then he walked up the aisle, fighting back the tears.

His successor was Herbert C. Cornuelle, age 37, who in a space of four years had risen from director of public relations to vice-president in charge of both plantations and manufacturing. Cornuelle, a tall, handsome man with an engaging manner (now president of Hawaii's Dillingham Corporation), says he was about the only person John Forbes had not talked to when he was dissecting Henry White's administration, so he was surprised when Forbes proposed him for the top post at Hawaiian Pineapple Company.

One of the first things Cornuelle did as the new president was to sell a long, black "mortuary" Cadillac that White often put at the disposal of VIPs and himself, and replace it with a beige station wagon. Another symbol of the old days was gone.

White retired as board chairman of the pineapple company in 1962 and moved to Florida. He died there in 1973 at the age of 76.

Chapter 17

New Ventures and Old

HAWAII'S GREATEST PERIOD OF CHANGE commenced March 12, 1959, when Congress passed legislation naming this small chain of islands, 2,400 miles offshore, the fiftieth state of the Union. Air raid sirens wailed the news at 10:04 A.M. Church bells began ringing, ships in the harbor let their whistles blast, and motorists leaned on their horns. That night there was dancing in the streets, both in Waikiki and at Iolani Palace, where Queen Liliuokalani had been deposed sixty-six years before. Bonfires and fireworks lit the sky. The next day, in a more solemn mood, government officials and the public marched to Kawaiahao—the mission church that Samuel Castle and Amos Cooke helped build—to thank the Lord for statehood.

In the years since, the momentum has occasionally slowed but never stopped, and Castle & Cooke and all other island companies have been closely involved in the amazing social and economic changes that have taken place in Hawaii since its people became first-class citizens.

That same year, at age forty-nine, Malcolm MacNaughton became C & C's president. He and his new management team decided that an entirely new corporate structure was essential to achieving real growth. They proposed that Hawaiian Pineapple Company and Columbia River Packers be merged into Castle & Cooke, thereby creating a single, widely held and readily marketable stock. The consolidation would provide minority stockholders in the pineapple and seafood companies with greater income stability through participation in other holdings. Expansion capital would be more readily available to the companies as well.

President Thomas F. Sandoz of Columbia River Packers quickly agreed to the merger, but Hawaiian Pineapple's president, Herbert Cornuelle, hesitated—"evidently fearful there might be a weakening of cherished semi-autonomous authority," according to MacNaughton.

"Herb seemed more concerned with preserving a maximum degree of independence than with developing a new combination, stronger and more profitable than the existing one."

That wasn't really it, according to Cornuelle. "I wanted to make sure that the pineapple company's stockholders got a fair break in any such merger, and I didn't want to see the Dole identity—the importance of the Dole Company—lost in the process." (By now, Hawaiian Pineapple had changed its name to Dole to take advantage of its brand identity.)

Before we could present the plan to stockholders," said MacNaughton, "we had to have the three managements in complete agreement. It wan't easy. Cornuelle was damned stubborn and remained so through a series of testy discussions.

"Rather than hold up the program indefinitely, we eventually agreed that Dole would continue to operate after the merger as a separate enterprise, with full authority to carry on its operations, and the president could act without 'interference.' " With this understanding, Dole's management supported the merger, and stockholders of all three companies overwhelmingly approved the joining on May 1, 1961. CRPA became Bumble Bee Seafoods, Inc., immediately following the merger.

The merger of Dole, with assets of $72 million, and Bumble Bee, with assets of $14 million, into Castle & Cooke created a single corporation with assets of $133 million and combined sales of $120 million. The now wholly owned subsidiaries retained their corporate identities and their own directors and management. The merger changed Castle & Cooke from a Hawaiian agency business to an important segment of the American food industry, in addition to its interests in shipping, stevedoring, and merchandising.

Immediately following the merger, Oceanic Properties was formed as a wholly owned subsidiary to manage and develop C & C's land holdings. It was a logical move for a company that now found itself with 155,000 increasingly valuable acres in Hawaii and a ranch in California. The island holdings were impressive:

Lanai: The entire island of 90,000 acres, except for areas dedicated for public use and some privately owned residential land.

Hawaii: 20,500 acres (half in sugar) at Kohala, plus 3,000 acres near Hilo, of which 1,100 were in a macadamia nut orchard.

Oahu: 42,000 acres (almost half in sugar and pineapple), plus property in the business, industrial, and waterfront sections of Honolulu.

Both Lanai and Kohala had excellent sites for resort development. The island of Oahu, with a greater population density than either Japan or Great Britain, would need an additional 15,000 acres for urban use over a period of time, and a sizable portion of the firm's land lay in the direct path of Honolulu's growth.

To head Oceanic Properties, the company selected Fred Simpich, who had been serving as vice-president for shipping operations in recent years. Oceanic was to become involved in a wide range of projects—a new town, golf courses, apartment and medical buildings, cemeteries, and small shopping centers—spread all the way from California to the Philippines. "They started out at 80 miles an hour and made some mistakes as a result," commented a senior company executive.

Oceanic's first major project was a large, new satellite city called Mililani Town, ultimately expected to cover 3,500 acres of former Dole pineapple land above Pearl Harbor, near Honolulu. The planning work had already been started by Dole president Cornuelle and was taken over by Oceanic after its creation in 1961. Using the talents of a prestigious group of planners and architects, it was to prove Oceanic's most successful project because it satisfied Oahu's great pent-up demand for housing by creating a sensitively designed, affordable new community of a type unique in Hawaii.

Earlier Castle & Cooke had bought the Blackhawk Ranch, a walnut and cattle spread east of Oakland, California, as its first mainland property investment. The ranch was later sold for a handsome profit and the proceeds used in the purchase of 11,000 acres of property near San Jose, with an eye toward the creation of a Mililani-type "new town" to serve the rapidly growing Santa Clara Valley. But before planning work was completed, the national money and mortgage picture turned sour, and the San Jose property was put on the shelf until a later date.

In still another type of venture, Oceanic bought the magnificent Sea Ranch, 5,200 acres of rugged coastline north of San Francisco. This country-home, recreation-oriented project has drawn international praise from architects and planners for its advanced and thoughtful approach.

To involve itself in the Southern California residential market, Castle & Cooke in 1969 acquired a major Los Angeles home-building company, Barclay Hollander Curci, Inc. (now Barclay Hollander Corporation).

Oceanic took the leadership in reversing the desertion of downtown Honolulu by bringing together six owners of the square block that was partially occupied by the Castle & Cooke headquarters building, designed and built by Tenney and Budge back in 1924. As manager of the project, Oceanic cleared the block and constructed a handsome three-building development known as the Financial Plaza of the Pacific. The centerpiece is the twenty-two-story Castle & Cooke building, headquarters of the company. Since the plaza was completed, other Hawaii corporations have followed suit, and a number of new high-rise headquarters buildings have been built, assuring downtown Honolulu's revitalization as the office and financial center of the island state.

Fred Simpich, who as Oceanic's first president spearheaded its "80 miles an hour" beginning, took early retirement and was succeeded by Warren G. Haight, who had been vice-president and treasurer of Oceanic.

HERB CORNUELLE REMAINED AS PRESIDENT of Dole until 1963, when he resigned to become executive vice-president and later president of United Fruit (now United Brands). Although there were occasional strains between MacNaughton and Cornuelle during that period, Cornuelle says that he feels Castle & Cooke, all in all, leaned over backwards to permit him to run his own show. During his five-year presidency, Cornuelle cut costs, surveyed more lucrative uses for Dole lands, laid out groundwork for the company's expansion to the Philippines, bought a 70 percent interest in a tomato cannery in Italy (which turned out to be a mistake and was later sold), and pushed a long-range program to effect technical advances.

"Cornuelle's leaving did not catch us entirely by surprise," says MacNaughton. "Though he had been doing a good job for us, he had not appeared too happy since the merger in 1961 and had met several times with a top United executive. Later, when hints were dropped about a possible sale of Dole to United, I told Cornuelle that 'United has nothing to offer us that we can't do for ourselves—and do it better.' We never heard anything more about it."

MacNaughton moved into Cornuelle's office before the effective date of his resignation, becoming president of Dole in addition to his presidency of Castle & Cooke.

"I didn't want to waste any time in clearing up possible misunderstandings and developing a better working basis with the Dole staff," says MacNaughton. "Unfortunately, for too many years, much of the thinking in the upper levels at Dole seemed to have been strongly influenced by their past semi-autonomy. Yet they were fine, experienced people, for the most part, and I hoped that among them I would find presidential material. As it turned out, each potential candidate was doing so well in his specialized field I didn't want to make a change. And I decided that what we needed at Dole was not a specialist in some single phase of the company but an experienced overall executive who could, at the same time, make a good public image for the organization.''

He chose William F. Quinn, a close personal friend, who had previously handled some of Dole's legal business. Quinn was a graduate of Harvard Law School and had been a partner in Robertson, Castle & Anthony. He had been appointed territorial governor in 1957 and two years later became the first elected governor of the new state.

Quinn had barely returned to private practice when MacNaughton recruited him for a career in business. He joined Dole as executive vice-president in mid-1964 and became president in April 1965. Quinn came into the company at a very busy time, for Dole was then well into establishing a plantation and cannery in the Philippines. "Labor costs in Hawaii were reaching the point where farming could eventually be forced out of business,'' said MacNaughton. "We had studied other areas of the world where it might be possible to produce quality pineapple at less cost than in Hawaii. The answer proved to be the Philippines.''

Dole Philippines was organized in 1963 to farm 18,000 acres 650 miles south of Manila on the island of Mindanao. While the first planting material was en route from Dole's Lanai plantation to the Philippines, construction was begun on roads and bridges, a port and warehouse facilities, a power plant and domestic water system, a church and a school, housing for thousands of future Filipino employees, and a cannery. Meanwhile, certain employees and their families, who were to be transferred from Hawaii and the cannery in Oakland, were sent to a Peace Corps training center in Hilo to learn the customs, languages, and living conditions of Mindanao.

The Philippine undertaking, now called Dolefil, ultimately cost over $50 million and supplies a major part of Dole's overall pineapple needs. The development has had a profound impact on what had been essentially underdeveloped lands with small native villages by offering employment, education, health care, and improved food supplies for thousands of residents and their families.

SINCE THE DAYS OF ED TENNEY AND CAPTAIN MATSON, Castle & Cooke had been Matson Navigation Company's alter ego in Hawaii. In addition to holding a substantial amount of Matson's stock, it had been the line's freight and passenger agent, its stevedore in the Port of Honolulu, and a strong influence in the operation of Matson's hotels in Waikiki. A substantial part of C & C's income had come from Matson fees and commissions, particularly in the years before MacNaughton began transforming Castle & Cooke from an agency-investment company to an operating firm. It was therefore an emotional as well as financial wrench when relations between Matson and Castle & Cooke began to unravel as the decade of the 1950s drew to a close.

Randolph (Joe) Sevier, a warm and hearty man and onetime Matson ship's purser, had been recruited by Budge during the Depression and had advanced up the management ladder until he was a C & C vice-president, in charge of activities relating to the company's representation of Matson in Hawaii. It was appropriate, therefore, that Sevier should be selected by Matson in 1948 as the heir apparent to John Cushing, who was soon to retire as the line's president.

Sevier's new task was anything but easy. Matson was finding the sailing getting financially rougher. Among many contributing factors were the rapidly rising labor rates as well as increases in all other operating expenses.

Sevier turned his top financial man, Stanley Powell, loose on costs, including those from Castle & Cooke. When the time arrived for the usually amicable renegotiation of the stevedoring and agency contracts, Powell came up with figures purporting to show that Castle & Cooke's costs, and therefore its charges, were too high. In fact, Sevier and Powell went so far as to assert that Castle & Cooke's stevedoring operations were less efficient than those of its competitors. The response from MacNaughton and his associates was vehement and volcanic.

Unlike the Atherton Richards fight, this one was waged behind closed doors of the Matson and Castle & Cooke board rooms, but it became far more bitter. MacNaughton produced his own figures showing Castle & Cooke Terminals to be the most efficient and lowest-cost stevedoring firm available anywhere in the islands and cited Terminals' winning of numerous competitive-bid contracts as evidence.

The contracts and the issues were complex, but in sum Matson and Castle & Cooke were completely at loggerheads. Matson took the first step toward rupture when in 1962 it abruptly canceled the freight and passenger agency agreement and opened its own Honolulu office—staffed largely with people from Castle & Cooke. The other shoe dropped shortly afterward when the stevedoring contract was canceled. The long and close relationship was sundered, leaving behind ill feeling and personal animosities.

It also left Castle & Cooke with a dilemma. The company owned 24 percent of Matson's stock, which it no longer wanted, but the stock, dampened by continuing poor earnings, was depressed far below its fair value; there was nary a buyer in sight to take the certificates off Castle &

Cooke's hands at anything more than a fire sale price. MacNaughton had no choice but to hang on.

The logjam finally was broken in 1964, when rescue came from a highly unlikely source—the U.S. Department of Justice. In a suit filed against Matson and its principal corporate owners, Castle & Cooke, Amfac, Alexander & Baldwin, and C. Brewer, the government charged that these firms had discouraged competition and should be forced to divest themselves of their Matson stock. The first word of MacNaughton's press release reacting to news of the suit was characteristic and to the point. "Good!" it said.

In a settlement approved by the Justice Department, Alexander & Baldwin bought out the other three owners for $65 per share, more than treble what the depressed Matson stock had been languishing at just a few months before. The sale netted Castle & Cooke a profit of well over $9 million. Three years earlier, in 1961, Honolulu Oil Corporation, founded by Captain Matson to provide fuel for his ships, had been liquidated at $100 per share; in that transaction Castle & Cooke's shares brought a net profit in excess of $16 million.

From the two sales, MacNaughton now had some walking-around money.

Consistent with the MacNaughton philosophy of seeking operating control, Castle & Cooke by now also had acquired majority ownership of Ewa Plantation and Waialua Sugar. The company had owned more than 50 percent of Kohala Sugar since 1916 and had increased its interest to almost 100 percent by 1960. That same year it increased its ownership of Waialua to 52 percent; two years later it owned more than 50 percent of Ewa.

Chapter 18

Banana Bonanza

IN FEBRUARY 1964, Henry Clark, then Castle & Cooke's vice-president–treasurer, addressed the New York Society of Security Analysts and in the course of his remarks noted that all of the company's new projects were going to "keep our people—and our money—busy." But, he added, the company would still be interested in acquiring anything that looked particularly good.

When Clark's remarks were later published and circulated in financial circles, William P. Green, a New York broker with the firm of H. Hentz & Company, read them and thought Standard Fruit & Steamship Company of New Orleans might look very good indeed. The suggestion was passed along to Malcolm MacNaughton, who agreed it could be interesting. "It sounded like an outfit that would fit very well into our organization."

How did it happen that Standard, then the nation's number two banana importer, was available for purchase? The opportunity came because Dr. Joseph S. D'Antoni, an expert in tropical medicine who had been drafted years before to head his family's banana business, now at age fifty-eight wanted more time for medicine and a bit more leisure.

"And there was no member of the family capable of running the company. My two sons were still in college and my cousin [B. C. D'Antoni]—the only one who might have been considered—had died suddenly. In addition, all of the family's assets were tied up in the business."

Dr. D'Antoni had been president of Standard since 1953. At the request of his mother, he had taken over the business upon the retirement of his brother, Blaise, who assumed the presidency at the death of their father, Salvador, one of the firm's founders. For eleven years this man of medicine turned banana merchant had seen his company through good times and bad. But finally he went to his mother with the suggestion that it was time to sell.

" 'Mama,' I said, 'the company has become too big a family responsibility. We should turn it over to someone else. Would you be willing to sell if the right party comes along?' she said, 'Yes, but only if the people we sell to are of good character.' Castle & Cooke seemed to be exactly the kind of buyer we were looking for.''

A meeting between top officers of Standard and Castle & Cooke was arranged for New Orleans. After hours of discussion and a sumptuous dinner, the host, Dr. D'Antoni, appeared to be only lukewarm to selling. Sometime "long, long after midnight," he did agree to think over a suggestion Alex Budge made, proposing that the companies send teams to look each other over. That was as far as Dr. D'Antoni would commit himself.

"I told Budge after we returned to our hotel near dawn," MacNaughton recalls, "that 'we had a nice trip to New Orleans, but I guess that's the end of it.' "

"I wasn't intentionally playing poker face with MacNaughton and Budge," says Dr. D'Antoni. "I enjoyed speaking with them and entertaining them. The reason for my lukewarm feeling was that I kept rolling over in my mind how this sale would affect the family financially. From 1953 until the first time I spoke with Castle & Cooke, there were at least six or seven individuals or corporations interested in buying Standard, but I noticed that this interest usually occurred when we had $10 or $11 million in cash in the banks, and I recognized their motives. This was not the case with C & C because, when I asked MacNaughton why he wanted to buy Standard, his answer was: 'We don't buy companies—we buy management.' "

A month later, Dr. D'Antoni phoned MacNaughton in Honolulu, inviting him to send a group to tour Standard's Central American properties, check its books, and meet its people. MacNaughton agreed, asking Dr. D'Antoni to send Standard men to Hawaii.

"Malcolm invited me to visit Dole and Bumble Bee and speak with anyone I wished as to C & C's interference in management. I didn't tell him at the time that I'd already made that investigation," says Dr. D'Antoni.

Both inspection teams liked what they saw, and negotiations got under way. "Standard was selling for $19 to $20 a share," MacNaughton recalls. "We offered $25. Dr. D'Antoni replied that he already had a higher offer from some Atlanta investment bankers but didn't like to turn Standard over to a bunch of investment people instead of practical operating people. Could I raise the price?

"Our directors authorized me to make a final offer of $26. Dr. D'Antoni agreed that $26 was fair, and he suggested that he be named chairman of the board and have executive vice-president Don Kirchhoff elected president. That suited us fine; it was exactly what we'd hoped for. Then there was one final detail: Dr. D'Antoni would have to talk it over with Mama."

That night she gave her blessing, saying, "Joe, your daddy would have liked and trusted these people and would have sold to them. Turn down the higher offer from the bankers and take this one."

In October 1964, with ready cash from the sale of its Matson and Honolulu Oil stock, Castle & Cooke initially purchased a 55 percent interest in Standard from the D'Antoni family and others for $14,600,000. Although control rested with the sellers, there were a number of other individual stockholders. Through a tender offer to them, and later an exchange of stock, Castle & Cooke acquired 100 percent of Standard Fruit in 1968.

BANANAS WERE NOT ALWAYS THE POPULAR fruit they are today, with annual U.S. consumption over eighteen pounds per person. The story is told of a ship captain who sold a cargo of the fruit to Massachusetts housewives in 1690 and never had the courage to return. The New Englanders boiled the strange, green oddities with their pork and beans and then threw the mess out in disgust.

At the Philadelphia Exposition of 1876, foil-wrapped bananas were sold as souvenirs at ten cents apiece. Buyers were dismayed when, days later, they opened their souvenirs to show the home folk and the bananas had turned black. They didn't know that the banana is one of nature's most delicate creations.

Standard, like Castle & Cooke, grew from the partnership of two pioneering families—Vaccaro and D'Antoni. Salvador D'Antoni was only twelve years old when he arrived in New Orleans from Sicily. He went to Baton Rouge to live with an uncle, helping him operate a riverboat that sold fruit along the Mississippi. Later the pair established a small fruit store in a sugar plantation town.

Salvador began purchasing fruit from Joseph Vaccaro, who was in the wholesale fruit business in New Orleans, and several years later opened his own small store. Everything was going along fine until the flood-swollen Mississippi broke through a levee and swept away the store.

Wiped out financially, D'Antoni went to New Orleans. One of the first people he visited there was Joe Vaccaro, who offered him a job operating a lugger that picked up fruit in New Orleans and sold it to plantations along the Mississippi. Later the partners shipped oranges to New Orleans from downriver groves, and Joe bought an old Louisiana orange farm, which he and his brother Carmelo fixed up. It was here that Salvador brought his bride, Mary, the daughter of Joe Vaccaro.

A month later a severe freeze wiped out the orange business. It was 1899, and by now the partners owned three luggers. But they had no cargo, so the families decided to try importing coconuts and bananas from Honduras. Joe Vaccaro's two younger brothers, Lucca and Felix, were in a separate produce business, and he prevailed on them to join Salvador and him in a business that was later to become Vaccaro Bros. & Co. ("My father being the 'Co.,' " explains Dr. D'Antoni.)

Honduras trade was a hazardous venture, requiring a bigger ship than the tiny luggers, so for $2,500 the partners purchased a weather-beaten two-masted schooner called the *Santo Oteria* and renamed her the *Frances* in honor of a Vaccaro sister.

Salvador was chosen to lead the first trip to Roatan, a small island off Honduras, and having little cash, he loaded the *Frances* with foodstuffs to use as barter. He would soon find this was a rough, tough business with ethics virtually nonexistent. Established traders called along the Honduras coast on no particular schedule, buying what fruit they might find stacked along the hot sands. At the first stop, the skipper would send messengers to notify growers that it was time to bring their fruit to the nearest beach to await the vessel's arrival on a certain day. A week or so might then be spent picking up odd lots of fruit. But if a ship got a full load before reaching some of the places that had been alerted, the vessel—without so much as an apology—would sail off to the States, leaving the growers' harvest to rot on the beach.

The Vaccaro-D'Antoni partners eventually changed this hit-and-miss routine by contracting with several of the larger growers, agreeing to take their entire crop at a fixed price and on specific dates. Even if the fruit wasn't picked up, it was paid for. Better shipping service helped to maintain schedules.

In 1900 the company acquired its first chartered steamship, the *Premier*, which was skippered from Baltimore to Honduras by Carmelo D'Antoni. A few years later the company began building a railroad into the jungle, thereby eliminating the slow transport by boat, muleback— or human back. Land was purchased, and the company began growing its own fruit to supplement what it purchased under contract from independent growers.

ALL THE MAJOR BANANA IMPORTING COMPANIES were growing the traditional Gros Michel variety of banana. It was a good shipping variety because of its tough, protective skin. The practice was to ship the fruit to market while still on the stalk. But "Big Mike" had some serious deficiencies, which became more critical as the years went on. It was a tall plant and vulnerable to being blown down in even moderate windstorms. Most serious of all, it was highly susceptible to Panama disease, a soil fungus that to this day has defied a cure. Once stricken with the fungus, thousands of acres were simply abandoned, and new ones replanted in uninfected lands. But Panama disease was relentless; it followed sooner or later, wherever bananas were planted, and all the growing countries of Latin America were pockmarked with abandoned fields totaling tens of thousands of acres.

A small but growing number of banana men were becoming convinced that the only solution was to find a new banana variety resistant to the disease. The Cavendish and its many subvarieties ultimately were to prove the answer, but a whole body of doubt, skepticism, and tradition had first to be overcome.

A. J. Chute, then Standard's manager in Honduras, was a strong advocate of a subvariety called the Giant Cavendish. To prove his point, Chute planted Giant Cavendish in Honduran soils abandoned to Panama disease by United Fruit Company in the 1930s. They flourished. But two more decades were to pass before the urgency of the Panama disease problem forced a major decision.

By the mid-1950s that time had come. Standard Fruit made the plunge, accompanied by much scoffing from the competition. Further studies had revealed additional desirable attributes of Giant Cavendish. The plant is shorter and therefore less vulnerable to blow-down, and production of fruit per acre is greater than Gros Michel.

Under the leadership of Dr. D'Antoni, Standard began the expensive and difficult task of switching all its plantings to Giant Cavendish. Standard was not the capital-rich firm that United Fruit Company was, and the effort with all its attendant risks put an enormous strain on the company. Then, as Standard's first stalks of Giant Cavendish reached the U.S. market, disaster struck. The fruit arrived in a mess. The skin of the Giant Cavendish is thinner and more delicate than that of Gros Michel. It could not stand the handling required in shipping and distribution of the fruit. It arrived bruised and battered.

Standard's answer was to pack the fruit in a corrugated cardboard box. More money was needed and with it the pioneering of a new system of handling the fruit. Out of much trial and error came today's system. Stalks of bananas are cut from the plant and gently transported to one of a series of fruit-handling stations strategically placed throughout each plantation. There workers grade the fruit, cut it into bunches, wash and cool it, and pack it in boxes, each weighing forty pounds. The fruit stays in the box from that point until it reaches the grocer's shelf.

Despite derision from the rest of the banana industry, this revo-
lutionary innovation was welcomed by produce buyers and grocers.
The fruit arrived in better condition, had a longer shelf life in the
produce department, and was much easier and cheaper to handle.
Pressure from customers soon forced the competition to swallow its
pride and follow suit. By 1962, Standard was fully converted to boxed
Giant Cavendish, and within a few years the familiar stalk of Gros
Michel was seen no more in U.S. grocery stores.

On the wall behind Dr. D'Antoni's desk is a plaque presented
to Standard by the United Fresh Fruit & Vegetable Association
for "originating and pioneering boxed bananas." The inscription
calls it "the biggest advance in the banana industry since the refrigerated ship."

WORKING CLOSELY with Dr. D'Antoni in the transformation of Standard was Donald J. Kirchhoff, his executive vice-president. Kirchhoff
had headed the Honduras division during much of the trying period of
conversion, then had been brought back to New Orleans headquarters.
Two weeks after control of Standard was sold to Castle & Cooke,
Kirchhoff, then thirty-nine, succeeded Dr. D'Antoni as president. Like
Budge many years before at C & C, Kirchhoff was the first "non-
family" man ever to head Standard.

Born in St. Louis, the son of an advertising man, Kirchhoff was
dark, good-looking, and soft-spoken. His strong suit was accounting
and finance. After graduating with an M.B.A. from Harvard Business
School, he had become an accountant with Kroger & Co. and later
controller of National Food Stores of Michigan, from whence Dr.
D'Antoni lured him to Standard in 1956.

There is no question that struggling Standard had scored a major
triumph with its pioneering of Giant Cavendish in a box. Kirchhoff was
determined to exploit that advantage by challenging the long-term
dominance of the banana market by the huge United Fruit Company.
Standard lacked the money to tackle United head-on, so Kirchhoff
concentrated first on building good relations with grocery stores by
training their personnel in the proper handling and display of boxed
bananas. In doing so, Kirchhoff embarked on a sustained program of
recruiting bright young management and professional people into the
Standard organization.

At first Standard's bananas were unbranded, while for decades
United had poured many millions of dollars into the "Chiquita" brand
name. Later Standard developed the "Cabana" label, a name derived
from a contraction of the "Cavendish banana." It was backed by only

modest advertising, the company's promotional efforts still being concentrated at the store level. In 1972 the big jump was made by shelving the Cabana label and beginning the nationwide marketing of Standard's bananas under the Dole label, backed by an accelerated advertising and promotion program.

In 1973, Kirchhoff achieved his goal. Castle & Cooke's banana operations wrested the leadership of the North American market from United and kept it.

It was always necessary for banana-growing companies to diversify their production areas as a hedge against unfavorable weather. While holding and expanding its operations in Honduras, Standard in earlier years had major growing operations in Mexico, Haiti, and the Caribbean coast of Nicaragua, but for various reasons had later closed them down. Under Dr. D'Antoni and Kirchhoff, two large plantations were established on the Caribbean coast of Costa Rica and more recently one on the Pacific side of Nicaragua. In Ecuador, the world's largest banana exporting nation, which prohibits foreign ownership of production facilities, Standard established a strong organization to buy fruit from Ecuadorian growers and further win their allegiance with technical help to improve quality and yields.

In its Central American growing areas, Standard also pioneered an "independent planter" program, under which citizens of those countries would develop banana plantations with financial and technical assistance from Standard in return for long-term purchase contracts (a practice that was carried to the Philippines when Standard established a banana plantation there).

This tied in directly with a basic tenet under which Standard had operated in Central America from the very first. The company was determined not to involve itself in the sometimes turbulent politics of its host countries. It involved itself generously in the social and economic welfare of the people in the areas where it operated, but it would not take sides in national or local politics.

Standard's long-standing posture is borne out by Dr. Thomas F. Karnes of Arizona State University, an authority on Central America. In a paper presented before the American Historical Association in 1972, Dr. Karnes traced the history of Standard and concluded: "I will pass no judgment on any other corporation, but I must so far conclude that Standard Fruit has taken nothing from Central America that cannot be replaced, that it vastly improved the living standards for thousands of people, and that it neither greatly impeded nor aided the processes of self-government in those places where it has been a guest."

Chapter 19

Seafood et Cetera

BUMBLE BEE MAY BE A STRANGE NAME for a seafood company, but it is a brand name that commands a premium wherever it is sold.

Bumble Bee was launched in 1899 (the same year Jim Dole went to Hawaii and Standard Fruit entered the banana business), when seven canneries operating near the mouth of the Columbia River joined forces as the Columbia River Packers Association (CRPA). Their target was the chinook salmon, for countless generations a favorite food of Pacific Northwest Indians living along the great river, as well as a commodity which the Hudson's Bay Company had preserved with salt and shipped to England and Australia in large wooden barrels.

Two years later CRPA acquired several sailing ships and built a cannery on Alaska's Bristol Bay, a huge estuary of the Bering Sea and home of the Alaska red salmon. CRPA was a participant, albeit a small one, in one of the most exciting eras of Pacific shipping. Until the 1920s whole fleets of magnificent sailing ships loaded with men and supplies would sail from Pacific Coast ports to Bristol Bay. There the men would catch and can the salmon, then race home under full sail, for the first vessels into port could command premium prices for the new pack of fish.

During CRPA's first season on Bristol Bay in 1901, some twenty-five thousand cases of salmon were processed. The company later built more plants in Alaska, and their production, together with that of the canneries on the Columbia River and Puget Sound, was shipped to New York and Boston. There was also a good market in England and other foreign countries.

For thirty years Columbia River Packers knew no marketing problems, only success. Until the crash of 1929, the firm had never gone out aggressively to sell its pack, preferring to sit back and wait for customers to come in. Buyers had the option of putting their own label on their purchases, and many of them did. Thus CRPA's pack was being marketed under as many as a hundred individual labels, including "Bumble Bee," which had been inherited from one of the founding companies.

As the depression deepened, CRPA, like Jim Dole, found its warehouses overflowing. So management pulled young Thomas F. Sandoz off his production job and told him to "get rid of this damned inventory." Sandoz, with eight years' sales experience before joining CRPA in 1928, became the first man in the firm ever to call on customers. He began building a better relationship with the trade and startled his bosses by selling seventeen carloads in the East, all for cash.

"Almost every buyer specified 'Bumble Bee' brand," Sandoz recalls, "so we began marketing more of our pack under that name."

Becoming sales manager in 1938, Sandoz sold most of each year's pack before it ever went into cans. Still, Columbia's growth was pretty much limited by lack of product—it had to find something else for its people to market.

That "something else," as it turned out, was swimming right off the Oregon coast, less than a day's sail from the cannery at Astoria. It was albacore, the prized white meat of the tuna family. "Discovered" in 1938 by salmon fishermen who had gone beyond their usual fishing grounds, it revolutionized Columbia River Packers' operations.

"Finding the albacore out there was pure happenstance and most of us were amazed when boatloads of it started coming in," says Sandoz. "It gave us the new product we needed to build up sales."

"Hell, those fish were there all the time," snorts W. B. Wootton, retired Bumble Bee executive. "We used to catch them while fishing for salmon off the mouth of the river. I remember my father catching them and throwing them overboard. We didn't know what they were and didn't much care. We were salmon fishermen, first and always."

Albacore were out there indeed, in vast schools. Tuna, unlike salmon, are unique because of their abundance and widespread distribution in the world's oceans. They are also high-speed travelers. Tuna tagged off Baja California have been found 175 days later at Midway Island, halfway across the Pacific. These fast fish are also extremely sensitive to water temperature, constantly migrating through the ocean to follow the changing warm surface currents.

Now that albacore had been found in large numbers off the Oregon coast, CRPA wanted to capitalize on this doorstep discovery. Within a year, it opened the first tuna cannery in the Northwest, adjacent to its salmon facility at Astoria. Acceptance of the new product under the Bumble Bee label was immediate; more tuna had to be found.

Sandoz went to Japan with one of the first groups of businessmen allowed there after the war and contracted for regular supplies of frozen Japanese-caught tuna for the Astoria cannery. "As sales increased we obtained a supply of light meat tuna from Hawaiian Tuna Packers which was processing more high-quality fish than the Hawaiian market could absorb," said Sandoz.

During all this activity in tuna, salmon had not been forgotten. Its big Alaska plant at Naknek on Bristol Bay was built in the early 1940s. Six years later CRPA built a cannery at Bellingham, Washington, to process fish from the Fraser River and Puget Sound, and in 1950 it joined with Pacific American Fisheries to form the Excursion Inlet Packing Company and build a plant sixty miles west of Juneau.

The biggest salmon deal of all was made in 1959, when CRPA and Ward's Cove Packing Company formed Columbia Ward's Cove Fisheries, Inc. (CWC). This subsidiary acquired all of Libby, McNeill & Libby's extensive salmon facilities in Bristol Bay, Kodiak Island, Cook Inlet, and several areas of southeastern Alaska. They followed this by forming another jointly owned subsidiary called Lake Union Terminals, thus acquiring valuable freshwater marine terminal properties within three miles of downtown Seattle. In 1968 CRPA's 50 percent subsidiary CWC acquired Kodiak Fisheries and Chignik Fisheries companies, which owned canneries on Kodiak Island and the Alaska Peninsula.

As a consequence, CRPA emerged as one of the largest canners of fancy Columbia River and Alaska red salmon, and a substantial packer of Puget Sound sockeyes and Alaska pink and chum salmon. By now renamed Bumble Bee, the big Oregon firm had become a major factor in America's seafood industry.

In 1961 it organized a new company, Maryland Tuna Corp., in partnership with a Japanese fishing company, to establish a $1.5 million cannery at Cambridge, Maryland. In 1967, Bumble Bee acquired full ownership. In addition to tuna gathered by foreign fishermen in waters off West Africa and Brazil, the Maryland plant processed tuna caught by fishermen off the East Coast of the United States.

In 1963, Sandoz, who had been president of the company since

1950, selected executive vice-president John S. McGowan to succeed him, but Sandoz remained as chairman and chief executive officer until his retirement in 1966. McGowan had grown up in the Columbia River fishing industry, in which his grandfather had established one of the early processing operations. Following his graduation from the University of Oregon, McGowan became active in the management of his family's business. He left to serve as a naval officer during World War II and, after his discharge, joined Bumble Bee.

Bumble Bee packs Figaro cat food, too, to utilize by-products of tuna canning operations. Once, to demonstrate its purity, Tom Sandoz stood before an audience and calmly ate a spoonful of the cat food, licked his lips with appreciation and smiled broadly.

Bumble Bee's product line was broadened in 1969, when the company bought control of Surinam American Industries, Ltd., which catches and freezes large tropical shrimp, commonly called "prawns," from a base in Paramaribo, the capital of Surinam (formerly Dutch Guiana), located on the northeast coast of South America. The product is sold almost entirely to the restaurant and hotel trade of U.S. eastern seaboard cities.

CONSOLIDATIONS AND ACQUISITIONS continued apace through the 1960s, as MacNaughton and his management team sought to remold and modernize Castle & Cooke. The company came full circle from its 1851 founding when it acquired in 1966 the San Francisco–based retail and wholesale firm of Ames Mercantile Company (since renamed Castle & Cooke Merchandising Corporation). By 1975 the company was operating a chain of twenty-five Value Giant junior department stores in Northern California, Oregon, and Washington, as well as merchandising concessions in other owners' discount stores in the same states plus Nevada and Hawaii, and a large wholesaling operation for health and beauty aids, hardware, housewares, and toys.

In 1969, Castle & Cooke bought the small but very profitable Arneson Products, Inc., based near San Francisco, manufacturer of an ingenious swimming pool cleaning device known as the "Pool Sweep," which was largely developed and patented by Howard Arneson, who stayed on to head the subsidiary.

Shortly afterward, Castle & Cooke acquired Libby, McNeill & Libby's Hawaii pineapple plantation, located on leased land on the island of Molokai, and its processing facilities in Honolulu. The purpose was to gain a larger fruit supply. It quickly became apparent that the operation would not pay under Castle & Cooke management any better than it had under Libby, and it was closed down a few years later. "We made a mistake," MacNaughton admitted flatly to the Honolulu press.

Located far out in the Pacific and with a large population of Oriental extraction, Hawaii had long felt a kinship with the nations of the Pacific Basin. "There are tremendous markets and opportunities out there," said MacNaughton, as he sent various members of his management group out to become better acquainted and look for expansion possibilities.

The first major thrust had been in 1963, when Dole established its large pineapple growing and processing operation on southern Mindanao in the Philippines. Then in 1963 and 1964, Castle & Cooke paid cash to buy a controlling interest in Republic Glass Corporation of Manila, the island nation's only window-glass manufacturer. In 1974, Philippine law required foreign companies to give up control of extractive industries. Agriculture isn't considered extractive, but glass-making is because it mines sand and other raw minerals. Rather than retain only a minority position in Republic Glass, Castle & Cooke sold its entire investment to Philippine buyers in 1975.

Beginning in 1967, Standard Fruit made a major move to satisfy the growing Japanese appetite for high-quality bananas by establishing new banana farms, also in southern Mindanao, under the name of Stanfilco. In the early 1960s, annual per capita Japanese consumption of the fruit was about three pounds, mostly from Taiwan. By 1975, consumption had skyrocketed to more than twenty pounds per person, and Dole-label bananas were among the leaders in that market.

Castle & Cooke men took a good look at the prospering nations of Thailand and Malaysia. In partnership with Thai businessmen, the company started a small and profitable steel pipe manufacturing firm in Bangkok in 1964. Later, looking for another low-cost source for Dole pineapple, the company set up, again with Thai partners, a new plantation and cannery, which went into operation in 1974.

Near Kuala Lumpur, the capital of Malaysia, a rock and gravel quarrying company was established in 1966 to supply the rapidly growing construction industry of the country; it was later expanded into other areas of the nation. The company's gaze swung north, and a minority interest was purchased in a food canning operation in South Korea.

Commenting on C & C's burgeoning Pacific Basin activities, MacNaughton said: "It's been our experience that, to succeed in foreign countries, the U.S. businessman must forget the obvious 'American Way.' The civilizations bordering the Pacific are far older than ours. These countries may have some things to learn from us, but we also have a great deal to learn from them. There must be a willingness to really understand the other fellow—and he to understand you. Above all, don't forget that you are a guest in the other man's country.''

A by-product of Castle & Cooke's Pacific expansion is that a large number of company executives spend long hours on trans-Pacific flights, carrying well-worn passports bearing numerous stamps from once exotic places that are now familiar.

Chapter 20

Looking to the Future

WHAT SORT OF MAN COULD TRANSFORM Castle & Cooke in less than twenty years from a small, almost placid investment and agency company into today's energetic international corporation with sales approaching $900 million?

Malcolm MacNaughton is concerned with problems existing both inside and outside his corporate headquarters, a joint concern that makes him typical of thousands of U.S. executives who today constitute "enlightened management." He has dynamism, a rasping epigrammatic way of speaking, and an inventive and versatile vocabulary that makes his listeners feel good. He's a "quick-study." He knows how to cut through verbiage and is impatient with people who don't. He can sometimes be forward to the threshold of rudeness, yet his thoughtfulness and compassion far outweigh these occasional lapses.

"He's not a simple man at all," says a C & C vice-president. "He is refreshingly outspoken with none of the doubletalk you too often hear out of businessmen. He doesn't think of himself as a business statesman making profound pronouncements on business. He's warm and human but sometimes he can be very rough."

He certainly can. C & C officers will testify he has violated the rule in all the management books that says you don't bawl people out in front of others. Sometimes he employs the Bronx cheer in expressing his sentiments.

"He can make you feel like an awful ass even in a crowded room," says one executive. Some officers tend to consider him impulsive, and among them there is sometimes a whispered early morning conference to ascertain what side of the bed MacNaughton got out of that morning.

"You've got to catch him on his good days," says another officer. "Some days he's just sort of cantankerous."

Yet for every incident of impulsiveness or cantankerousness, his associates will cite two examples of thoughtfulness. He is meticulous in sending flowers in observance of birthdays and anniversaries. Like Ed Tenney, he will inquire with genuine concern about a relative's arthritis, and is one of the first to call when a friend is in the hospital. He is considered a "soft touch" when someone needs money, and his monetary gifts to schools and charities are numerous and generous. He makes it a point to commend people for jobs well done and to express consideration for the feelings of underlings.

He has strong likes and dislikes and opinions on all subjects, and he seldom hesitates to tell a person off. He quickly recognizes man's foibles—the ridiculous, the pompous, the ludicrous, the fatuous—and cuts such practitioners down to size with dispatch. Yet he can be sentimental—even maudlin—about people. His loyalty to his friends, business associates, and family is unflinching. And all of C & C's executives—and almost anybody else who knows him—will agree that he is an engaging conversationalist and a past master at telling a droll story.

MacNaughton recalls with affection his parents in Portland, and his participation in the affairs of his community follows in their mold. His mother was active in the Congregational church and the YWCA, and "E. B." was in everything. He was a civic leader with strong beliefs, and he acted accordingly. His interests were especially strong in the field of civil liberties.

For his time, E. B. MacNaughton was considered extremely liberal and his active participation in the Unitarian church (he was a national lay moderator) and Reed College were, in the eyes of many, proof of his radicalism. He didn't care what other people thought. Once he was widely criticized by his associates for sitting on the same platform with Henry Wallace in the days when Wallace was considered a "pinko" by almost everyone in Portland's business community. But the people of Oregon have long since come to agree with the headline used by the *Portland Oregonian* in an April 1971 retrospective article about "E.B.": he was a "Businessman with Soul."

Young Malcolm MacNaughton attended Washington High School in Portland. He was a mediocre student, but already he was playing a good game of golf and getting his name on the local sports pages.

Malcolm's grades were not high enough for Reed College, but he convinced a panel of faculty members that he had an inquiring mind, which is what the school seeks. ("I was pretty well Christianized by the end of those two hours.")

Reed College, known for its small classes and provocative professors, provided the stimulation Malcolm needed. "I became a student—and it was hard for me because I hadn't had much practice." His grades at Reed were good enough to make possible his enrollment at Stanford as a junior. He was graduated in 1931, after which he earned an M.B.A. at Stanford's Graduate School of Business.

MacNaughton wears clothes immaculately on his six-foot frame, and in his buttonhole often wears an orchid from his own collection. His style is basically conservative, although brighter colors have recently been noted among his shirts, and he has a Hong Kong sports coat that could be called "mod." He disdains a Honolulu Chamber of Commerce suggestion that corporate executives wear aloha shirts during summer months as a gesture to the "Hawaiian spirit." When he plays golf on a Wednesday or Thursday afternoon, his sports clothes are also conservative.

MacNaughton has flown as many as 150,000 miles a year on business trips to San Francisco, New York, Alaska, Central America, and Asia. He believes in being visible and available to people everywhere in the Castle & Cooke organization.

In Honolulu he plays a stellar role in community affairs. He was a leader in establishing a single United Fund drive and one of the founders of the Oahu Development Conference (a fifteen-year-old planning organization that was looking to the future before the word *ecology* was heard outside the classroom). He is chairman of the board of Iolani School and president and a director of Queen's Medical Center. He also serves on the board of the Hawaii Council on Economic Education and is a director of the Bank of Hawaii and Hawaiian Airlines.

On the mainland he has at various times served as a trustee of Reed, Mills, and Pepperdine colleges and was awarded a Doctor of Laws degree by Pepperdine in 1974. He is a director of Wells Fargo Bank and Wells Fargo Mortgage Investors, and is a member of the Business Council and the advisory councils of Stanford Research Institute and the Stanford University Graduate School of Business.

MacNaughton's cultural interests have been somewhat limited, although in 1974 he joined the board of directors of the Honolulu Symphony Society. In earlier years he gave full support when Castle & Cooke guaranteed a Honolulu appearance of the New York Philharmonic, a ballet performance by Margot Fonteyn and Rudolf Nureyev, an opera season for Honolulu, summer starlight concerts, and an art acquisition program for the company. In 1966, Castle & Cooke was chosen by a national magazine as one of the twenty outstanding companies in the nation for its support of the arts.

Summing up MacNaughton, one of his long-time associates commented: "He is the most interesting and stimulating man to head Castle & Cooke since Ed Tenney, and when the final returns are in, he may surpass Tenney."

"MY FUTURE ROLE WITH THE COMPANY will be like that of a village priest. From now on, I don't want to hear any of your complaints, but I'll listen to all your confessions." With that characteristic benediction, MacNaughton announced at a Castle & Cooke management meeting in early 1975 that on April 1, following his sixty-fifth birthday, he would be stepping aside as chief executive officer of the company. He would continue, he said, as chairman of the board and would remain active on the company's behalf, particularly in corporate and community relations. But he would no longer be the boss.

That job was being passed to the company's forty-nine-year-old president, Don Kirchhoff. The announcement was no surprise to the audience. MacNaughton had announced at a 1969 management meeting that Kirchhoff, then president of Standard Fruit, would move from New Orleans to Honolulu to take over a new function as executive vice-president in charge of all company food activities except sugar. Henry B. Clark, Jr., vice-president and treasurer, would at the same time become executive vice-president for sugar and all non-food operations. Kirchhoff became president in 1973, and MacNaughton moved up to chairman of the board. The line of succession was set. But the company's management would have to adjust to another style of doing business on the part of their new boss.

MacNaughton and Kirchhoff are both dynamic, energetic leaders, but there the resemblance ends. MacNaughton's articulate, free-swinging, visible style is not for Kirchhoff. He is quieter, much less in evidence to employees, but in his soft-spoken way just as direct and unequivocal as his predecessor. He practices management through tight, highly centralized internal controls. Seemingly every scrap of information about the company's far-flung operations crosses his desk to be read, digested, then checked off with a large, soft pencil. His work is his hobby as well as his vocation. When not traveling, which he does frequently, he usually spends part or all of the weekend at his desk in the Honolulu or San Francisco offices. His analytical mind quickly digests the voluminous operating reports he requires of his subordinates. He was shaped by the tough, competitive, and ever-changing banana business. "We are running on a much faster track than we used to," comments one of his executives.

By the beginning of the 1970s, Castle & Cooke had gathered under its corporate wing a diverse collection of formerly independent companies. Each had its own management structure, its traditional ways of doing business, and its own identity in its community and industry. As Castle & Cooke's corporate form evolved, each component retained a high degree of autonomy, pretty much running its own show, with MacNaughton or one of his top managers acting as the principal liaison man with headquarters in Honolulu.

"We were in an evolutionary period and we quickly came to realize that our loose-knit structure wasn't as effective as it should be," MacNaughton explained. For one thing, he said, too much of the company's debt was in the form of expensive short-term credit lines with banks and not enough in long-term debt with fixed interest rates and maturities. There was not enough equity in relation to debt, and the demands of the component units for capital were insatiable.

"First, we put our financial house in order by issuing additional common stock and convertible bonds, then converting the short-term bank lines into longer-term loans with a major insurance company," he continued. "The result was a much stronger balance sheet. Then Don and I and a small team of top men tackled the structure of the company itself." The result was a sweeping revamping of the entire company in 1972, with more far-reaching changes than most other corporations ever go through.

After months of analysis and numberless charts of organization drawn and rejected, the decision was made to centralize food marketing and corporate financial administration in San Francisco because of its more central location but to retain headquarters in Honolulu. All food activities except sugar were brought into a single group, dubbed Castle & Cooke Foods. Later, real estate activities and manufacturing-and-merchandising were organized into two additional groups. Tight central controls were established over budgets, which had to be prepared and approved in minute detail and then reviewed quarterly against performance—a favorite Kirchhoff management tool. Operations were structured along functional lines. Men and women whose careers had been exclusively with bananas or pineapple or seafood, for example, found themselves functioning across the whole spectrum of Castle & Cooke food activities.

"Some companies are successful with a decentralized structure," says Kirchhoff, "but our decision was purely pragmatic. Centralization was the answer for us.'' Scores of managers and their families were moved from New Orleans, Honolulu, and Astoria to the San Francisco area. Others, whose functions had been duplicated, were left behind and let go. It was a traumatic experience for a lot of people, moving to a new location and many into essentially changed jobs.

"Despite all the problems of taking the organization apart and putting it back together in a new form,'' commented one employee, "we suddenly found it a hell of a lot easier to solve problems quickly by walking into the next guy's office, rather than writing or phoning him a couple of thousand miles away. Before, there was too much of an 'us and them' feeling in and among the different parts of the company. Now we know we're all working for Castle & Cooke.'' Millions of dollars were saved by elimination of duplicate efforts, reduction of staff, more stringent financial practices, and countless smaller measures.

Top management was further strengthened with the addition of Leonard Marks Jr. as executive vice-president and chief financial officer in 1972. He had been senior vice-president of Wells Fargo, assistant secretary of the U.S. Air Force, and professor of finance at the Stanford Graduate School of Business. Executive vice-president Henry Clark, a twenty-six-year veteran with the company, continued as head of Castle & Cooke's sugar operations in Hawaii and all of its non-food activities. These included the company's real estate and merchandising operations in Hawaii and on the West Coast, the California "Pool Sweep" manufacturing subsidiary, four transportation-related subsidiaries in Hawaii, and the several majority-owned manufacturing affiliates in the Far East.

With the consolidation of Dole's operations into Castle & Cooke Foods, Bill Quinn, still a lawyer at heart, resigned in 1972 and joined one of Honolulu's leading law firms as a senior partner.

THE RESTRUCTURING OF CASTLE & COOKE also brought into focus some company strengths and weaknesses, which the new consolidation made it possible to act upon effectively for the first time. One problem concerned the future of its Hawaiian sugar companies. Waialua was one of the most productive and profitable in the islands and was expanding. Earlier the company had sold Ewa Plantation to Amfac, Inc., and operations had been consolidated with the latter's adjacent Oahu Sugar Company. Ewa was located entirely on land whose lease would expire in 1978. Company officials were certain that exploding land values in the Ewa area would result in much higher land rent, assuming that a new lease could be negotiated. In addition, the owners of the land had indicated that they intended to withdraw acreage for other uses. This

would reduce Ewa's acreage to a point where operation of the plantation and mill might not be viable. On the other hand, acquisition of
the Ewa leasehold combined with other lands it leased would assure
Oahu Sugar of being able to operate economically at its mill in Wai-
pahu for years to come.

Kohala was another story. For the past forty years, it had been
marginally profitable at best. Frequently it lost money or barely broke
even because of its location on the windy north cape of the island of
Hawaii, whose extremes of dry or wet weather made the plantation less
productive and more costly to operate. Since World War II Castle &
Cooke had invested millions in attempts to improve profitability, including the testing of alternative crops, but finally the company realized that
nothing more could be done. In 1971, it was announced that Kohala
would be closed. It harvested its last crop in 1975.

"We have the world's best marketing organization for fresh produce," Kirchhoff once told a luncheon meeting of financial analysts.
Dole had proven it, he pointed out, by wresting away the banana market
leadership in North America and carving out a healthy chunk of the
tough western European and Japanese markets. One major opportunity
was "in house"—fresh pineapple.

From the early 1960s Dole had been shipping small but slowly
increasing quantities of fresh Hawaiian pineapple to the Pacific Coast in
refrigerated containers. In adapting pineapple developed for canning to
the fresh market, there were some problems in growing and shipping;
but the biggest was in marketing, because the channels of distribution to
the grocery store require separate sales forces and methods for canned
and fresh products. The strategy was to concentrate sales of surface-
shipped Dole fresh fruit in the western states initially while developing
techniques to assure high quality when it was distributed east of the
Rockies in the future. Meanwhile, smaller volumes of fruit at necessarily higher prices were air-freighted to the eastern half of the country.

Another combination of factors concerned Hawaiian pineapple.
With ever-increasing costs of labor and operating supplies, pineapple
canning in the islands could survive only with the most efficient plantation operation. It was decided that the former Libby plantation on
Molokai should be shut down, and the growing of pineapple for canning
should be concentrated on the island of Lanai. Meanwhile the Wahiawa
plantation on Oahu, where Jim Dole started, was gradually converted
to the growing of fruit for the fresh market. The shift of a major part of
Dole pineapple production from Hawaii to the lower-cost Far East
began to pay off as pineapple earnings climbed to levels never before
achieved in the company.

Having brought Dole bananas to dominance in the North American market, Kirchhoff could see great promise for Dole fresh pineapple. In a Honolulu address in 1975, he pointed out that per capita consumption of fresh pineapple nationally was only eight-tenths of a pound (though higher in the West than in the East). If consumption could be increased to the level of fresh peaches, which are only a seasonal fruit, the volume would equal 462,000 tons a year. To supply that kind of tonnage, he said, 35,000 acres would be needed, compared to the 5,000 presently allotted to pineapple for the fresh market.

"Obviously," he concluded, "this isn't going to happen tomorrow—maybe never—but it does mean if we can keep our product economics in line, and we have labor available, there is a future for pineapple in Hawaii."

Kirchhoff's fresh produce marketing organization could add still more arrows to its quiver. The search began for other fresh products to be marketed along with bananas and pineapple. One answer was mushrooms.

In 1973, Castle & Cooke acquired the privately owned West Foods, Inc., the largest mushroom producer in the western United States. West Foods' "Shady Oak" label was well known on canned mushrooms. The company had growing facilities at Salem, Oregon, and Soquel and Ventura, California. At the time, West Foods sold 68 percent of its production to the fresh produce market; the balance was canned, though the fresh was far more profitable. In two years Castle & Cooke brought fresh sales to more than 90 percent of production.

In 1974 two additional mushroom facilities were purchased. One was in southern Illinois, near St. Louis, where mushrooms were grown in the caves of a limestone quarry; the other, a much smaller one, was in Brazil. And the Dole label was added to fresh mushrooms.

Bumble Bee's seafood products had been good earners, but Castle & Cooke management saw further opportunities to broaden that product line, too. Further, they recognized a basic defect in the method of tuna procurement. The company bought most of its raw tuna from international fishing companies—most of them Far Eastern—in what was, in effect, a volatile auction market. Many of its principal·competitors filled their requirements with the catch from their own fishing fleets. The economics was strongly in favor of "catching 'em rather than buying 'em." But modern tuna fishing vessels are enormously expensive to build, and there were none to be bought.

Out of the collapse of San Diego–based Westgate-California, Inc., in 1973 came the opportunity. Edmund Gann, member of an old Southern California fishing family, had built one of the most modern tuna fleets on the coast and had later sold it to Westgate-California. After the latter's bankruptcy, the fleet was returned to Gann, and he was interested in selling it again, this time for cash. After protracted negotiations, Castle & Cooke in 1975 paid $30.5 million for twelve Gann vessels. Together with the two modern vessels already operating under the Bumble Bee house flag, it gave Castle & Cooke one of the three largest fleets controlled by U.S. tuna canners, with a total carrying capacity of 13,000 tons of raw fish. Thus the groundwork was laid for further growth of the Bumble Bee label in the tuna business.

The tremendous growth in the number of Americans eating away from home suggested a further expansion into the institutional seafood market, beyond the prawns from Surinam. Thus, shortly before the Gann fleet purchase, Castle & Cooke bought the long-established Pan-Alaska Fisheries, Inc., freezer of king crab, snow crab, and shrimp from Alaska.

Under Kirchhoff's leadership, Castle & Cooke was committed to continued growth. In 1970 its sales had passed half a billion dollars. By the end of 1975 they were approaching $900 million.

THE SOMNOLENT VILLAGE IN THE SANDWICH ISLANDS first seen by Samuel Northrup Castle and Amos Starr Cooke on that Sabbath morning in 1837 is no more. It has been replaced by a sprawling state capital vibrant with a mixture of races and cultures.

The coral-block depository they helped to build is also gone. Some distance away there is now a handsome twenty-two-story tower that serves as the heart of the corporation founded by two lay missionaries when the United States was only seventy-five years old. That company today, in the year of the nation's bicentennial, has operations in locations ranging from the gale-swept Aleutians to the hot and humid lowlands of several Latin American republics, from the broad Columbia River to the klongs of Bangkok, from Brussels to Tokyo.

The more than thirty thousand employees in fields and canneries, on fishing boats and construction sites, in quarries and offices are as diverse as the products and services their energies generate. The company's accounts are figured in marks, guilders, colones, lempiras, yen, and baht, as well as dollars.

Underlying all the money and energy is still a spirit brought by the missionaries and perhaps best expressed by Jim Dole: "We have built this company on quality, and quality, and quality." Much has changed, but that spirit remains.

SAMUEL NORTHRUP CASTLE AND AMOS STARR COOKE—*this is what they and their successors have wrought.*

Expansion, 1948-1976

Castle & Cooke's present banana business was begun in 1899 by Vaccaro Brothers & Company, predecessor of the Standard Fruit & Steamship Company. The founders were Joseph Vaccaro, his brothers Felix and Lucca, and his son-in-law, Salvador D'Antoni. Castle & Cooke purchased controlling ownership in Standard Fruit in 1964, and increased this to 100 percent four years later. The bananas are marketed under the Dole label.

In 1901, before railroads, Honduran banana growers had to float their fruit downriver to the port at La Ceiba.

The Ceiba, a high-speed banana ship, was built in 1911.

Castle & Cooke bananas are grown in Honduras, Costa Rica, Nicaragua, Ecuador, and the Philippines. The fruit comes from company farms and independent planters.

Freshly harvested bananas are carried to flatbed trailers, which are padded to protect the tender fruit for transport to the packing sheds.

Standard pioneered boxing of bananas to protect the fruit.

Previously, bananas on the stem were shipped unprotected.

The year 1899 saw the beginning of Columbia River Packers Association, forerunner of Castle & Cooke's Bumble Bee Seafoods operations. CRPA resulted from the merger of seven salmon canners along the Columbia River. Samuel Elmore was the firm's first manager.

Above: C & C's seafood line includes Alaskan king crabs.

Right: Tuna in Hawaiian waters are caught with poles.

Left: Columbia River salmon once were caught by dip-netting.

Lower right: CRPA's first Alaskan cannery was built in 1901.

In the 1960s, C & C expanded into many new fields. Its Philippine pineapple operation, started in 1963, paved the way for its growth in the Far East.

Mushrooms were a 1973 addition to the company's food products. Domestic production, bearing the Dole label, is focused on the fresh produce market.

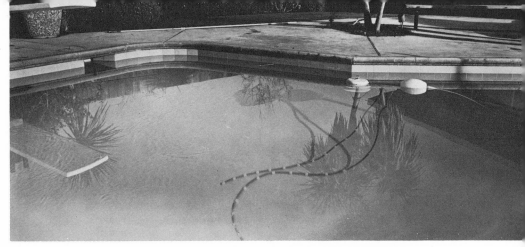

The Pool-Sweep (Arneson Products) manufacturing firm was acquired in 1969.

Castle & Cooke reentered the mercantile field, its original line of business, when it acquired a West Coast self-service merchandising firm in 1966.

Real estate has been part of the world of Castle & Cooke since 1961. Mililani Town on Oahu is a development of its Oceanic Properties subsidiary.

Corporate headquarters occupy the top floors of the 22-story Castle & Cooke building in the Financial Plaza of the Pacific, located in the heart of downtown Honolulu. These quarters have been occupied since 1968 when the new structure replaced the former headquarters—on the same site—which had been occupied since 1924. The Financial Plaza, covering an entire block, was the first commercial condominium in the world. It was developed by C & C's Oceanic Properties.

Malcolm MacNaughton (left), president of Castle & Cooke from 1959–73 and chairman of the board since then, set the pattern for the company's growth into a major international food producer. His successor, D. J. Kirchhoff, president, is expanding on the MacNaughton foundation.

The Castles—a

Married November 10, 1836

Samuel Northrup Castle
Born August 12, 1808
Died July 14, 1894

Married October 13, 1842

Charles Alfred Castle   1844-1874
M. Claire Eloise Coleman
1847-1917

Harriet Angeline Castle   1847-1924
M. Charles Carson Coleman
1845-1935

William Richards Castle   1849-1935
M. Ida Beatrice Lowrey
1854-1926

*Castle & Cooke
Auditor 1901-1902
Vice President 1918-1934
Director
1901-1902, 1918-1934*

George Parmelee Castle   1851-1932
M. Ida Mary Tenney   1856-1944

*Castle & Cooke Partner
1886-1894
Vice President
1895-1903, 1917-1932
President
1903-1917
Director 1895-1932*

Samuel Castle   1843-1843

Samuel Northrup Castle   1880-1959
(took mother's maiden name)
M. Anna Ellison Haviland

(dates unknown)

*Castle & Cooke
Vice President 1957-1959
Director 1941-1959*

Alfred Lowrey Castle   1884-1972
M. Ethelinda Schaefer 1886-1970

*Castle & Cooke
Auditor 1919-1923
Director
1919-1941   1958-1967*

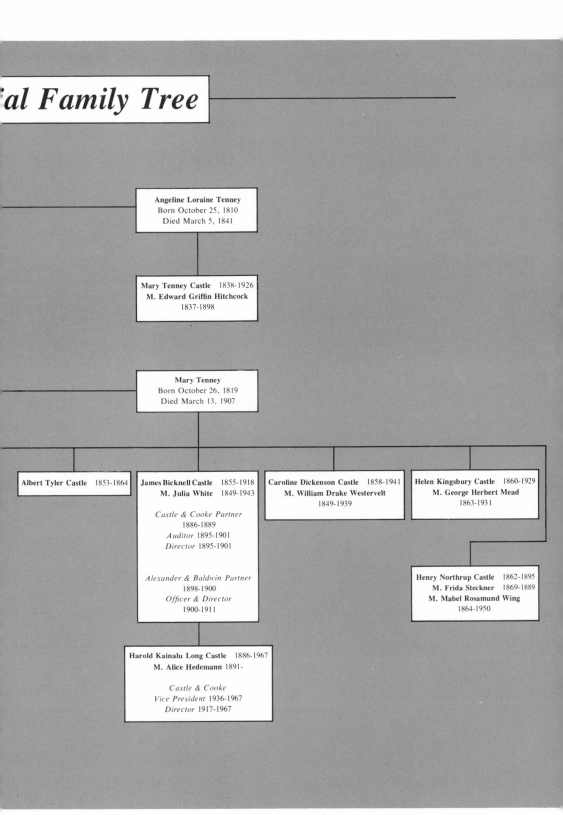

Angeline Loraine Tenney
Born October 25, 1810
Died March 5, 1841

Mary Tenney Castle   1838-1926
M. Edward Griffin Hitchcock
1837-1898

Mary Tenney
Born October 26, 1819
Died March 13, 1907

Albert Tyler Castle   1853-1864

James Bicknell Castle   1855-1918
M. Julia White   1849-1943

Castle & Cooke Partner
1886-1889
Auditor 1895-1901
Director 1895-1901

Alexander & Baldwin Partner
1898-1900
Officer & Director
1900-1911

Caroline Dickenson Castle   1858-1941
M. William Drake Westervelt
1849-1939

Helen Kingsbury Castle   1860-1929
M. George Herbert Mead
1863-1931

Henry Northrup Castle   1862-1895
M. Frida Steckner   1869-1889
M. Mabel Rosamund Wing
1864-1950

Harold Kainalu Long Castle   1886-1967
M. Alice Hedemann 1891-

Castle & Cooke
Vice President 1936-1967
Director 1917-1967

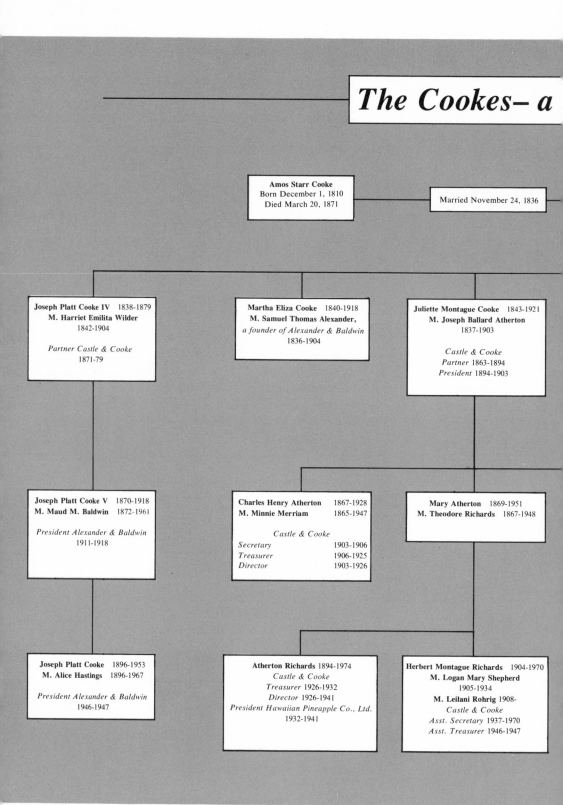

The Cookes– a

Amos Starr Cooke
Born December 1, 1810
Died March 20, 1871

Married November 24, 1836

Joseph Platt Cooke IV   1838-1879
M. Harriet Emilita Wilder
1842-1904

Partner Castle & Cooke
1871-79

Martha Eliza Cooke   1840-1918
M. Samuel Thomas Alexander,
a founder of Alexander & Baldwin
1836-1904

Juliette Montague Cooke   1843-1921
M. Joseph Ballard Atherton
1837-1903

Castle & Cooke
Partner 1863-1894
President 1894-1903

Joseph Platt Cooke V   1870-1918
M. Maud M. Baldwin   1872-1961

President Alexander & Baldwin
1911-1918

Charles Henry Atherton   1867-1928
M. Minnie Merriam   1865-1947

Castle & Cooke
Secretary   1903-1906
Treasurer   1906-1925
Director   1903-1926

Mary Atherton   1869-1951
M. Theodore Richards   1867-1948

Joseph Platt Cooke   1896-1953
M. Alice Hastings   1896-1967

President Alexander & Baldwin
1946-1947

Atherton Richards 1894-1974
Castle & Cooke
Treasurer 1926-1932
Director 1926-1941
President Hawaiian Pineapple Co., Ltd.
1932-1941

Herbert Montague Richards   1904-1970
M. Logan Mary Shepherd
1905-1934
M. Leilani Rohrig 1908-
Castle & Cooke
Asst. Secretary 1937-1970
Asst. Treasurer 1946-1947

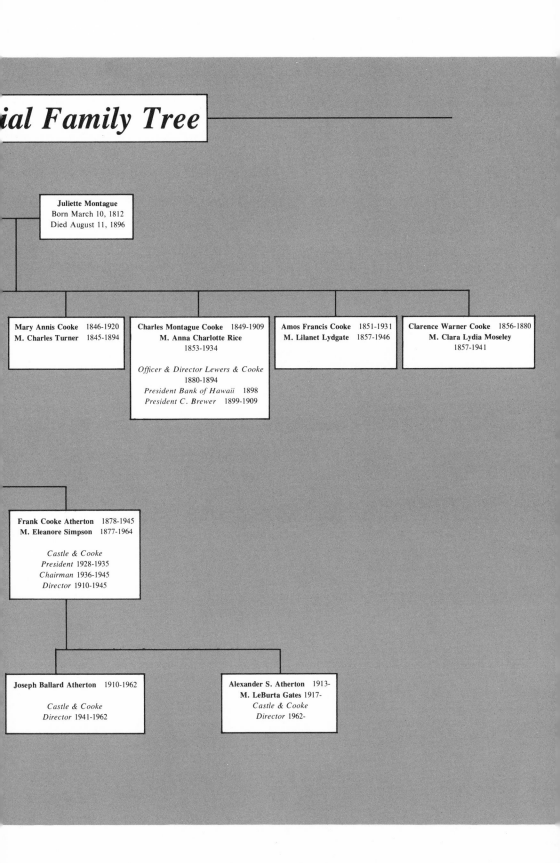

ial Family Tree

Juliette Montague
Born March 10, 1812
Died August 11, 1896

Mary Annis Cooke 1846-1920
M. Charles Turner 1845-1894

Charles Montague Cooke 1849-1909
M. Anna Charlotte Rice
1853-1934

Officer & Director Lewers & Cooke
1880-1894
President Bank of Hawaii *1898*
President C. Brewer *1899-1909*

Amos Francis Cooke 1851-1931
M. Lilanet Lydgate 1857-1946

Clarence Warner Cooke 1856-1880
M. Clara Lydia Moseley
1857-1941

Frank Cooke Atherton 1878-1945
M. Eleanore Simpson 1877-1964

Castle & Cooke
President 1928-1935
Chairman 1936-1945
Director 1910-1945

Joseph Ballard Atherton 1910-1962

Castle & Cooke
Director 1941-1962

Alexander S. Atherton 1913-
M. LeBurta Gates 1917-
Castle & Cooke
Director 1962-

Monarchs of Hawaii

	SUCCESSION TO THRONE	DEATH
Kamehameha I	1795 (exact date not known)	May 8, 1819
Kamehameha II (Liholiho)	May 20, 1819	July 14, 1824
Kamehameha III (Kauikeaouli)	June 6, 1825	December 15, 1854
Kamehameha IV (Alexander Liholiho)	December 15, 1854	November 30, 1863
Kamehameha V (Lot Kamehameha)	November 30, 1863	December 11, 1872
Lunalilo (William Charles Lunalilo)	January 8, 1873	February 3, 1874
Kalakaua (David Kalakaua)	February 12, 1874	January 20, 1891
Liliuokalani (Lydia Liliuokalani)	January 29, 1891	November 11, 1917 (Deposed: January 17, 1893)

GOVERNMENTS OF HAWAII*

	FROM	TO
Monarchy	1795 (exact date not known)	January 17, 1893
Provisional Government	January 17, 1893	July 4, 1894
Republic of Hawaii	July 4, 1894	June 14, 1900†
Territory of Hawaii	June 14, 1900	August 21, 1959‡
State of Hawaii	August 21, 1959	

*Source: Hawaii State Archives
†Hawaii was annexed on August 12, 1898, but territorial government was not established until June 14, 1900.
‡Although the statehood bill passed Congress on March 12, 1959 and was signed into law six days later, Hawaii was not officially proclaimed a state until August 21, 1959.

GLOSSARY

algarroba: (*Sp.*) *carob tree. In Hawaii the Kiawe tree.*   al gah roh' bah

bagasse: (*Fr.*) *fibrous residue of sugarcane after juice has been extracted*   bah gas'

braguinha: (*Port.*) *Portuguese four-stringed musical instrument, later called the ukulele.*
     brah gee' nah

haole: (*Haw.*) *a person not of Hawaiian blood; a Caucasian.*   how leh

hui: (*Haw.*) *a club, association.*   hoo ee

kahili: (*Haw.*) *feather standard, symbol of royalty.*   kah hee lee

kahu: (*Haw.*) *honored attendant, guardian.*   kah hoo

kalo: (*Haw.*) *taro, edible starchy plant of the arum family.*   kah loh

kamaaina: (*Haw.*) *a person born in Hawaii. (Lit. child of the land)*   kah mah ah ee nah

kapu: (*Haw.*) *taboo, forbidden.*   kah poo

luau: (*Haw.*) *a Hawaiian feast.*   loo ow

luna: (*Haw*) *foreman.*   loo nah

malihini: (*Haw.*) *a newcomer or stranger among the people of Hawaii.*   mah lee hee nee

nei: (*Haw.*) *here or this Hawaii nei—Hawaii, here.*   neh ee

okolehao: (*Haw.*) *an alcoholic beverage distilled from the ti root.*   oh koh leh how

pilikia: (*Haw.*) *trouble.*   pee lee kee ah

poi: (*Haw.*) *a staple Hawaiian food made of taro root which has been cooked,*
     pounded, kneaded to a paste, and often then allowed to ferment.   poh ee

rajao: (*Port.*) *a five-stringed musical instrument, originally Portuguese.*   rah djow'

tabi: (*Jap.*) *a Japanese stocking with separate compartment for the large toe.*   tah bee

tanomoshi: (*Jap.*) *a Japanese-American system for raising investment capital.*
     tah noh moh shee

tapa: (*Tah.*) *a course cloth made from bark which is often decorated.*   tah pah

taro: (*Tah.*) *a plant of the arum family, cultivated for its edible starchy, tuberous*
     rootstocks.   ta roh

ti: (*Tah.*) *a woody tree or shrub of the lily family.*   tee

A GUIDE TO THE PRONUNCIATION
OF HAWAIIAN WORDS

Every syllable in Hawaiian ends in a vowel, and each vowel is pronounced separately.
There are no silent vowels or diphthongs. The vowels are pronounced:

> *a*: as the *a* in *above*
>
> *e*: as the *e* in *bet*
>
> *i*: as the *i* in *it*
>
> *o*: as the *o* in *sole*
>
> *u*: as the *u* in *rule* or the *oo* in *moon*

The consonant *w* is pronounced as a *v*. (Thus, Ewa=*Eva*.)

Chief Executives of Castle & Cooke

S.N. Castle
Founder & Partner 1851–1894

A.S. Cooke
Founder & Partner 1851–1871

J.B. Atherton
Partner 1863–1894
President 1894–1903

George P. Castle
President 1903–1916

E.D. Tenney
President 1916–1928
Chairman 1928–1934

F.C. Atherton
President 1928–1935
Chairman 1935–1945

A.G. Budge
President 1935–1959
Chairman 1959–1970

M. MacNaughton
President 1959–1973
Chairman 1973———

D.J. Kirchhoff
President 1973———

Castle & Cooke, Inc.

Profit and Dividend History since incorporation on December 29, 1894

	Profits	Dividends		Profits	Dividends
1894	$ -	$ -			
1895	31,000	-	1936	1,939,000	1,155,000
1896	60,000	48,000	1937	1,532,000	1,210,000
1897	131,000	72,000	1938	1,236,000	581,000
1898	95,000	75,000	1939	1,224,000	629,000
1899	1,403,000	69,000	1940	1,079,000	823,000
1900	288,000	138,000	1941	1,516,000	871,000
1901	213,000	120,000	1942	1,129,000	581,000
1902	94,000	95,000	1943	1,507,000	871,000
1903	160,000	60,000	1944	1,354,000	978,000
1904	133,000	80,000	1945	1,485,000	980,000
1905	147,000	180,000	1946	1,360,000	784,000
1906	150,000	150,000	1947	1,246,000	878,000
1907	236,000	150,000	1948	1,043,000	784,000
1908	322,000	200,000	1949	946,000	641,000
1909	382,000	240,000	1950	1,816,000	1,172,000
1910	427,000	240,000	1951	1,579,000	966,000
1911	476,000	240,000	1952	1,046,000	752,000
1912	404,000	240,000	1953	1,268,000	827,000
1913	253,000	210,000	1954	1,087,000	798,000
1914	299,000	200,000	1955	1,880,000	1,221,000
1915	415,000	360,000	1956	1,973,000	1,194,000
1916	951,000	420,000	1957	1,994,000	1,331,000
1917	811,000	400,000	1958	1,170,000	1,406,000
1918	498,000	280,000	1959	3,032,000	1,539,000
1919	827,000	400,000	1960	2,991,000	1,566,000
1920	1,314,000	615,000	1961	(329,000)	2,912,000
1921	586,000	300,000	1962	4,592,000	1,026,000
1922	584,000	324,000	1963	2,813,000	2,776,000
1923	619,000	393,000	1964	7,801,000	3,465,000
1924	948,000	523,000	1965	8,160,000	3,476,000
1925	684,000	399,000	1966	9,687,000	3,656,000
1926	807,000	498,000	1967	10,079,000	3,987,000
1927	866,000	618,000	1968	10,692,000	4,317,000
1928	1,094,000	633,000	1969	15,178,000	5,719,000
1929	961,000	633,000	1970	20,368,000	6,254,000
1930	840,000	535,000	1971	10,072,000	6,609,000
1931	795,000	538,000	1972	11,596,000	7,273,000
1932	577,000	321,000	1972*	12,080,000	5,525,000
1933	1,197,000	419,000	1973	26,876,000	7,884,000
1934	985,000	421,000	1974	42,661,000	11,071,000
1935	1,196,000	1,013,000	1975	38,160,000	12,303,000

*Second listing for 1972 covers only a 9-month period resulting from a change in fiscal year to one ending on the Saturday closest to December 31.

Bibliography

BOOKS

Adler, Jacob, *Claus Spreckels: The Sugar King in Hawaii*, Honolulu: University of Hawaii Press, 1966.

Alexander, Mary Charlotte, and Dodge, Charlotte Peabody, *Punahou 1841–1941*, Berkeley: University of California Press, 1941.

Ashley, Clifford W., *The Yankee Whaler*, Boston: Houghton Mifflin Co., 1926.

Bingham, Hiram, *A Residence of Twenty-one Years in the Sandwich Islands; or the Civil, Religious and Political History of Those Islands*, 3rd ed., rev., New York: Praeger Publishers, 1969.

Bird, Isabella L., *Six Months in the Sandwich Islands*, Honolulu: University of Hawaii Press, 1964.

Black, Cobey, and Mellen, Kathleen Dickenson, *Princess Pauahi Bishop and Her Legacy*, Honolulu: The Kamehameha Schools Press, 1965.

Castle, William Richards, Jr., *Life of Samuel Northrup Castle*, Honolulu: Samuel N. and Mary Castle Foundation in cooperation with the Hawaiian Historical Society, 1960.

Conde, Jesse C., and Best, Gerald M., *Sugar Trains: Narrow Gauge Rails of Hawaii*, Felton, California: Glenwood Publishers, 1973.

Cooke, Mary, *To Raise a Nation: Historical Novel of Hawaii*, Honolulu: Hawaiian Mission Children's Society, 1970.

Daws, Gavan, *Shoal of Time: A History of the Hawaiian Islands*, Toronto: The Macmillan Company, 1968.

Day, A. Grove, and Stroven, Carl, *A Hawaiian Reader*, New York: Appleton-Century-Crofts, 1959.

Dean, Arthur L., *Alexander & Baldwin, Ltd., and the Predecessor Partnerships*, Honolulu: Alexander & Baldwin, Ltd., 1950.

Deere, Noel, *The History of Sugar*, Vol. I, London: Chapman and Hall, 1949.

Emory, Kenneth P., *The Island of Lanai*, Honolulu: Bernice P. Bishop Museum Bulletin 12, 1969.

A Feasability Study and Report on the Old Stone Depository at the Mission Houses Museum, H. Lockwood Frost and Rossie Moodie Frost, architects, Honolulu, n.d.

Feher, Joseph, *Hawaii: A Pictorial History*, Honolulu: Bishop Museum Press, 1969.

Hawaiian Pineapple Company, Ltd., *What It Means to Grow Big in Twenty-five Years*, Honolulu, 1927

Hedemann, Meta M., *Meta M. Hedemann: From 1878*.

Ii, John Papa, *Fragments of Hawaiian History*, Honolulu: Bishop Museum Press, 1959.

Judd, Gerrit P., IV, *Hawaii, An Informal History*, New York: Collier Books, 1961.

Kamakau, Samuel M., *Ruling Chiefs of Hawaii*, Honolulu: The Kamehameha Schools Press, 1961.

Kent, Harold Winfield, *An Album of Likenesses: Princess Bernice Pauahi Bishop and Charles Reed Bishop*, Honolulu, 1962.

———, *Charles Reed Bishop: Letter File*, Honolulu: 1972.

———, *Charles Reed Bishop: Man of Hawaii*, Palo Alto, California: Pacific Books, 1965.

Krauss, Bob, and Alexander, William P., *Grove Farm Plantation*, Palo Alto, California: Pacific Books, 1965.

Kuykendall, Ralph S., *The Hawaiian Kingdom 1778–1854: Foundation and Transformation*, Honolulu: The University of Hawaii Press, 1938.

———, *The Hawaiian Kingdom 1854–1874: Twenty Critical Years*, Honolulu: The University of Hawaii Press, 1953.

Lyons, Cicely, *Salmon: Our Heritage*, Vancouver, British Columbia: British Columbia Packers, Limited, 1969.

MacDonald, Alexander, *Revolt in Paradise*, New York: Stephen Daye, Inc., 1944.

Men and Women of Hawaii—1954, Perry Edward Hilleary, ed., Honolulu: Honolulu Business Consultants, 1954.

Men and Women of Hawaii—1966, Gwenfread E. Allen, ed., Honolulu: Honolulu Star-Bulletin, Inc., 1966.

Men and Women of Hawaii—1972, Betty Finley Buker, ed., Honolulu: Star-Bulletin Printing Co., Inc., 1972.

Missionary Album, Sesquicentennial Edition 1820–1970, Honolulu: Hawaiian Mission Children's Society, 1969.

Nellist, George F., *The Story of Hawaii and Its Builders,* Honolulu: Honolulu Star-Bulletin, Ltd., 1925.

Porteus, Stanley D., *A Century of Social Thinking in Hawaii,* Palo Alto, California: Pacific Books, 1962.

Richards, Mary Atherton, *The Hawaiian Chiefs' Children's School,* Rutland, Vermont: Charles E. Tuttle Company, 1970.

Scott, Edward B., *The Saga of the Sandwich Islands,* Vol. I, Crystal Bay, Nevada: Sierra Tahoe Publishing Co., 1968.

Sullivan, Josephine, *A History of C. Brewer & Company Limited, 1826–1926,* Boston: Walton Advertising & Printing Co., 1926.

Vandercook, John W., *King Cane: The Story of Sugar in Hawaii,* New York: Harper & Bros., 1939.

SERIALS, PAMPHLETS, ETC.

Castle & Cooke Report, Honolulu, 1965–1975.

Castle & Cooke, Inc., *Annual Report,* 1924–1974.

Hawaiian Sugar Planters' Association, *Hawaii's Sugar Islands,* Honolulu, 1974.

Kohala Sugar Company (1862–1887), Castle & Cooke, Inc., private.

Thrum's Hawaiian Annual and Standard Guide, combined with All About Hawaii for 1945, Donald Billam-Walker, ed., Honolulu: Honolulu Star-Bulletin, Ltd., 1945.

Thrum's Hawaiian Annual and Standard Guide, combined with All About Hawaii for 1945–1946, Clarice B. Taylor, ed., Honolulu: Honolulu Star-Bulletin, Ltd., 1946.

Thrum's Hawaiian Annual and Standard Guide, combined with All About Hawaii for 1946–1947, Clarice B. Taylor, ed., Honolulu: Honolulu Star-Bulletin, Ltd., 1947.

Thrum's Hawaiian Annual and Standard Guide, combined with All About Hawaii, 90th ed., Charles E. Frankel, ed., Honolulu: Star-Bulletin Printing Co., 1968.

NOTE: Juliette Cooke is quoted extensively in this book, whereas there are virtually no quotations from either Angeline or Mary Castle. Letters or journals written by them are almost nonexistent in the files of the Hawaiian Mission Children's Society, and the few in possession are, in contrast to the record left by Juliette Cooke, quite prosaic.

Illustrations

Most photographs and other illustrations are from the collections of **Castle & Cooke, Inc.** *and its affiliates. We also gratefully acknowledge the assistance of these sources in supplying pictorial material:*

Hawaiian Mission Children's Society: Juliette Montague Cooke, *49*; Plan of the interior of the bark Mary Frazier, *50*; Sketch of bark Mary Frazier, *50*; Kamehameha III, *51*; Letter by Juliette Montague Cooke, *54*; Cooke family home, *56*; Castle family home, *57*; Letter by Juliette Montague Cooke, *102*; Letter by, S.N. Castle, *105*; Letter by S.N. Castle, *111*; Castle family, *116*; Cooke family, *117*. **Bernice P. Bishop Museum:** Bernice P. and Charles R. Bishop,*'55*; Queen Street in 1850, *56*; S.N. Castle home, *181*; Chinatown fire, *192*. **Hawaii State Archives:** Kamehameha IV, Kamehameha V, William Lunalilo, *107*; King Kalakaua, *112*; Queen Kapiolani's crown, *113*; Coin, postage stamp and currency, *115*; Queen Liliuokalani, *118*. **Hawaiian Historical Society:** The first and second Lurlines, *178*, *179*; Moana Hotel and Waikiki Beach in 1900, *188*, *189*. **Matson Navigation Company:** Royal Hawaiian Hotel and Waikiki Beach in 1946, *188*, *189*; Royal Hawaiian Hotel, *189*; Boat Day, *190*. **Robert Morse, TIME-LIFE Picture Agency © Time, Inc.:** Honolulu Municipal Building sandbagged and guarded,*217*; Royal Hawaiian Hotel—Navy rest center, *217*.

Index

KAUAI

NIIHAU

OAHU

Honolulu